THE TOUR IS WON ON THE ALPE

THE TOUR IS WON ON THE ALPE

Alpe d'Huez *and the* **Classic Battles** *of the* **Tour de France**

Jean-Paul Vespini

Translated by David V. Herlihy
Translation edited by Mark Deterline

VELO
press

Boulder, Colorado

Chapters 1–22 and front and end matter were published in France as *Le Tour se gagne à l'Alpe: Des aventures et des hommes* by Mango Sport in 2003. First published by Éditions Romillat in 1995. This translation and all subsequent chapters are published in agreement with the author, Jean-Paul Vespini.

1830 North 55th Street
Boulder, Colorado 80301-2700 USA
303/440-0601 · Fax 303/444-6788 · E-mail velopress@insideinc.com

Distributed in the United States and Canada by Publishers Group West

Library of Congress Cataloging-in-Publication Data
Vespini, Jean-Paul.
 [Tour se gagne à l'Alpe. English]
 The Tour is won on the Alpe : Alpe d'Huez and the classic battles of the Tour de France / Jean-Paul Vespini; translated by David V. Herlihy; translation edited by Mark Deterline.
  p.   cm.
 ISBN-13: 978-1-934030-23-3
 1. Tour de France (Bicycle race)—History.   2. Alpe d'Huez (France)—History.
I. Deterline, Mark. II. Title.
GV1049.2.T68V4713 2008
796.6'20944—dc22
2007050364

Cover design by Jason Farrell; interior design by Jane Raese
Cover photograph by Getty Images
For information on purchasing VeloPress books, please call 800/234-8356 or visit www.velopress.com.

08 09 10 / 10 9 8 7 6 5 4 3 2 1

To Fabienne

It is good to follow one inclination as long as it rises.
—ANDRÉ GIDE

In 1977, I experienced the greatest joy of my career
when I kept the yellow jersey by 8 seconds.
I could have died happy that day on my bike.
—BERNARD THÉVENET

Contents

Foreword

The Tour de France is part of France's national heritage. This epic sporting event includes a cultural dimension that has not escaped the interest of educated people—a bonus that naturally appeals to the organizers as well.

Those who celebrate the Tour's virtues love to point out that it is a much better teacher of geography than schoolbooks. Moreover, the Tour offers added advantages: It reveals the true face of France's heartland, invites fans to share in this discovery or rediscovery, and promotes the cities along its route.

This exposure is particularly valuable when the stop happens to be a mountain resort such as L'Alpe d'Huez. This alpine ski mecca owes some of its fame to the bicycle. It has now entered the Annals of Cycling History (La Légende des Cycles) so dear to the French writer and sports columnist Antoine Blondin, taking its place alongside the famous peaks of the Galibier, the Tourmalet, and the Ventoux.

The formidable challenge of the Alpe, and others like it in the Alps and Pyrénées, has greatly enhanced the prestige of the Tour. With its especially severe hardships, the famous climb of L'Oisans occupies a privileged position. It foments epic battles among the climbers and shakes up the standings of the race.

In fact, the Tour's first mountaintop finish was witnessed on the Alpe. To put it there, Élie Wermelinger, at the time the general commissioner of the Tour, reconnoitered the Alpe's sinuous road months in advance aboard a Panhard Dyna motorcar that had to clear its own way through the snowdrifts.

It fell to Fausto Coppi to inaugurate the tradition of Alpe d'Huez, and his great victory in the dizzying heights of L'Oisans belongs to cycling legend. It evoked the fervent admiration of Jacques Goddet, the Tour's director from 1936 to 1986, who made a spontaneous association between the man and the mountain in an editorial published in *L'Équipe* that began as follows: "Facing us, on the other side of the enormous crevasse which forms the valley of La Romanche, rises the Pelvoux chain, which majestically dominates all of its neighboring peaks, just like the great and solitary Coppi towered over his adversaries."

Over the years, the incomparable Campionissimo, and the equally impressive Lance Armstrong, are the only two who have won the Alpe stage and the Tour in the same year. That may seem surprising, yet this high point of competitive cycling has always shaken things up, producing unexpected and unforgettable moments such as the breakaway of Hinault and LeMond; the repeat victories of Zoetemelk, Winnen, and Bugno; and the triumph of Lucho Herrera, who sent all of Colombia into a frenzy.

One cannot speak about the Alpe without commenting on its surroundings, its ambience, its twenty-one turns, its boisterous crowds, and its inevitable Dutch contingent, which has led to it being called "Dutch Mountain"—the Low Country's highest peak. Today Dutch fans are no longer the only foreigners who flock to the Alpe for the big event. German, Belgian, and Danish campers amass along the road days ahead of time, joining the French aficionados and attesting that the climb up Alpe d'Huez has become a de rigueur stage in the Tour. This is a place of sport, celebration, and passion that fosters the formidable popularity of cycling and forges a worldwide community of fans.

All these images, all these exploits, have inspired our good friend Jean-Paul Vespini to write this book with love and skill. It is a unique contribution, faithful to reality and well-documented. It's the work of a journalist who should be complimented and thanked for his remarkable accomplishment and for the tribute he has paid the Tour de France.

—Jean-Marie Leblanc
Director of the Tour de France, 1989–2005

Prologue: The Pinnacle

The Tour de France and Alpe d'Huez have become such inseparable icons that their union transcends the race's everyday logistics. It's virtually an unwritten rule, for example, that if the Tour goes through the Pyrénées, it must traverse the Aubisque; if it passes through the Alps, it must make an ascent of the Galibier. An ascent of Alpe d'Huez, however, is another matter altogether: It sets the bar much higher and has become part of the very essence of the Tour. Today the question is not whether the Tour de France will include the Alps, and with or without them Alpe d'Huez, but simply whether or not the Tour will include Alpe d'Huez. The difference is significant.

The imposing peaks of eras past still have our utmost respect. But they are more or less wedded to their particular regions, with the possible exception of the treacherous Mont Ventoux. Today these strategic cols of yesteryear, vestiges of a distant era and commemorated feats, are practically steamrolled by pelotons that cross them largely intact. That's not true of the stubbornly selective Alpe d'Huez.

Great traditions take time to develop. In 1952, when the Tour made its first stop at the summit of the Alpe, no one could have predicted that the world of professional cycling had just discovered its Fenway Park, its Wimbledon, its stadium of reference.

Oddly enough, this first ascent, dominated by Fausto Coppi, the Campionissimo, who donned the yellow jersey following his stunning performance, was quickly forgotten. A few venomous pens even dared suggest that the Tour organizers were crazy to have sent the racers up there in the first place. And yet, without knowing it, the Tour had laid the foundation for cycling's modern temple.

Following the 1952 Tour, the riders and the organizers would forget Alpe d'Huez for eighteen years. Then, in 1976, Alpe d'Huez returned, this time to win the hearts of the masses. It was something of a revelation:

The entire cycling world began talking about this terraced spectacle of a climb, its every switchback numbered.

Since then, it has been referred to simply as the Alpe, known on this first-name basis throughout the cycling world. It is difficult to imagine a Tour without it, much as there could be no ski World Cup without Kitzbühel, no Formula One sans Monaco.

This devotion of the cycling faithful is shared by the riders, who go there in search of their Holy Grail. For them, winning atop the Alpe's lofty peak means as much as a world championship or a yellow jersey. It brings them closer to paradise. In times past, the Tour's heroes rode into the Casse Déserte of the prestigious Izoard. Today they set their sights on victory at L'Alpe d'Huez, chasing the imaginary wheel of Coppi, their great predecessor.

Alpe d'Huez has become the rite of passage, the key stage, the queen of all climbs, and the day of reckoning on which the Tour is won or lost. That is the true secret of the Alpe's success: It is a climb that delivers a verdict—absolute, impartial, and final.

Simple statistics do not reveal the Alpe's true stature. After all, how many riders have prevailed at the summit of Alpe d'Huez and gone on to win the Tour in the same year? So far, only two: Fausto Coppi in 1952 and Lance Armstrong in 2001 and also 2004, the year the stage served as an uphill time trial finish.

Should we therefore conclude that Alpe d'Huez rarely determines the eventual winner of the Tour? Definitely not. To truly gauge the significance of this climb in determining overall victory, we must focus our attention on the yellow jersey. By so doing, we see that in seventeen of twenty-five ascents, the winner of the Tour was in yellow following Alpe d'Huez.[1] In general, Tour winners must make a supreme effort there to either save the jersey or consolidate their lead. And as you will see in the following chapters, even in years when the Tour is not decided on the Alpe, the race can certainly be lost there.

Alpe d'Huez is known by many nicknames: the Platform of Huez, the Fortress of L'Oisans, the Mountain Temple (in fact, a splendid church near the summit made of wood and mortar has long offered journalists a makeshift pressroom; it once even hosted a boxing match before the building was completed). The Alpe is also referred to as Dutch Mountain, not because the parish priest happens to be Dutch but because, paradoxically, riders from the Netherlands' endless expanses of flat country distinguished themselves on the Alpe's climbs at the beginning of this modern era. Dutch riders claimed six victories between 1976 and 1983 and have amassed eight victories in all. That might not seem sufficient to warrant the nickname, but there is no denying that the Batavians[2] have shown a strange affinity for this ascent. Joop Zoetemelk, Hennie Kuiper, Steven Rooks, and Gert-Jan Theunisse all found their wings here. They come, it seems, to rise majestically and dominate the competition in the Tour's most decisive stage. On behalf of an entire people, they make up for the lack of hills in their own country and proudly demonstrate that the Dutch know how to spin more than just windmill blades.

This passion draws scores of rabid Dutch fans to the Alpe each year, where they overrun every twist in its twenty-one switchbacks days before the actual stage. It is a pilgrimage that also attracts fans from all over the world, transforming the Alpe into cycling's Tower of Babel. At night, hundreds of cars, campers, and motorcycles cruise the road in an effort to nab the best spots. In the pale beams of their headlights, the most fanatical paint the names of their favorite stars across the road. Others stake out their territory with signs proportional in size to the admiration they feel for their champion so that they can be certain to keep their spot.

From the first to the last of the twenty-one turns, each deserves mention, but three in particular stand out:

Turn 16, at Garde: A flat section enables the fans to see the racers recuperate a bit.

Turn 8: A massive inscription of "Holland" in the rocks sets the tone, ambience guaranteed.

Turn 7: At the entrance of Huez, next to the small cemetery on the left, this spot offers an ideal view of a section of road with an 8 percent grade.

These five-star vantage points are hard to come by, but they are where you can see the racers best. Proud fans are up late into the night, looking forward to the craziness of the next day.

At Alpe d'Huez, cycling disciples enter their sanctuary. Exactly how many will be there on race day, jumping and yelling as the riders pass? At least 200,000 and perhaps as many as 300,000 as passions in the world's largest natural stadium, this overheated cauldron, come to a boil. From switchback to switchback, the crowd will chant the name of the first rider to pass, the chosen one.

The Alpe bubbles with emotion as all eyes focus on the passing riders to gauge their positions and prospects. Meanwhile, cars in the caravan honk their horns incessantly at the imprudent and irreverent fans who have strayed into the champions' path of glory. The fans holler and gesture. This grand, colorful spectacle celebrates the mountain in a ritual that has become legendary. The public relishes this epic struggle, and the racers draw enough strength from the delirium to will themselves up the mountain.

Marco Pantani, the stage winner in 1995 and 1997, remarked, "I climbed it without ever seeing the road. The crowd guided me. I only had to listen to the fans who, meter after meter, watch you and yield just enough room to let you pass through a narrow opening. They show you where to go. In 1995, I did the entire climb without ever seeing any pavement. All I could see in front of me were thousands of boisterous fans who yelled out my name. I ascended like a blind man in the middle of a sea that opened up for me."[3]

Andy Hampsten, the winner of the 1992 stage, recalled, "People didn't clear a path until the last second. I felt like I was going 60 kilometers an hour. The sensation of passing through a narrow opening in the crowd was the most beautiful and emotional thing I've ever experienced in my life."[4]

What are the key elements that make this such a sacred cycling ritual? For starters, it's the geography. The 14-kilometer (8.7-mile) climb is truly hellish as the elevation rises from 800 meters (2,625 feet) at Bourg d'Oisans to 1,860 meters (6,102 feet) at the summit. The grade averages 8 percent, a rise of about 50 meters (164 feet) from one hairpin to the next. The brutal slope becomes especially taxing after the bridge at Romanche, where some sections reach a 14 percent grade before the hamlet of La Garde. For the uninitiated, it's a voyage into the depths of hell.

The inspired concept of numbering the turns helps riders keep track of their time, provides a countdown, and heightens the suspense. For some years now, a new aspect has come into play, similar to the hour record: the winner's time, both overall and at each switchback. It was always a close match between Pantani and Armstrong.

There is history in the turns as well. The climbs up Alpe d'Huez have generated great drama: surprising surges by the raging bull Joaquim Agostinho, a yellow-jersey-driven Ronan Pensec, an angelic Andy Hampsten, a haughty Laurent Fignon. And there have been moments of great triumph: the soaring breakaway of the Colombian Lucho Herrera; the dominating performance of Bernard Hinault and Greg LeMond, hand in hand; and Joop Zoetemelk's act of defiance.

Of course, there have been low points as well, such as the stunning defeats of a dehydrated Eddy Merckx, an exhausted Jean-François Bernard, or a tortured Gianni Bugno.

There have also been plenty of memorable misadventures, like Lucien van Impe's fall after an automobile clipped his bicycle, Michel Pollentier's drug bust, and the arrival of an exhausted Jean-Marie Leblanc outside the time limit.

Alpe d'Huez is a place that demands great emotion and sacrifice. Theunisse, for one, was obsessed with it. After a suspension, he went there to revive himself, repeating the climb over and over as if doing penitence. He scaled it something like twenty-four times in just a few days.

Every July, all eyes focus on this dream stage. And if by chance the organizers neglect to include it in the program, the fans let them have it. Even the racers protest; they were more upset when the Tour bypassed Alpe d'Huez in 1993 than when the Pyrénées were omitted altogether the previous year.

You just don't mess with the Alpe. It is irreplaceable. In 1993, at the finish in Isola 2000, each of the imposter's twenty-one turns was numbered and given the name of a cycling great as if to make up for the appalling absence of Alpe d'Huez. Immediately thereafter, Isola was all but forgotten and has not reappeared on the Tour itinerary.

There is only one Alpe. This is its story.

CHAPTER ONE

Birth of
a Legend

TWENTY-ONE SWITCHBACK TURNS, FOLDED AND DRAPED ACROSS A forested mountain face. Almost 14 kilometers—about 8.6 miles—of relentless climbing up an average grade of 8.1 percent. A finish in thin air at 1,860 meters (6,100 feet). Who could conceive of putting mortal cyclists on such a monster?

Who, in fact, but a local hotelier, searching for a way to fill rooms at his ski lodge in the off-season.

Although virtually unknown to the public, Georges Rajon is a celebrity in the ski-resort village of L'Alpe d'Huez. Ask any native how to get to his home, and you'll be quickly directed to a distinctive chalet with hunting trophies proudly displayed above the balconies.

In 1950, Rajon built a hotel at the foot of the Alpe's future ski trails, calling it the Christina in honor of his daughter. An ardent promoter of the resort, he did everything he could to support its development. He became so influential and widely respected that he surely could have appointed himself mayor at any time. Instead, he chose to limit his public service to a six-year stint as a town council member. "I was never much of a diplomat," he explained. "I'm too accustomed to speaking my mind, holding nothing back."

Still, Rajon was so active in town affairs that many assumed he really was the mayor. Thus, it's no surprise that when Élie Wermelinger, the onetime general commissioner of the Tour de France who was in charge of mapping out each edition of the race, came to L'Alpe d'Huez in late 1951 to scout a potential stage, he made the same assumption. "I was riding along in a Dyna Panhard with [André] Renard, a veteran of the 1911 Tour, at the wheel," Wermelinger later told *L'Équipe*. "At the Bourg d'Oisans exit, we had to stop to put on chains. Meanwhile, up at the summit, the mayor of L'Alpe, Rajon, waited for us."

Of course, Rajon—innkeeper, not mayor—was just trying to get the Tour to pass through town. In his view, the visit would inject some cash into the local economy and help promote the budding resort. He also had a selfish interest: He loves sports. Built like a lumberjack, with an iron constitution, he was once an Olympic-caliber skier. He is also a huge cycling fan who has never missed an Alpe stage. When the peloton arrived at the Alpe for the first time, in 1952, he was the official scorer, scribbling the names of the racers on a large chalkboard as each crossed the finish line.

The idea for hosting a Tour stage was first proposed by the late Jean Barbaglia, a painter and artisan from nearby Bourg d'Oisans who was also a lover of cycling and winter sports. "Jean came to see André Quintin [another hotelier at L'Alpe d'Huez] and me one day in 1951," Rajon told *L'Équipe* some years later. "He asked, 'Why don't they bring the Tour to the Alpe?' That's how it all began."

Together, Rajon and Barbaglia approached Wermelinger, who happened to be a close friend of the painter. The Tour architect was intrigued and promised to consider the idea, which appealed to his sense of adventure and his nose for business. In 1952, he published the first edition of his famous annual guidebook for Tour enthusiasts, *Le Petit Wermelinger*. He continued to publish it until his death in 1993. It was so practical and informative that copies were always hard to come by. Jacques Goddet, the longtime director of the Tour, once admitted that he lifted passages regularly from *Le Petit* for his columns in *L'Équipe*. "Many of my colleagues like to sprinkle a few factoids here and there for the benefit of their readers, or plunk an opportune quote in the middle of an article, just to show off their erudition," Goddet confessed. "I do that a lot myself—thanks to Élie, my faithful collaborator."[1]

Still, finishing a stage atop a mountain was a radical proposition, even to Wermelinger. Nothing like it had ever been done before in the history of the Tour. In fact, the first time racers would finish at a summit was in

1952 atop the Alpe, which barely beat out Puy-de-Dôme, another summit destination during the same Tour, for the honor.

As quirky as the proposition sounded at first, it began gaining favor with other local hoteliers, who were among the first to grasp the magnitude of the Tour and to appreciate its potential impact on the local economy. They realized that the Tour offered a unique opportunity to market their beautiful resort to a broader public. Although L'Alpe d'Huez offered up-to-date skiing amenities, the French were not yet bitten by the winter sports bug, and the town could not afford to ignore a potential boost.

It was a different era, the early 1950s. Dwight Eisenhower was about to be elected president of the United States, Raymond Kopa led the French soccer team to victory over the Germans, and the English biochemist Jack Drummond and his wife and daughter were brutally murdered in the French Alps, a sensational case that became the subject of a movie, *L'Affaire Dominici*, twenty years later. Skis were still generally made of wood—hickory for the most fortunate. And there were just a handful of sleepy ski resorts in southeastern France catering to a fortunate few.

So the prospect of bringing the Tour to town struck many local businessmen as a welcome shot in the arm. To be sure, the Tour at that time did not command the worldwide coverage it receives today. But it was already captivating all of France, thanks to the magic of radio. Every July, thousands sat with their ears glued to their transistors throughout the Tour as they strained to hear the commentary of Georges Briquet on the French channel or Alex Virot on Radio Luxembourg.

Although L'Alpe d'Huez was still a comparatively young resort, it was already sufficiently developed that it could seriously entertain the thought of hosting a Tour invasion. Since the construction of the Bel Alpe almost twenty years earlier, the number of local hotels and inns had surged to more than thirty. The primary catalyst was the opening of the Grand Hôtel in 1935. With its sixty rooms and excellent services, it sparked the construction of other splendid establishments, especially after the war, including the Trois Dauphins, the Edelweiss, and Rajon's Christina. Travelers could also stay with local entrepreneurs who had transformed their private chalets into comfortable guesthouses.

High society was already frequenting L'Alpe d'Huez to take in its charm and fresh mountain air. Among the favorite haunts was the famous Ménandière, which opened its doors in 1947 (today it's a restaurant with a piano bar). Its comfortable and elegant ambience, featuring sumptuous bedrooms, attracted some of the biggest names in show business—stars such as Charles Aznavour and Elizabeth Taylor. Artists and politicians also came to L'Alpe d'Huez. Jean Monnet, the architect of European unity, often retreated there to escape the public's eye. The French president, Albert Lebrun, was a regular at the Ours Blanc, whose famous chef, Raymond Olivier, had trained at the Grand Véfour in Paris (and, a few years later, would teach cooking to millions of television viewers).

The resort also boasted a marvelous road, a veritable boulevard compared to the deadly paths of the Pyrénées. Ah, the road to the Alpe! It deserves a chapter unto itself. As late as 1881, according to town documents, the summit road was nothing more than a mule path. By the early 1930s, the road from Bourg d'Oisans to Huez measured a good 4 meters (13 feet) across. But the continuation to the summit was still just a narrow strip of earth, barely 2.5 meters (8 feet) wide. That was not enough to support a Tour stage, let alone the development of a major winter resort. Yet at the time, the local economy, though growing, could not support the cost of constructing a real road.

Fortunately, the situation would soon take a turn for the better, permitting not only the inaugural ascent of 1952 but also a construction boom in the 1960s. The guiding light was a man named Joseph Paganon.[2] Born in 1880 in the nearby region of Isère, this chemist and freemason became a deputy of the district. He loved L'Alpe d'Huez so much that he built a chalet there. When he became minister of public works in 1933, he initiated the construction of a new road from Bourg d'Oisans to the summit of the Alpe that would measure a full 7 meters (23 feet) wide. In 1966, when the Olympic Games came to Grenoble, some sections were widened another 1.5 meters (5 feet). The section between Huez and the summit, however, is still the original road. Tour racers go left at the upper fork.

"Paganon was a true visionary who anticipated the ski resort boom," affirmed Rajon, adding with a chuckle, "but to finance the project, he had to draw from funds earmarked for the Pyrénées." Fourteen firms participated in the project, with each covering the costs of paving exactly 1 kilometer (a little over .5 mile). Collectively, they completed the road within the 1935 calendar year.[3] That, along with the concurrent introduction of the first ski lifts, cleared the way for the Tour and unprecedented development.

The Town Didn't Pay a Dime

Although local businessmen were keen on bringing the 1952 Tour to town, local officials were markedly less enthusiastic. There was, after all, the small matter of paying Tour organizers 2 million French francs ($4,000 today) for the privilege of hosting the affair, and August Chalvin, the real mayor, had little in the way of discretionary funds. But he was not oblivious to the potential payoff. "We can't pay anything," he bluntly informed the steering committee. "But if you folks want to bring the Tour here, be my guest."

Three men took it upon themselves to negotiate a deal with Tour organizers and oversee the entire event: Jean Barbaglia, the mastermind behind the idea; Georges Rajon, who would also orchestrate the second ascent in 1976; and André Quintin, the owner of the Ménandière.

"We met with all the local shop owners and hotel managers," Rajon recalled, "and put it to them straight: 'You will have to pay, but you will earn it all back, and then some!' We also got the Tour organizers to agree to a rest day immediately after the stage, to ensure a significant influx of cash. The town didn't pay a centime, and it worked out perfectly for everyone."

When the inaugural climb finally concluded at the summit of the Alpe, Fausto Coppi had registered a victory for the ages. Still, another twenty-four years would elapse before the second ascent established the great love affair between the Tour and Alpe d'Huez. Perhaps that was because in Coppi's time, a vital element of the Alpe's full magic was missing: the famous markers that enumerate in descending order all twenty-one turns of the summit road. Here's how that ingenious idea came about.

An Idea from Yugoslavia

Rajon has always loved the great outdoors. Not surprisingly, given his athletic makeup, he is partial to vigorous exercise. Over the years, he has traveled throughout the world—Alaska, Canada, Africa—to hunt a wide variety of animals. In his living room, he proudly displays an assortment of wildlife trophies, notably a gigantic bearskin. He is also fond of fishing and has reeled in some remarkable prizes.

In the summer of 1964, Rajon made his annual trip to Slovenia to hunt chamois. Jacques Anquetil had just won a record fifth Tour—his fourth in a row. Rajon was hoping for good results too. But as he began the drive up Mont Vrsic, 2,700 meters (8,860 feet) high, his thoughts were far from the Tour. Since the first ascent, the Tour had never again set foot on the Alpe. Rajon was simply looking for chamois and focusing on the beauty of the countryside near the borders of Italy and Austria.

But as he climbed the fifty-three turns of the Vrsic Pass, Rajon began to think about the future of the Alpe and its development as a tourist destination. The turns he was negotiating were numbered in increasing order. What a brilliant idea! "Why don't we number the switchbacks from Bourg d'Oisans to the Alpe?" he asked himself. Better yet, number the turns in descending order so that visitors would know exactly how many remained before the summit.

Upon his return from Yugoslavia, Rajon encountered little difficulty selling the idea to his friends. Later that same year, for the first time, the 14-kilometer road to L'Alpe d'Huez labeled its curves, starting with number 21 at the base and ending with number 1, just 2.5 kilometers (1.6 miles) from the summit. Little did Rajon realize at the time that these markers were also destined to benefit future Tour contestants.

A dozen years later, when the Tour finally returned to the Alpe, the racers could, for the first time, gauge their progress on the summit road as soon as they began their ascent. They could even pace themselves according to the amount of work left to do, as indicated by the markers. Ever since 1976, in fact, racers have focused on those markers as if they were part of a giant hourglass.

At present, each marker indicates, in addition to the number of the curve, three numbers set against the backdrop of the French flag: 1,450, 1,860, and 3,350. These correspond to the altitude, in meters, of the town of Huez (4,760 feet), the resort (6,100 feet), and the mountain peak (10,990 feet). Each marker also gives the altitude at that particular spot as well as the distance to the nearest emergency phone. That last bit of information is useful for tourists but for Tour riders provides an endless source of jokes.

Today those twenty-one markers add an element of magic to this high destination of the Tour. Every year a few overzealous fans go so far as to dig up and cart off markers as souvenirs of their summer pilgrimage. For obvious reasons, the town should erect a monument to the glory of Georges Rajon. After all, many Legion of Honor medals have been issued for less deserving contributions to a country's national heritage.

CHAPTER TWO

1952

Fausto Coppi Climbs
to the Heavens

I T WAS THE AFTERNOON OF JULY 4, 1952, AND THE 266-KILOMETER (165-mile) stage to the Alpe was nearing its climax. Just past Bourg d'Oisans, an important tourist center about 15 kilometers (9 miles) from the finish line where the road begins to rise to the summit, Jean Robic of team France took off. Raphaël Géminiani, his teammate, followed close behind. But "Gem" quickly faded, partly asphyxiated by the brutal pace. Meanwhile, Robic, nicknamed "Leatherhead" (though he was not wearing his trademark helmet that day), continued his furious charge. The car carrying reporters from *France-Soir* followed in his wake.

Three kilometers (1.9 miles) later, Fausto Coppi, who had complained that boisterous fans outside his hotel had disturbed his sleep the night before, burst forward like a bolt of lightning and joined the Frenchman. The road got steeper, the gaps widened, and on the otherwise quiet mountain, where an occasional "viva" was shouted by his compatriots, Coppi set the pace.

He drove his bike through every turn, his torso upright as he concentrated on his work, without giving the impression that he was really pushing himself. While Robic stood on his pedals to hold the Italian's rear wheel, the Campionissimo pedaled in the saddle, caressing the top of his handlebars. The little Breton panted, his muscles taut, his eyes fixed on the asphalt, as if he had already accepted his imminent defeat.

For 7 more kilometers (4.3 miles), Coppi turned his large chainring, pulling Robic behind him. The spare tire wrapped around the Frenchman's neck was looking more and more like a yoke. Finally, 6 kilometers (3.7 miles) from the summit, Coppi decided to take off, leaving Robic behind. Jacques Goddet, director of the Tour, recalled the moment in *L'Équipe:* "Coppi was unyielding and untouchable, thanks to his extraordinary biomechanical dexterity. Robic kept trying to attack, but Fausto simply accelerated without ever turning back to gauge his lead, as if he were oblivious to any other rider. And when Coppi sensed that Robic was at a breaking point, he accelerated even more. Before anyone knew it, he had a 25-meter lead, and that was that."

A powerless Robic let the Campionissimo go. As Coppi confided later, "I knew he wasn't there anymore, since I no longer heard his breathing, or the crunching of his tires on the ground behind me." He added, "I prefer not to look behind me. It's an exercise of will that I often practice when I find myself at the front in the mountains. I only allow myself a quick sideways glance at turns in the road. I could have dropped my French rival earlier, but it would have meant making a bigger effort than I did when I finally decided to go."

In *Miroir-Sprint*, Charles Pélissier, winner of sixteen Tour stages between 1929 and 1935, wrote in his weekly chronicle, "Coppi didn't seem to exert any extra effort at all. Going up the mountain, he even kept enough energy in reserve to direct traffic, signaling to the cars when to pass or wait. That was really amazing!"

André Leducq, winner of the 1930 and 1932 Tours, was equally stunned. Writing in the weekly print newspaper *But et Club*, he said, "I watched Coppi accelerate through the turns of Alpe d'Huez while Robic, whom he had just caught, was still in his slipstream. Coppi had rosy cheeks, bright eyes, and supple legs. Everyone else looked like they were suffering. It must be a wonderful feeling to soar like that, to have everyone at your mercy."

Perhaps Carlo Perioni summarized Coppi's mastery best in his cartoon published in the Italian biweekly *Il Guérin Sportivo*. In it, his main character, Marino, suggested that Robic try a radical new approach the next time he had to chase Coppi up a mountain: Ride a motorcycle.

War of the *Miroirs*

The postwar period was a wonderful time for cycling fans, and the sports press was at its best. Two French weeklies were particularly focused on cycling, and they were bitter rivals. One was *Miroir-Sprint*, later replaced by the monthly *Miroir du Cyclisme*, directed from the start by Maurice Vidal (sadly, it folded in 1994). Billed as "the best-selling sports weekly," it was known especially for its cartoons by René Pellarin, known simply as Pellos. The other journal, directed by Gaston Bénac, was called *But et Club: Le Miroir des Sports*. Bénac, a prominent reporter for the more mainstream publications *France-Soir* and *Paris-Presse*, was also the creator of the famous Grand Prix des Nations time trial, held annually from 1932 to 2004. *But et Club*'s editor-in-chief was Félix Lévitan, who was also codirector of the Tour. He would later direct *Parisien Libéré*.

Miroir-Sprint and *But et Club* shared the same format and price (35 francs) and were surprisingly similar in other respects. In particular, the color of their pages alternated between tan and green, and they both dedicated ample space to the Tour, with superb photographs. Each review employed a former Tour champion to provide commentary—Pélissier in the case of *Miroir-Sprint* and Leducq in the case of *But et Club*. Many of their contributors eventually wound up writing for *L'Équipe*, notably Pierre Chany (formerly with *Miroir-Sprint*) and Marcel Hansenne (formerly with *But et Club*). Both reviews featured flamboyant prose and evocative headlines. "You can't stop a meteor" was how Bénac summed up Coppi's dominance that day.

Television Arrives

The Italian did indeed put on a beautiful show on the slopes of the Alpe—not only for the fans who were there to see it live but also for television viewers. For the first time, a cameraman filmed the actual race close-up, from the back of a motorcycle. Bernard Gensous, a television technician who began his career in 1941 and ended it as a director with TDF1, recalled, "That year, thanks to Pierre Sabbagh [an early French television reporter] and the birth of daily televised reports, we covered the entire Tour. Every evening, we sent the day's footage to Paris, where it was developed, edited, and broadcast with the commentary of Georges de Caunes."

That was quite a leap forward when one considers that only four years earlier, in 1948, television coverage of the Tour was limited to the finish at the Parc des Princes in Paris. Three television cameras covered the race, and the images were sent to a truck where all the reporters huddled. The images were then relayed via an observation balloon to the Eiffel Tower for public broadcasting.

Certainly the cameraman who followed the stage that day had no shortage of interesting images to capture. There was Coppi, alone and airborne, and Alfredo Binda, the Italian team's director. Binda stood in his car to assess Coppi's position before turning his attention to the beauty of the countryside. At the summit, where the crowd was finally able to cheer for Coppi, the champion was awarded a bonus of 1:40 (which he didn't need!). He then donned the yellow jersey, sponsored by the wool manu-facturer Sofil. Jean Masson, the French minister of sport, who had come to follow this key stage, extended his congratulations.

Behind Coppi emerged Robic, who had held up remarkably well under the circumstances, conceding "only" 1:20. As a collective reward for their respective efforts to conquer the mountain, Coppi and Robic split the 100,000-franc prize ($285 in 1952, or about $2,500 today) for combative-ness offered by the French sugar industry.

In third place, 3:22 behind Coppi, was the Belgian Constant "Stan" Ockers, who would finish second overall in this Tour. His technical direc-tor, Sylvère Maès, the winner of the 1936 and 1939 Tours, pushed him hard, going so far as to simulate with his hands the pedaling rhythm he demanded from his racer.

Coppi's faithful and astonishing *gregario*,[1] the eagle-nosed Andrea Carrea, finished sixth, 3:29 behind his leader. The evening before this stage, in Lausanne, Carrea had temporarily claimed the yellow jersey, al-most by accident. Like a good teammate, he had immersed himself in a breakaway to keep his leader in the race. But by the end of the day, his ad-vantageous position had catapulted him to number one in the overall stand-ings. Embarrassed, he had apologized profusely to the Campionissimo. "He didn't know what to say," Coppi recalled. Coppi quickly reassured his teammate. Half a century later, when Carrea spoke of this sublime moment from his home in Novi-Ligure, one could detect a certain pain in his voice: "He told me, 'Tomorrow, we will be the *domestiques* and you will be the champion.'"

Another standout that day was Jan Nolten (eighth), a 23-year-old who was competing in his first Tour de France. As it turned out, he would be the first in a long line of Dutchmen to distinguish himself in this stage, setting a precedent for Joop Zoetemelk, Hennie Kuiper, Steven Rooks, and Gert-Jan Theunisse. Nolten also won a prize for composure, awarded by the maker of an aperitif. Later in the Tour, he would prevail in Monaco, depriving Jean Dotto of a beautiful victory, and would also stand out on the slopes of Puy-de-Dôme, finishing second behind Coppi.

A subpar Géminiani (13th) temporarily fell behind the Spaniard Antonio Gélabert, the 4th-place finisher, in the best climber classification. Although there was as yet no distinctive polka-dot jersey to designate the leader in this discipline, the St. Raphaël Quinquina Trophy awaited the eventual winner in Paris—who turned out to be none other than Coppi.

As for Gino Bartali (12th), he fell twice in this Tour, losing any shot at the overall win. The first fall took place in Switzerland, near the French border, when he collided with the Luxembourger Bim Diederich. The second occurred when a car in front of him stalled and began to roll backward, knocking him off balance. As a consolation, he received the prize for least lucky rider, worth 20,000 francs ($57 in 1952, or about $550 today), offered by an insurance company.

Rounding out the pack was Jean Delahay. He finished last in 23rd place, having lost over half an hour over the final 14 agonizing kilometers (8.7 miles) of this crucial stage, which had begun that morning in Lausanne.

The Crazy Plan to Climb the Alpe

The pen manufacturer Bic, which awarded a prize based on overall performance in what it considered the toughest stages of the Tour, promptly added the Alpe to its list. Still, many observers did not look favorably upon its inclusion. In *L'Équipe*, Claude Tillet complained, "This day comes down to just 15 kilometers at the end, and it doesn't really reflect who the true 'top' finishers are." Jean Denis, writing in *Le Méridional*, offered even blunter criticism of Tour officials: "What a strange idea it was to schedule a rest day up there. Those people should have their heads examined."

By 1993, forty-one years later, the prevailing attitude had changed considerably. When the Alpe d'Huez stage was omitted from the Tour that year, cycling journalists howled in protest, as if some vital appendage of the Tour had been severed, rendering it meaningless. Still, the widespread misgivings about the inaugural ascent are understandable in retrospect. Never before had racers faced such a steep climb as the Fortress of L'Oisans. And this daunting prospect, after the accumulated fatigue of ten days, raised serious concerns—even among the racers themselves.

Breakaways Threatened with Frame Pumps

The day after the stage, Tour organizers summoned a number of riders to the Grand Hôtel and demanded an explanation for their bizarre behavior the previous morning. The accused included some of the most prominent competitors: Bim Diederich and Jean Goldschmidt of Luxembourg; Géminiani, who had been a great force in the Vosges and would shine again at Mont Aspin; Lucien Lazaridès; and Raoul Rémy, who would go on to win the stage at Aix-en-Provence. The charge: that they had brandished their bicycle pumps in the early part of the stage to prevent anyone from launching a breakaway. The consequences were potentially severe; at that time the organizers showed little tolerance for tomfoolery. The Swiss racer Carlo Lafranchi had just shelled out a fine of 200 francs after he had swiped a tall hat off a spectator and worn it while leaving Geneva.

If the peloton indeed conspired to save its energy for the climb, it succeeded. During the initial flat stretch from Lausanne to Bourg d'Oisans, the racers cruised along at a leisurely pace, falling a full 40 minutes behind official predictions. The 332 journalists and photographers who covered the route, meanwhile, spent much of their time admiring the countryside. The public, for its part, was free to devote its attention to the twenty-four vehicles that formed the publicity caravan, and the forty or so cars and trucks that were transporting race-related equipment. Even then, the Tour was an impressive spectacle, a colorful cortege moving through the French heartland.

But the loafing would not last. As some critics had predicted, the stage would indeed hinge on the final 15 kilometers (9.3 miles) leading to the summit of the Alpe. And that final stretch loomed as one of the most trying ordeals in a difficult Tour that captured magnificently the contours of France, from the cobblestones of the north to the canal paths of the south to the mountains of the Vosges, Alps, and Pyrénées. Included in the daunting series of climbs were the Ventoux, Peyresourde, Aspin, Tourmalet, and Aubisque, and even the Puy-de-Dôme.

"This edition scares me," confessed Maurice Vidal to the readers of *Miroir-Sprint* the day before the Alpe stage. "Even if these guys are truly giants of the road, they still have their physical limits." Vidal complained that the route was excessively severe and had imposed an insane pace ever since its start in Brest. "Every day," he asserted, "numerous racers finish the stage demoralized, declaring that they have reached the limits of human endurance. Whether or not he is victorious, Coppi's face is so worn that one must wonder, despite all his heroic efforts, if even he will reach a breaking point."

As if the steep climbs and blistering pace weren't enough, the weather was taking its toll as well. This superhuman Tour began on the June solstice in sweltering heat. It was so hot, in fact, that road tar stuck to tires. The riders gulped down bottles of water—one fellow from Bordeaux reportedly drank forty in a single day! Others doused their faces and necks with beer and lemonade from glass bottles. The riders could barely eat in the stifling heat. According to Chany, the temperature "subjected the caravan to extreme devastation."

Pellos, the cartoonist for *Miroir-Sprint*, depicted the brutal conditions in a memorable cartoon titled "The New Enemy of the Racers." It showed the sun god Phoebus transformed into a devil as he mercilessly cast his rays onto the backs of the wilting riders. Meanwhile, the peloton's traditional foes, fatigue and bad luck—personified respectively by the "hammer man" and the "witch with green teeth"—looked on incredulously.

And the heat continued. As the Tour unfolded, newspapers carried dramatic headlines: "40 degrees Celsius in Italy. 18 dead. Heat wave invades all of Europe." And to think that the organizers had gone out of their way to design an excruciating course! Their intention was to spark a battle among the top contenders, but as it turned out, many were missing out on the fun. Absent from the start were Louison Bobet, who would win the next three Tours; Hugo Koblet, the previous winner, who suffered from back pain; and Ferdi Kübler, the hero of the 1950 Tour. The Tour's torrid pace soon claimed more casualties. Rik van Steenbergen, the first in this race to wear the yellow jersey, suffered a mechanical breakdown and then sunstroke on the road to Metz. More dropouts followed in subsequent stages, notably Robert Chapatte, who suffered a throat infection and would therefore never tackle the Alpe as a racer, and Louis Caput, Poulidor's future *directeur sportif*, who injured his left arm.

The contest was increasingly shaping up as a duel between France and Italy, for it was the golden age of national and regional teams. The French favorites, from the national team coached by Marcel Bidot (who had taken over from his brother Jean), were Géminiani (2nd in 1951) and Robic (27th in 1951). The Italian favorites, coached by Alfredo Binda, were Coppi (who had been ailing since the death of his brother the previous year), Gino Bartali (4th in 1951), and Fiorenzo Magni (7th in 1951).

The Campionissimo, despite the high expectations, was barely in fourth place when the Alpe stage began in Lausanne, 5:04 behind team-mate Carrea, the surprise leader. Yet when the stage ended on the summit, it was Coppi who wore yellow, now ahead of Carrea in the overall standings by 5 seconds, Magni (in third) by 1:50, and Lauredi (in fourth) by 5:01. Alpe d'Huez had allowed Coppi to make up his entire deficit.

Usually modest and reserved, a beaming Campionissimo made no effort this time to conceal his pride. "I don't really understand why we, the climbers, were not attacked more violently before Bourg d'Oisans," he mused. "No one approached me asking for permission to get a head start. I guess they could see from my face that I wasn't about to let anyone get ahead of me." Then Coppi explained his winning strategy. "I had promised myself that I would not be the first to deliver a deadly blow; rather, I would wait for the attackers. That would give me a triple advantage. First, I would not have to break my rhythm. Second, I could see who my top rivals were that day. Finally, I could demoralize them by jumping on their wheels, if possible."

When the Tour resumed with a stage to Sestrières, Coppi delivered an impressive encore. He would go on to dominate the 1952 Tour. Well before the end of this epic race, the organizers decided to classify the Italian as untouchable, "beyond category." They then increased the prize for second place, with the runner-up, Ockers, ultimately collecting almost as much as the winner.

Coppi Prefers Room 28

When Robic crossed the finish line of the Alpe stage, falling to 10th place in the overall standings, he was eager to call it a day and get to his hotel room. Of all the racers staying at the Christina, including teams France and Italy, he was the first to reach the front desk. Behind it was Rajon's good friend Marchusio, who had agreed to fill in while regular staff assisted race officials. Robic was still wearing his sweaty Colomb jersey, with his shorts hiked halfway up his thighs and his spare tire dangling from his neck. With his tired face, he looked like someone who had just given his all in a losing battle. He nevertheless summoned up sufficient strength to ask for his room key in a firm voice. Marchusio, as it happened, knew nothing about bike racing, nor could he recognize any of the sport's stars. He eyed Robic with thinly veiled disdain, as if the grubby individual before him were some hapless amateur out for a Sunday spin.

"And you are, sir?" Marchusio responded politely but firmly.

"What?" barked a stunned Robic. "You mean you don't recognize me? Why, I'm Robic of course."

Unfazed, Marchusio opened the large reservation book and took his time looking for Robic's name. "Ah . . . here it is," responded Marchusio at last. "Robic, room 6."

Robic grabbed the key and stormed off to his room, grumbling all the way.

A few minutes later, another tired racer made his way to the front desk. "I would like room 28," intoned a calm voice. It was Coppi. When Binda had visited the Christina in preparation for this event, he had asked Rajon to reserve that room for his star. Curiously, it was far from being one of Rajon's best rooms, all of which featured a bath, balcony, and stunning view of the mountains. It was a small room on the third floor facing the back of the building, with no elevator access.

"It was the least requested room in the entire hotel," Rajon remembered. "But Fausto wanted peace and quiet, not frills, especially since he had the next day off to rest. So he positioned himself as far away from his fans as possible, so as not to hear their shouts. He was happy to give up his view in return for greater privacy, and no doubt he hoped his relative inaccessibility would stem the steady stream of visitors."

A Walk around Lake Besson

The next day, before the stage to Sestrières via the formidable Galibier, the racers had a chance to relax. The Campionissimo, true to form, spent most of the morning in bed resting his legs, receiving an occasional visitor. At one point Aldo Zambrini, the owner of Bianchi, dropped by, and he

THE TOUR IS WON ON THE ALPE

persuaded his star to join him for a drive to Lake Besson along a dirt road. A few teammates went along as well, including the faithful Carrea, who looked like a tourist with his shorts and checked shirt. Coppi wore a polo shirt and slacks and held a cap in one hand, as if ready to shield his head from the sun. Through his dark glasses, he admired the surrounding snow-capped mountains and the crystal-clear water that sparkled under the sun like the yellow jersey he had worn the evening before—an exploit that had earned him, once again, a pile of congratulatory letters and telegrams.

Miroir-Sprint produced a marvelous post-stage edition with a host of unusual snapshots capturing the scene at the Alpe. Team doctors, far from resting, were busy tending to tired legs. One photo depicted Robic looking rather worried as his wife served him breakfast. The Bordeau sisters did their best to enliven the atmosphere for team France. Pierre Molineris, a local boy from Voiron, stretched his legs in a tub of tepid water as his wife and young son lovingly looked on. Jean Dotto, who was driving around town in his Citroën, caused a sensation when he stopped at the local cobbler to get new metal plates nailed to the soles of his cycling shoes.

But et Club offered much the same fare, including photos of Coppi and Bartali as they signed post-Tour contracts under the watchful gaze of general manager André Mouton. There was also a portrait of Géminiani and Lucien Lazaridès seated in an official Tour vehicle, taking in some accordion music.

The ambience at the Christina that evening was likewise relaxed as both the Italians and the French tried to recover from their recent ordeal and prepare for the next. Marchusio, a gifted professional magician, dutifully entertained the French team in the hotel dining room. When the Italians, led by Bartali, descended for their meal, they too were amused by Marchusio's wizardry—especially Bartali. After all, Gino "Il Pio," a devout Catholic, was a firm believer in miracles.

CHAPTER THREE

1976

How Alpe d'Huez
Became "Dutch Mountain"

ONE OCTOBER NIGHT IN 1975, GEORGES RAJON WAS WATCHING television in the living room of his chalet on the Alpe, as he always did in the evening. Suddenly the phone rang. He picked up the receiver and immediately recognized the voice of his friend Roger-Louis Lachat, a cycling enthusiast and journalist with *Dauphiné Libéré*.

"Hello, Georges? Guess who I'm having dinner with right now?"

"I don't know, who?" replied Rajon.

"Félix Lévitan, the codirector of the Tour."

In fact, the two were dining at La Poularde, a restaurant in Grenoble, and discussing the route of the 1976 Tour. Lévitan had just revealed to Lachat that the anticipated stage to Grenoble had fallen through and that he needed to find an alternative mountaintop finish.

"Go to Alpe d'Huez!" Lachat had blurted without a moment's hesitation. He was from that region and knew something of the Tour, having followed twenty-five to date.

"You think?" the intrigued Lévitan had asked, a sparkle of hope in his eyes.

The proposition stunned Rajon, the man who had brought the Tour to Alpe d'Huez in 1952. He lowered the volume of his television and raised the only concern that kept him from immediately saying yes: "How much will it cost us?"

"About 100,000 francs," replied Lachat (approximately $21,000 in 1976, or $76,000 in today's dollars).

Rajon mulled it over. *The town should pay the Tour fee this time around,* Rajon thought. *But even if it won't, I'll come up with the money through the sports club I direct. We can't let an opportunity like this just slip away.* With a firm voice, he said, "All right, let's do it." They set up a meeting in Cannes, where Lévitan lived, to work out the details. As soon as he hung up, Rajon hustled over to see his friend Émile Bory, the deputy mayor and owner of the Hôtel des Bruyères, to enlist the town's support.

"Please call the mayor right away and tell him I said the city should invest in this," Rajon said. "If he refuses, I'll try to get my club to underwrite it."

At that time, Rajon was not on particularly good terms with the mayor, Monsieur Mauchamps, a dentist from Grenoble. Nonetheless, he hoped that his vow to find alternative funding if necessary would compel the mayor to accept the Tour's proposal.

The next morning at about nine o'clock, Bory knocked on Rajon's door to bring him the welcome news: The mayor had approved the project. At last a second finish at Alpe d'Huez was in the works.

The Flight of the Four Musketeers

Three months later, Lévitan called Rajon to arrange their rendezvous in Cannes. They decided to meet at a villa that belonged to the father of Rajon's close friend and then sports club president Alain Aro, who would become mayor of L'Alpe d'Huez two years later.

The day of the meeting, Rajon headed to the local airport. He boarded a small plane with the resort's resident navigator, "the pilot of the glaciers," Henri Giraud, at the controls. The other passengers were Lachat, the journalist, and Bernard Gauthier, winner of four editions of Bordeaux-Paris, who had been brought on board as technical adviser.

It was Gauthier who in 1952 had described Alpe d'Huez in detail for Fausto Coppi, who had been trying to get information about the steepness of the grade. The Campionissimo was later quoted in the weekly publication *But et Club: Le Miroir des Sports* as saying, "I had no idea what to expect at first. I consulted a number of French riders, but Gauthier was the only one who professed any familiarity with this new 'giant' of the Tour. He recommended a very small gear, which I found reassuring; if Alpe d'Huez called for such a small gear ratio, my chances were pretty good. I looked forward to what promised to be a real confrontation, and the night before the stage, in Lausanne, felt like the night before a battle."

Twenty-four years after that first ascent, plans for a second one were laid under the sun of the Riviera and the pines of the backcountry. The stage would start at Divonne and establish Alpe d'Huez once and for all as the strategic high ground of the Tour. Credit goes to Lachat—one of Jacques Goddet's favorite cycling journalists[1]—and to Rajon, the man who had helped bring the Tour to the Alpe in the first place.

Over the years, that fortuitous pairing would establish a rich tradition. Little wonder that the organizers of the 2003 Tour—the centennial edition—made sure that, along with finishes in cities and towns that had been part of the very first edition, Alpe d'Huez figured prominently in the program. They even created an immense color-coded parking lot just before the plateau of the resort and charged 5 francs per vehicle. But they woefully underestimated the stage's appeal. A huge traffic jam, stretching from Grenoble to the summit, impeded the race itself. "It was a bad idea in retrospect," conceded Rajon, and the makeshift parking lot has never made another appearance.

The 1976 Tour promised to be the big rematch between Eddy Merckx and Bernard Thévenet. July 13 of the previous year had proved a most unlucky day for the great Belgian, who was in yellow at the time (and for the last time, it would turn out, in his incomparable career). The Cannibal made a huge effort to pull away from the pack and claim a record sixth Tour. But Thévenet ultimately caught and passed him on the ascent to Pra-Loup, some 217 kilometers (130 miles) north of Nice.

Perhaps you remember that day? I do—I was there. I was twenty years old at the time and will always cherish the memory. It was one of those thrilling moments that make you happy to be alive. Right before my eyes, Merckx dropped Thévenet just a few meters before the summit of Col d'Allos, the last obstacle before the final climb to Pra-Loup. The Cannibal hurtled down the descent at breakneck speed while we listened to reports of his increasing lead over Nanar, our ears glued to transistor radios.[2] Unbelievable! Eddy was sailing toward another Tour victory.

Then all hell broke loose.

The Belgian bonked—which was later attributed to side effects from a medication he had taken the day before—signaling the demise of his lead.

The ascent toward the summit of Pra-Loup suddenly became a great injustice, a shattered dream, and a living hell. Merckx ultimately slipped to fifth place overall, nearly 2 minutes behind Thévenet, the winner.

Now the 1976 Tour, which would start from Saint-Jean-de-Mont, offered Merckx another shot. Oddly enough, the considerable pre-race hype included practically no mention of the ninth stage from Divonne-les-Bains to Alpe d'Huez, except that it would cap off nine days of flat riding and one rest day. The ascent of '52 had been long forgotten. Instead, this would be the year when the famous resort would explode onto the scene.[3]

Merckx Forfeits

It was no secret that Tour organizers had tailored the 1976 route to highlight the anticipated showdown between Merckx and Thévenet. They included five mountaintop finishes and twenty-four major climbs—first in the Alps and then in the Pyrénées—without a single transitional stage, save for one rest day. You could smell the gunpowder before the first shot was even fired.

But alas, the great duel was not to be. Merckx was in the midst of a troubled season. Early on, he had won Milan–San Remo, joyfully punching his fist into the air as he crossed the finish line to collect his seventh title, eclipsing the record of Costante Girardengo. As it turned out, however, that would be his last major victory. The great Belgian was already facing the beginning of the end. He would suffer through a painful Giro after falling victim to a bad saddle sore and would then retreat to recuperate. Merckx saw the 1976 Tour start without him.

Thévenet was also having a turbulent year, missing the races he had targeted early in the season due to injury. He eventually returned to competition and managed to beat out Vicente Lopez-Carril for first place in the Dauphiné Libéré, but at the Tour he no longer appeared to be a top contender. The highly anticipated Tour of Revenge was now wide open.

Once the race got under way, the first to wear yellow was the somewhat aging thoroughbred Freddy Maertens (Velda-Flandria). Under the able supervision of Guillaume Driessens, who had coached Coppi, Rik van Looy, and Merckx himself, Maertens had already won an impressive six stages at Paris-Nice that season and would pull off an even more amazing performance at the Tour. He would wear the yellow jersey for eight days and win an unprecedented eight stages before falling to a still respectable eighth place. Most impressively, he would keep the green jersey until the very end. As if to prove that his strong Tour showing was no fluke, he donned the rainbow jersey later that year in Ostuni, Italy, and won thirteen out of twenty-one stages the following year at the Vuelta.

A Tour for Old-Timers

Maertens was certainly not the only veteran to distinguish himself at the 73rd Tour, a race plagued by an extraordinary heat wave. The top two finishers, Lucien van Impe and Joop Zoetemelk, were both pushing 30. Forty-year-old Raymond Poulidor, making his 14th and final appearance, finished a surprisingly strong third. Wearing the striped jersey of the insurance company Gan (and cosponsors Mercier-Hutchinson), he had earned the nickname "the Calm One" well before François Mitterrand claimed to be a "calm force" in the French presidential election of 1981.

Ferdinand Bracke (Lejeune-BP), who had set an hour record in Rome eleven years earlier (averaging an impressive 48.093 kilometers [28.798 miles] per hour), won the 17th stage from Fleurance to Auch. Wladimiro Panizza (Scic-Fiat), the veteran sprinter, dominated at Pau. Raymond Delisle (Peugeot), the ex-champion of France, arrived first at Pyrénées 2000 and, for the first time in twelve Tours, wore the yellow jersey. He had signaled his color preference a few weeks earlier at the Dauphiné Libéré, where he had donned that race's yellow jersey following the Salève stage.

Other notable performers over 30 were Jean-Pierre Genet, Poulidor's faithful lieutenant; Luis Ocaña (Super Ser), who was admittedly a far cry from the conquistador of 1973; Herman van Springel (Flandria), second in the 1968 Tour and winner of the green jersey in 1973; and Domingo Perrurena, the champion of Spain (Kas). Also competing was a youngster of 27, Roger Legeay (Lejeune-BP), who finished 58th at Alpe d'Huez and 35th overall. Years later, he would serve as *directeur sportif* to Greg LeMond, the first American to win the Tour.

Maertens Loses the Jersey

When the peloton stopped at Divonne for a rest day prior to the first alpine stage, finishing at L'Alpe d'Huez, Maertens was still in yellow. Even when the race resumed and the peloton climbed the fearful Luitel under a scorching sun, Maertens was holding on to his slim lead.

But then came the climb up the Alpe. Maertens would finish a distant 22nd that day, almost 5 minutes behind the winner, Zoetemelk. In just 14 kilometers (8.7 miles), to the chagrin of his many fans, the plucky Belgian not only relinquished his handsome jersey but also lost any hope of winning the Tour. Pierre Chany, writing in *L'Équipe*, aptly summed up the situation: "A shepherd lost amidst the flock."

At the first turns up the Alpe, Delisle (Peugeot) attacked in order to set up his captain, Thévenet, for an offensive. But in a scene eerily reminiscent of the inaugural running in 1952, when Coppi had caught and dropped Robic, Van Impe immediately jumped on Delisle's wheel, then came around him to take the lead, imposing his own blistering pace. The little Belgian was no slouch on the hills; his climbing prowess had already earned him three stages, and he would win three more by the time the race reached Paris. Close behind these two were Pollentier (Flandria), with his choppy pedaling style; Thévenet; and Zoetemelk.

But Thévenet, trying to hold that blistering pace to the summit, soon cracked under the intense pressure. This was not to be his day. Delisle and Pollentier fell behind as well, and the stage turned into a duel between a surging Van Impe, known for his explosive attacks and whose supple cadence evoked the great Charly Gaul, and Zoetemelk. Just before the first switchbacks, the Dutchman, with the help of his *directeur sportif*, Louis Caput, had changed to a lighter bike equipped with 42/53 chainrings and a 13-23, 6-speed cogset.

Van Impe rode with his hands on the brake hoods as he alternated between sitting and pedaling out of the saddle. Occasionally the Belgian cast a furtive glance at Zoetemelk to assess how his adversary was holding up. The Dutchman, hunched over his bike, seemed to push as hard with his arms as he did with his legs. More often than not, the two found themselves side by side while the frenzied crowd yelled its encouragement, caught up in the magic of Alpe d'Huez.

Poulidor's Sacrifice

Farther back, his chin sinking below his handlebars, his cadence irregular, Thévenet did the lion's share of the work in pursuit of the two fugitives. But

Nanar steadily lost ground. Ten kilometers (6.2 miles) from the summit, he had fallen a minute off pace. By the 7-kilometer (4.3-mile) banner, the gap had widened to 1:25, and by the finish line it totaled 1:48. Maertens, meanwhile, fell even farther behind, accompanied by his Siamese twin, Michel Pollentier. Kuiper, wearing the jersey of world champion, latched on to the twosome, while Ocaña languished.

With 7 kilometers to go, Zoetemelk, by order of his *directeur sportif*, refused to alternate pulls with Van Impe, who was closing in on a Tour victory with every turn of the pedals. Meanwhile, far behind, Poulidor rested his hands on the top of his handlebars as he cruised along beside Thévenet like a recreational cyclist.

Poupou would receive high praise the next day from the press for not challenging his teammate Zoetemelk. Still, many regretted that the French veteran had passed up this golden opportunity, the last of his career, to (finally) wear the yellow jersey, the emblematic garment that would always elude him. In fact, Poulidor began the day in fifth place overall behind Maertens, Pollentier, Kuiper, and Danguillaume—who would all languish on the mountain—and led Van Impe by 23 seconds and Zoetemelk by 34.

Riding next to Poupou, Nanar would roar again, finding a second wind to limit his losses over the second half of the climb. The winner of the previous Tour was now virtually on his own, battling against all the others, who let him do most of the work. Pushing himself to the limit, the courageous Thévenet pulled away on his own, leaving behind his companions in misfortune, who were unable to follow this locomotive from hell. They included Delisle; Lopez-Carril (Kas-Campagnolo), the Spaniard who was actually a renowned climber; Martin (Gitane); and the Italians Bergamo, Battaglin (Jollycéramica), and Bellini (Brooklyn), who wore the polka-dot jersey of best climber.

Meanwhile, 1,860 meters (6,102 feet) above sea level, Zoetemelk took the stage in a final sprint (a feat he would repeat in 1979) ahead of Van Impe, who would never win on the Alpe, despite his six titles as the Tour's best overall climber.

Van Impe, who had made the Tour his primary objective, pulled on his first yellow jersey on the summit of Alpe d'Huez. Ironically, he would lose the Tour the following year on the same inclines that had proven so decisive this time around. On the way to Paris, he would give his fans an exceptional performance on the slopes of Plat d'Adet (Saint-Lary Soulan), eclipsing Zoetemelk by more than 3 minutes; Poulidor by more than 11; and the ailing Thévenet, who would drop out the next day, by 15.

Still, the memorable day on the Alpe belonged to Zoetemelk. In winning this stage, the Dutchman definitively erased the bad memories of 1974, when he had fallen at Valras-plage during the Midi-Libre and bruised his temporal bone, triggering, for lack of proper care, a bout of meningitis. The next day, at the top of Montgenèvre, he would again prevail.

Although he failed to win the Tour that year, Zoetemelk had come alive on the Alpe, and the legend of "Dutch Mountain" was born. The reign of the House of Orange had begun.

CHAPTER FOUR

1977

Thévenet Can't Climb the Stairs

THE TOUR DE FRANCE ALMOST ALWAYS INSPIRES GREAT RIVALRIES. The 1977 edition, like the one before, promised early on to boil down to a race involving Eddy Merckx. The previous winter, the Cannibal had suffered a spell of mononucleosis and signed with a new team, Fiat, whose director was Raphaël Géminiani, the brainy competitor who had ridden in service to Fausto Coppi and Louison Bobet, masterminding their many victories. Merckx had not won anything since taking Milan–San Remo in March the previous year; he was eager to get back to his winning ways in this Tour and to atone for his disappointing no-show the year before. This time his anticipated rival was not Bernard Thévenet but a fellow Belgian and the reigning world champion, Freddy Maertens.

Alas, once again an anticipated showdown failed to materialize due to an unexpected withdrawal. But this time it was not Merckx who disappointed—it was Maertens who made a stunning announcement in February, when the details of the Giro were revealed in Milan: He would not compete in the upcoming Tour. Surprisingly, health issues had nothing to do with his decision. It was rather a question of team Flandria's poor planning (or perhaps greed). A few weeks before, Guillaume Driessens, Maertens's *directeur sportif*, had signed a contract with the Spaniards guaranteeing the star's participation in the Vuelta. Meanwhile, one of the team owners had signed a similar deal committing the Belgian to the Giro.

Maertens was being asked to compete in the Vuelta a España, the Giro d'Italia, and the Tour de France, all in the same year! It was suicide. Bound by contract to the other two races, he bowed out of La Grande Boucle.[1]

Tour aficionados were devastated. True, Maertens was no great climber. But he was fast, and he was the reigning world champion; the prospect of the two Belgian thoroughbreds battling it out over the flat portions of the route was the stuff of high drama. As was to be expected, when the contest finally got under way without Maertens, it was something of a Tour of Monotony. That is, until the race reached Alpe d'Huez.

Handsome Didi in Yellow

The 1977 Tour started in Fleurance, with a counterclockwise route calculated to deliver the racers to the foothills of the Pyrénées as early as the second stage—an order not exactly to their liking.

Dietrich Thurau, a 22-year-old German with Ti-Raleigh, won the prologue and took control the next day in the Pyrénées, conquering the Aspin, the Tourmalet, and the Aubisque peaks in succession. At the time trial in Bordeaux, Didi dominated the competition once again, then kept the yellow jersey for more than two weeks. The young leader basked in the glory and endeared himself to all of France, especially the young girls. But despite his glitter, he turned out to be a mere bottle rocket in the sport's long history. Like that of many cycling prodigies, his flame burned early and brightly, only to flicker and fade prematurely.

A fate equally swift and cruel awaited the ailing Merckx in the Alps. The 32-year-old, who had been forced to abandon Paris-Nice after an acute sinus infection, kept a low profile in the early part of the Tour. Alpe d'Huez promised to be brutal, deadly, and pitiless. The Cannibal would nonetheless launch one last heroic effort.

Meanwhile, Tour followers sat bored in their cars. Fourteen stages had produced only one serious attack. Jacques Goddet, the Tour director, tried to stir things up with an editorial that appeared in *L'Équipe* after the Freiburg stage, just before the Alps. Under the headline "A Plea for a New Tour," the successor to founding father Henri Desgrange entertained ways to enliven the program. He suggested new attractions, like a 100-kilometer (62-mile) team time trial and a motorcycle-paced event, along with increased incentives, such as a greatly enhanced prize for "competitiveness," and stiffer penalties, such as annulling all stage-specific prizes if the average speed fell below a set minimum.

The debate over the Tour format erupted during a season that had already been rocked by doping scandals. Thévenet had tested positive at Paris-Nice, and the Belgian cycling federation had nailed numerous racers in a series of controls, including some of the biggest names in the sport: Merckx (in Flèche-Wallonne), Maertens (in the Tour of Flanders, Flèche-Wallonne, and the Tour of Belgium), Michel Pollentier (in the Tour of Belgium), Willy Tierlinck (in Flèche-Wallonne), and Walter Planckaert (in the Tour of Flanders).

Professor Patrick de Backere of Ghent University, a renowned Belgian specialist, had overseen the tests, detecting ample traces of Stimul, an amphetamine-based cocktail. A photograph of the busted racers appeared in the first tabloid edition of *Miroir du Cyclisme*, along with the caption "They all stand accused—and are fed up."

Too Many Mountaintop Finishes?

Prior to the Tour, on the eve of the Giro in Milan, Merckx had called the racers to an impromptu meeting in which they demanded that the list of banned substances be revised to distinguish medicines that cause little or no harm from those that are truly dangerous. The former were to be tolerated and the latter "rigorously forbidden." This was a far cry from the Festina scandal that would erupt in 1998, but events like these already illustrated the overriding need to conduct antidoping campaigns differently.

Those events were still fresh in everyone's mind and weighed heavily on the Tour. The syringe cast its long shadow over the peloton. Marc Jeuniau, a Belgian journalist and Merckx's longtime confidant, called for fewer mountaintop finishes in order to decrease the racers' incentive to use drugs. "Whatever happened to all those promises to humanize the Tour?" he fumed in the pages of *Miroir*. "Instead, the organizers have increased the number of mountaintop finishes. They've shamelessly eliminated the transitional stages and have even hauled the racers from the end of the Alps straight to the foothills of the Pyrénées.[2] It is difficult, even inconceivable, to be a professional cyclist in 1977 and not resort to taking stimulants."

Jeuniau's protest did not fall on deaf ears. The Tour's own head doctor, Philippe Miserez, made waves when he conceded, "Never before have drugs posed as great a threat to the health of the racers." In this climate of suspicion, a rumor began to circulate that Joop Zoetemelk, the winner at the summit of Avoriaz, had tested positive.

Now the brutal Alpe d'Huez loomed. It is perhaps the most breathtaking of all the mountains ever to figure in the Tour—a great tool of selection when the Tour hangs in the balance.

The previous day, at Chamonix, Thévenet had vaulted into first place overall, leading Thurau by 11 seconds; Van Impe by 33 seconds; Kuiper by 49 seconds; and Zoetemelk, the winner of the previous Alpe d'Huez stage, by 1:13. Merckx, who was about to climb the formidable mountain for the first and last time, trailed by over 3 minutes.

The fearsome summits of the Madeleine and then the interminable Glandon, a 25-kilometer (15-mile) haul, would serve as warm-up exercises before the final assault on the Alpe. From the first switchbacks of the Col de la Madeleine, Merckx showed the effects of food poisoning. He had consumed bad celery root (of all things) on his rest day in Freiburg some days before and had been unable to undergo proper treatment, as the most effective medications were—naturally—on the list of forbidden substances. Once again, the specter of doping hovered over the peloton like an eagle over its prey. Stuck at the back of the pack, the Belgian desperately held on.

Merckx's Miraculous Climb

As Merckx struggled up the Glandon, his suffering was so apparent that most observers expected him to quit at any moment. His eyes were haggard, his head slightly tilted, his face contorted, and his mouth agape. He held out his hand for a water bottle as he sat glued to his saddle, laboring up the middle of the road, crying but unrelenting. An adoring crowd cheered on its hero, still celebrating the greatest athlete of the age. But the Cannibal had been tamed, falling behind by over 10 minutes. The champion had become human.

That evening, Merckx changed his bicycle, consulted his doctor, and dug deep within himself to find the will to stave off defeat, like a sick man determined to defy death. Still, everyone sensed that the champion's defeat was at hand on the Tour's steamy slopes. It was a moment that epitomized both the grandeur and the mortality of those kings of the road: worshipped by the crowds, rejected by the gods.

Those following the Tour expected the worst for Merckx, sharing intimately in his agony as he advanced toward the cauldron of the Alpe. He seemed to stick to the mountainside like gravel to a tire. He was spilling his guts onto the road for all to see.

In Abel Michea's book *Alors Gem Racconte*, Géminiani, the Big Gun, would later shed light on Merckx's plight: "At Chamoix [the eve of the Alpe stage], an exhausted Merckx was randomly selected for a drug test. He was unable to urinate, so he was forced to drink two liters of mineral water. But that was not the ideal way to treat his dysentery. As a result he was up half the night in his hotel room."

Yet a miracle would resuscitate Merckx. As he inched toward the summit of the Alpe, he suddenly regained his smooth pedal stroke and finished strong. At the summit, a rejuvenated Merckx gushed with pride, "I'm the one who climbed Alpe d'Huez the fastest." Goddet agreed. In his recap of the stage, published the next day in *L'Équipe*, the journalist wrote, "Merckx was the fastest of all the finishers. The Tour doctor, who followed him for some time, even concluded that Merckx could have benefited from one more mountain." The proud Cannibal nonetheless finished the stage a distant 20th, 13:51 off the pace.

This legendary stage had heated up earlier in the day on the climb over the Glandon. Seven kilometers (4.2 miles) from the summit, Lucien van Impe (Lejeune-BP), wearing the polka-dot jersey, went on the offensive. He dropped Thévenet (Peugeot), who was just ahead of Kuiper (Ti-Raleigh), Zoetemelk (Miko Mercier), and Francisco Galdos (Kas). Meanwhile, the once mighty Thurau, who was now wearing the white jersey of best young rider, was languishing and about to self-destruct.

Van Impe, the little man from Flanders, launched a long breakaway à la Merckx and would surprise observers, who were convinced he would crack on the flat 15-kilometer (9-mile) run-up to the foot of the Alpe. Not at all! Van Impe reached the summit of the Glandon with a 1:25 lead over his nearest rival, Thévenet, whose yellow jersey was virtually being peeled off his back at that moment.

During the long 19-kilometer (11.4-mile) descent, with some of the roads in disrepair, Van Impe pushed his lead to 2 minutes. The fans could only marvel at his audacity. He was having a superb day and was skillfully constructing his second straight Tour victory—or so everyone thought. He reached the foot of Alpe d'Huez with a 2:45 advantage and was about to enter terrain much to his liking. That was when everything turned upside down again.

As Van Impe surged ahead, Thévenet was the only one chasing, with Kuiper and Zoetemelk on his wheel. Kuiper used the pretext that he had to stay behind to look after Thurau, his faltering teammate. The resentful Zoetemelk had not forgotten how, after his fall in Iffendic in the Lorient-Rennes stage, Thévenet and the other leaders had immediately gone on the attack to capitalize on his misfortune.

"Those two weren't working," Thévenet recalled, "and I wasn't feeling very good. Whenever I slowed down, they slowed down. Then I said to myself, 'If Van Impe can stay out there all alone on the flat, then so can I. And since these two want to bury me, I'm going all out on my own.'"

Thévenet's Reply

From the first turns at Huez, the crammed spectators, leaning into the road to get a better view of the oncoming battle and yielding to Van Impe only at the last minute, realized that the little Belgian was now paying the price for his efforts.

In the valley, Van Impe had summoned all his strength in an attempt to pull off this grand exploit. In doing so, he had expended much of his energy. The gifted climber tried to find his rhythm. His once smooth pedaling motion had become choppy and his breathing labored. It was now a time trial between him and the chasers.

Kuiper, who had sucked Thévenet's wheel since the summit of the Glandon, now launched an offensive of his own, followed by Zoetemelk. Thévenet hesitated for a moment and fell behind his two antagonists. Courageous and stubborn, he fixed them in his sights, as if to latch on to their shadows and limit the gap to 50 meters.

But there's no place to hide on Alpe d'Huez.

Thévenet continued at his own pace, applying powerful strokes as if drawing strength from his yellow jersey. He cut the distance with every pedal stroke and eventually caught the two attackers, who promptly got back on his wheel. Once again, Thévenet took off in relentless pursuit of

Van Impe, whose lead had shrunk to 1:20 with 5 kilometers left before the finish.

At that moment, Kuiper launched another offensive and set off like a rocket in search of a stage. Zoetemelk faltered. Thévenet showed signs of weariness but still managed to drop the Dutchman, who had won the Alpe stage the year before. Only Van Impe and Kuiper were now ahead.

"The fans kept me informed about my position in the overall standings," recounted Thévenet, "and they let me know I was steadily losing time to Kuiper. Some of them were mocking me, I could tell. In that surreal moment, I could guess what they were saying and their disposition by the tone of their voices. I knew some were yelling, 'Up yours!' and I could see their obscene gestures. In moments like that you either go on automatic pilot or you fall."

Up ahead, a trailing car, trying to avoid the sprawling crowd that was choking off the road, accidentally clipped Van Impe's rear wheel, flinging the exhausted Belgian to the wayside. He howled in anger and pain, his feet held captive by his toe clips. He managed to get up and start again but soon had to stop when he realized that his rear wheel was damaged. Fuming, he waited on the side of the road for his support vehicle, his right arm extended. But help was slow in coming. His team car was boxed in at the rear of the procession. It seemed like a flashback to the early days of the Tour.

Van Impe watched helplessly as Kuiper zoomed past like a missile. Then came the magnificent, courageous Thévenet, making a supreme effort, slumped over his machine, his nose glued to the handlebar stem.

"When I passed Van Impe," Thévenet recalled, "he was very gracious and yelled out, 'Keep going, it's not far.' At the red pennant signaling the last kilometer, Daniel Pautrat, a television reporter, blurted out, 'If you continue at that pace you'll keep the yellow jersey by a second.' I rode the last kilometer as if my life depended on it. I knew that the fans were pulling for me, and I felt that I had no right to let them down by losing the yellow jersey."

In that final kilometer, another time trial battle for the yellow jersey ensued between the swift Kuiper and the gritty Thévenet. In the end, Kuiper took the stage by 41 seconds. But Thévenet, who finished his sprint in an outrageously tall 54x17 gear, managed to hang on to the jersey by the slimmest of margins. He would wear it into Paris as well, winning his second Tour in three years. "The greatest joy of my career," Thévenet would later confide, "was at Alpe d'Huez in 1977, when I kept my yellow jersey by 8 seconds. I could have died a happy man on my bicycle that day. I gave it everything I had."

At the foot of the climb, Van Impe had been leading the Tour. Over the Alpe's twenty-one switchbacks, he lost his shot at victory for good.

Thirty Riders Eliminated

At the final turn, an exhausted Zoetemelk fell, as did an equally spent Thurau a short time later. Fortunately, both escaped serious injury. Then along came Merckx, and thousands of stupefied television viewers witnessed his dramatic resurrection. But that evening, Merckx was so psychologically spent that he wanted to abandon the race for good.

"It was painful just to look at him; he was a real wreck," wrote Rik Vanwalleghem.[3] "The next day, Jos Janssens, Merckx's masseuse, came to tell me that Eddy wanted to talk to me. It was extremely unusual for Merckx to seek out a journalist like that. 'Yesterday I told you certain things,' Merckx confided to me. 'That I was going to quit racing, that I had had enough. But now I've changed my mind. I was so sick yesterday that I didn't know what I was saying.'"

As for Thévenet, he had a tough time getting to his hotel room that evening. "You had to climb a staircase to access the Christina," he recalled.[4] "I took one look at it and said to my masseuse, 'Pierrot, I'll never make it up those stairs. I'm completely spent.' So he got out of the car and threw his arms around my upper torso as if he were congratulating me. Then he discreetly propped me up from under my shoulders and practically dragged me up the stairs to my room, which I shared with Michel Laurent.

"As usual, we hung our jerseys by the window," Thévenet continued. "When the fans outside saw my yellow jersey, they chanted my name to get me to come out. But I was already in bed, exhausted. I simply couldn't get up. I wasn't faking it; I really was knocked out. Even Laurent thought I was joking around. 'Go ahead, show yourself,' he urged. But it would have been impossible! I'm sure my fans were disappointed, but I was so exhausted that I didn't eat a thing that evening. I just stayed in bed the entire time."

Later on, in the middle of the night, he arose from bed wracked by hunger. "I woke up the masseuses," Thévenet recalled. "I had to eat something, but the kitchens were closed. All I had was bread to restore myself, and I ate as much of that as I could get my hands on. That was the most taxing stage of my entire career, and no one ever knew."

That year, the legend of Alpe d'Huez was permanently inscribed in gold letters on the temple of cycling lore. Thirty riders were eliminated on Alpe d'Huez when they finished outside the time limit. In the Pyrénées a few days before, thirty-five racers had already been threatened with expulsion for falling beyond the 40-minute cutoff, based on overall time, only to be reinstated. But this time the organizers showed no mercy and booted out the stragglers, including five from the Bianchi team alone, along with Thévenet's teammates Patrick Béon, Régis Délepine, and Georges Talbourdet.

Despite vigorous protests from the *directeurs sportifs*—the Bianchi team even threatened to boycott the Tour—the organizers held firm. Some believed they were determined to punish the peloton for its lethargic performance during the earlier flat stages—as if the climb up the Alpe weren't punishment enough.

CHAPTER FIVE

1978

Pollentier, or the Story of a Toad's Trickery

FOLLOWING HIS BITTERSWEET PERFORMANCE ON THE ALPE IN 1977, with the yellow jersey hopelessly out of reach, a defiant Eddy Merckx declared, "I wasn't beaten squarely. I was sick. I'll come back to the Tour next year to prove it." It was a burst of pride from an incomparable champion, and few doubted that he would make his presence felt in the 1978 edition.

Sadly, however, the Alpe would smile on him no more. On May 18, 1978, the 33-year-old veteran unexpectedly announced his retirement. It was a severe blow to his fans. The greatest cyclist of all time was quitting, and his shocking announcement set off wild rumors. There was talk— once again—that substance dependency was the real reason Merckx's doctors had forbidden the champion from racing again.

In his memoirs,[1] Jacques Goddet, longtime director of the Tour, wrote, "One couldn't help but notice that no sooner had yesterday's beautiful athlete stopped training and competing than his body became heavy and his face bloated. . . . I think he must have been the victim of imprudent counsel, that is, poor medical advice from people who considered themselves experts at prescribing medical products not forbidden by the federal lists, and supposedly without risk of side effects for the user."[2]

For his part, Merckx attributed his premature retirement to "serious health issues" that had developed during his long and fruitful career, notably a fractured vertebra suffered in a fall at Paris-Nice in 1972, a concussion and coma following a fall in Blois in 1969, and repeated infections suffered during his final years of competition. The Cannibal would nonetheless climb the Alpe that year—in an automobile. He accepted a position as technical assistant with the C&A team, working with Lucien van Impe, who was still racing.

With Merckx gone from the peloton (and also Raymond Poulidor, who bowed out after the Criterium of Wambrechis in December 1977), the Tour would welcome in 1978 a newcomer with the dark, moody air of a predator. His name was Bernard Hinault. After his exploits the previous year in Ghent-Wevelgem and Liège-Bastogne-Liège, which he had won handily, as well as his fresh victory in the Vuelta, he was widely expected to fill the void left by Merckx's departure.

The two previous years, following the advice of his friend Cyrille Guimard, with whom he would have a falling-out a few years later, Hinault had passed on La Grande Boucle. But now, at 24 and with a string of victories under his belt, he felt ready for this beautiful adventure. As if to signal that he was a serious contender, the Breton from Yffiniac had captured the red-white-and-blue jersey of champion of France just a few days before the start of the Tour's 75th-anniversary edition.

A 156-Kilometer Time Trial

As part of the Tour's birthday celebration, the organizers had the questionable idea of making the fourth stage a 156-kilometer (93-mile) team time trial from Evreux to Caen, just like in the good old days. Ti-Raleigh prevailed with Hennie Kuiper, Gerrie Knetemann, Klaus-Peter Thaler (who donned the yellow jersey), and Henk Lubberding. C&A, with Van Impe and Joseph Bruyère, finished second.

Kuiper thus built up a 1:20 advantage over Hinault and a 3-minute lead over Bernard Thévenet, who would eventually abandon the race during the 11th stage, at the foot of the Tourmalet. A few days after the team event, during the individual time trial through the vineyards of Saint-Émilion, Hinault proved that he had the stuff of a champion by beating Kuiper by 3 minutes, Zoetemelk by almost 1, and Thévenet, who was already sick, by over 4.

After several stages in the Pyrénées came the 52.5-kilometer (31.4-mile) individual time trial from Besse en Chandesse to Puy-de-Dôme.

Hinault finished 1:40 behind the winner, Zoetemelk. At that point, the Belgian Bruyère, Merckx's faithful ex-lieutenant, still wore the yellow jersey. Zoetemelk was in second place, 1:13 behind, and apparently in the best position to snatch the yellow jersey. Directly behind him was Hinault (1:50), followed by Michel Pollentier (4th at 2:38), Joaquim Agostinho (5th at 6:20), and Kuiper (6th at 7:15). Van Impe, who had fractured his clavicle at the start of the season in the Tour of Flanders, was a distant 17th, more than 15 minutes behind.

Once again, Alpe d'Huez would turn everything upside down.

The race began in earnest that day just before the summit of Luitel. Pollentier, robbed of the polka-dot jersey of best climber, launched an attack to regain it by quickly changing gears and rapidly opening a gap in an all-out bid for the climber's title. At that point, his principal rivals, Zoetemelk, Hinault, and Kuiper, let him go because—in virtual terms—Bruyère had already lost his golden fleece,[3] lagging behind by more than 4 minutes.

"Bruyère had enjoyed a weeklong jaunt in yellow that was about to come to an abrupt end, though he had paid full price for the adventure, considering the amount of energy he had expended," wrote Antoine Blondin.[4] "For him, the climb up Alpe d'Huez was like a descent into hell. He was completely cooked at the finish."

A Gift for Pollentier

The driving Pollentier, now ahead of the pack, was starting to get ideas. He lowered his head to the handlebars and plunged through the village of Séchillienne, rushing toward the first turns of the Alpe. His lead rose to over 3 minutes. Meanwhile, fans were taken aback by the apparent lethargy of his main rivals. Kuiper was content to follow, while Hinault used the pretext that he was not sufficiently well-placed in the standings to take the initiative, letting Zoetemelk lead the chase. It was a subtle, effective battle tactic designed to wear down his Dutch adversary both physically and mentally.

Meanwhile, the mouse pedaling away furiously out front was starting to annoy the cats in the peloton. Pollentier was using his trademark jerky pedaling style, putting all his weight on one leg at a time, a style more befitting a toad than a cyclist. When he reached the foot of the resort, "Pollentier le Polio," as Hinault called him in reference to his dislocated style, still held an advantage of nearly 2 minutes, enough to make him think he could pull on the yellow jersey. Over the course of the climb, he carefully rationed his energy, displaying a level of discipline entirely absent from his unseemly form on a bike.

Pollentier hung in there. He had lowered himself over his machine, his back hunched, his elbows and knees sticking out, in a sort of uncoordinated skating motion. There he was, intent on wringing his body and torturing his bike, as Pierre Brambilla had insulted his machine and cursed himself back in the late 1940s. Pollentier's clumsy effort, made even uglier by his evident suffering, bordered on the pathetic. It was the public display of a talent that had languished all too long at the service of Freddy Maertens.

Pollentier's performance was part of a logical progression stretching back to the 1977 Giro. Maertens, carrying momentum from his recent victory in the Tour of Spain, had been leading the Giro when he'd been forced to withdraw after a fall. Pollentier, a model *domestique* and friend of Maertens since their childhoods, had refused to drop out and won the Giro as leader of the team, ahead of Francesco Moser, before going on to win the Tour of Switzerland and the championship of Belgium.

Pollentier was newly infused with confidence, having proven unbeatable in the Dauphiné Libéré, just a few weeks before the start of the Tour. That victory, which he had constructed over alpine turns, had taken on the symbolic value of a liberation now complete. It was substantially different from his pair of Tour stage victories, one at Super-Lorian (beating Merckx) in 1975 and the other at Fleurance in 1976.

Behind Pollentier, a battle raged. In close pursuit were Zoetemelk, wearing a yellow cap awarded then to the best-placed team in overall standings; Hinault, decked out in his tricolor jersey, like the fiery musketeer d'Artagnan wearing a cape; and Kuiper, "the Leech." The Dutchman from Germigny-l'Éveque attacked Hinault just beyond the resort but soon gave up, leaving the Frenchman to struggle on his own. Hinault was often out of the saddle, his torso cantilevered over the front wheel, his face tense.

A few turns higher, Pollentier was steadily losing ground, although he gamely pushed on. By the time he crossed the line—exhausted, losing his cap—his lead over the second-place Kuiper had shrunk to only 37 seconds. But thanks to a 20-second sprint bonus he had at Bourg d'Oisans, the margin proved sufficient to claim the yellow jersey by a mere 4 seconds over Zoetemelk and 18 over Hinault. The suspense would last all the way to Paris.

Shortly after the finish at Alpe d'Huez, journalists gathered to file their reports in a makeshift pressroom. It was located in the Alpe's modern church, watched over by Our Lady of the Snows and the parish priest, Father Japp Reuten, an enterprising Dutchman who helped finance this house of God by selling beer in cans.

Suddenly word of a scandal rocked the Tour: Pollentier, the yellow jersey, had reportedly tried to cheat and was about to be kicked out of the race! The full story gradually emerged. After crossing the finish line, Pollentier had gone to his hotel to change. He'd put on the jersey of champion of Belgium, rather than the yellow jersey, as well as a jacket. Under his armpit, Pollentier had placed a small bag containing urine from a third party. Connected to that was a narrow plastic tube that was taped down his back, ending right below his penis. He presented himself at the drug test with this hidden paraphernalia.

The doctor on duty that day was not the same one who had presided over previous controls. He adhered strictly to the rules, as his predecessor had undoubtedly failed to do, and ordered Pollentier to urinate with his jersey raised and his pants lowered. The racer's trickery was quickly discovered, especially because the tube was blocked, preventing Pollentier from submitting the substitute urine. It seemed he had been the victim of sabotage, though the identity of the perpetrator was never discovered.

In any event, the news exploded like a bomb. The revelation forced journalists, tired after a long day and ready for the showers, to scramble for information and rewrite their reports. Only a short while earlier, a calm Pollentier, accompanied by his *directeur sportif*, Fred de Bruyne, had left the medical caravan confidently asserting, "Everything is fine." But both knew otherwise.

Word that something serious had happened quickly reached the Hôtel des Cimes, where Pollentier's team, Flandria, and Hinault's team, Renault, were staying. In room 32, Noël Couëdel, *L'Équipe*'s special correspondent, interviewed the cheater as he lay in bed. He had thrown his yellow jersey haphazardly into a nearby suitcase, as if to express his contempt for the verdict. Incredibly, Pollentier stubbornly denied everything. "I took a long time to urinate, but the doctor said nothing to me. I signed and countersigned all the usual papers. How could it be that fraud was not discovered until an hour later? I just don't get it."

Pollentier, who had finally produced his own urine under the watchful eyes of a federal doctor, no doubt hoped that the scandal would just blow over. After all, he hadn't actually tested positive for any banned substance. He admitted only to using Alupin, a product designed to improve breathing. He had had no problem using it in Italy, Belgium, and Switzerland, but he feared that if Tour officials found traces, he would be disqualified.

Pollentier would never again wear the yellow jersey he had donned just two and a half hours earlier. That evening, he was relegated to the last place in the stage, penalized 10 minutes in the overall standings, fined 5,000 Swiss francs, and suspended from competition for two months. As the racers prepared for their day off, he was the talk of the town.

Gutierrez Too

As it turned out, Pollentier was not the only cheater nabbed that day. Antoine Gutierrez (Lejeune-BP), chosen at random to meet drug-testing requirements, had left the doping control only moments before Pollentier. He had also used a sachet filled with urine to fool the doctors, but once again, the deception had been discovered.

Unlike Pollentier, he was not ousted from the race until the following day, a delay that further angered the directors of Flandria, who maintained that Pollentier was being unfairly treated. Maertens, Pollentier's staunch ally, and Marc de Meyer, Pollentier's *domestique*, threatened to drop out of the race the following evening as they awaited approval from Pol Claeys, the CEO of Flandria, who was present at the race.

This affair followed a similar incident in the Midi-Libre, when the Spaniard Pedro Vilardebo of team Teka had been nabbed after sending Eulalio Garcia to take his place at testing! But Vilardebo had not been disqualified and was competing in this Tour (wearing number 70), as was Garcia (number 64).

According to Flandria, Pollentier was the victim of a double standard and was paying for the sins of others. At least, that was how many racers saw it, and they knew full well how easy it was to cheat the system.

In the monthly publication *Vélo*, the talented journalist Roger Bastide wrote, "A rubber sack hidden under clothes and filled with a healthy organic liquid intended to substitute for one's own, ah well! Let's face it, as shameful as that sounds, it's common practice. We are quite certain of that, even if we can't prove it."[5] It was a precursor to the revelations of Festina's masseuse, Willy Voet.[6] In *Miroir du Cyclisme*, Maurice Vidal, an ardent defender of the sport, concluded, "It is in any case difficult to finish a Tour on mineral water alone.[7] But it's absolutely impossible at the current pace."

Pollentier and Alpe d'Huez, both Tour icons, paid the price by serving as examples. Meanwhile, Gutierrez was suspended for two months.

All this took place just days after annulment of the prologue results—it had been run in the rain but did not count in the overall standings—and the infamous strike at Valence d'Agen. That day, Hinault, in his first Tour, led the march with his fellow racers to protest the excessively early starts and the transfers necessitated by the ludicrous half-stage from Tarbes to Valence d'Agen.

Pollentier's Letter

The day after the stage was a rest day on the Alpe, but it was anything but calm. Pollentier, the former wearer of the yellow jersey, acknowledged his fault and begged for forgiveness. In a long, moving letter addressed to the directors of the Tour, he asked for indulgence while listing all of his excuses. "I am accused of fraud when I did not, in fact, commit any fraudulent acts," he wrote. "The presence of a receptacle was interpreted as such, when in my opinion it was at most an attempt at fraud. I never committed the act of substituting urine, as I filled a vial with my own urine in front of the doctor, in the most natural manner." But Pollentier, who lost all of his post-Tour appearance contracts (about forty in all), remained expelled.

With Pollentier out, Kuiper wound up winning the most prestigious stage of the Tour for the second consecutive year. When the Tour left the Alpe, with team Flandria still present but sans Pollentier, Zoetemelk was wearing the yellow jersey Hinault would steal from him in the time trial from Metz to Nancy, just two days before Paris. Joop would wait until 1980 for his victory. Maertens, meanwhile, handily collected his second green jersey as points leader.

Three months later, Thévenet made headlines when he sounded the alarm of the dangers of cortisone with admirable frankness and courage. From the heights of Alpe d'Huez, Our Lady of the Snows smiled her approval.

CHAPTER SIX

1979

Two Climbs for
the Price of One

I'LL NEVER COME BACK TO THE TOUR," CRIED MICHEL POLLENTIER during the rest day at Alpe d'Huez in 1978. Evicted from the race for his attempt to cheat, he presented himself as a martyr. Yet when in 1979 Tour organizers doubled the stakes and offered participants no less than two ascents of Alpe d'Huez, Pollentier, of course, was back.

Riding now in the Splendor team colors alongside Sean Kelly, Pollentier would in fact climb Alpe d'Huez only once. High atop the mountain where a year before he had won the yellow jersey—if only for a few hours—he abandoned the Tour because he couldn't keep pace. Pollentier would never again be seen on the Alpe.

That anyone could manage two ascents of the Alpe in as many days seemed doubtful. Had the organizers, in a fit of pique over doping scandals, decided to punish the peloton in a particularly diabolical way? The riders may well have thought so, but in fact this double whammy was more the result of chance than any Machiavellian maneuvering by the organizers.

Originally, the Tour was to stop at the Alpe just once, summiting at the culmination of the Vars–Alpe d'Huez stage on July 16, following an ascent of the Col du Lautaret. The riders were to spend the night in Les Menuires, start from there the next morning, and finish atop the Col de Vars (a Tour first) after having climbed the Col de la Madeleine, the Col du Télégraphe, the Col du Galibier, and the Col d'Izoard—quite a lineup before Alpe d'Huez the following day. But then the Vars stage was thrown out.

"Three weeks before the Tour, I received a phone call from one of the organizers," recounted Georges Rajon. "He was nervous. He said, 'Monsieur Rajon, could we do two stages at Alpe d'Huez? Because the one to Vars has to be canceled.' I was surprised. But I immediately responded, 'The resort is open. Everyone will be happy to welcome the Tour two days in a row. But how much extra will it cost us?' The commissaire, obviously happy to have resolved this serious issue, replied without hesitation, 'We're not asking you for anything!'"

The cancellation of the mountaintop finish at Vars had nothing to do with the Tour—it was the result of a real estate dispute. "During the planning of the Tour," Rajon remembered, "a large developer promised the mayor of Vars that he would make all of his apartments and offices available to riders and the Tour entourage. A lucky break because the big disadvantage ski resorts have is their limited lodging capacity. In return, the developer asked the mayor to authorize a construction permit to erect a new building in the town. That document was denied! Furious, the real estate agent withdrew his offer, and the Tour organizers suddenly found themselves in trouble."

In the end, the Tour would spend three days at the Alpe: first in the stage from Les Menuires—which figured in the Tour for the first time—with the Madeleine, Télégraphe, and Galibier cols, followed by the Lautaret descent before the climb up Alpe d'Huez. The following day would include a circuit around the Alpe (the start and finish being held at the resort), with riders traversing the Côte de la Morte, the Col de Malissol, and the Col d'Ornon by way of the Alpe—at only 120 kilometers total (75 miles), the shortest stage of this Tour. On the third day, the riders left the Alpe and headed toward Saint-Priest in the Rhône region.

New Teams, Old Faces

With the 1979 season under way, even the best-informed of the Tour's entourage strained to recognize the riders after an especially frenetic off-season game of musical chairs. Lucien van Impe had moved, along with future world champion Claude Criquielion, to Kas, a Spanish team chartered in Belgium. Joseph Bruyère, the hero of the 1978 Tour, preferred Flandria. Didi Thurau opted for Ijsboerke, whose handsome yellow-and-blue jersey would be showcased during his stage win at Vitrolles in Paris-Nice. Herman van Springel, for his final season, chose the colors of Marc Zeepcentrale–Supéria. And Freddy Maertens, with his fuller face and longer hair, went to Savone. Maertens, almost unrecognizable, was upset with Pollentier, his ex-teammate. The brothers-turned-enemies had rocked the off-season with shocking accusatory statements.

Meanwhile, Bernard Hinault was dreaming of a second Tour victory. He was an attacker, this "Badger," as he was nicknamed by teammate Maurice Le Guilloux. He jumped into the lead early and was already in yellow after the second stage, a 23-kilometer (14.3-mile) time trial from Luchon to Superbagnères. Behind him by only 11 seconds was the lovable old bear, Joaquim Agostinho. Now 36, as untiring as he was clumsy, an unconditional admirer of Eddy Merckx, under whose reign he had debuted, and adored in his own country, the Portuguese perennial would show his strength on the climb up Alpe d'Huez.

In the end, Hinault would win seven stages, the last on the Champs-Élysées, after breaking away with rival Joop Zoetemelk. Earlier in the race, the Badger and his teammates had tried out the much-anticipated "aero" bikes in the time trial between Captieux and Bordeaux. The event had been won by team Ti-Raleigh, led by notables Gerrie Knetemann, Henk Lubberding, Dutch champion Jan Raas, and Johan van de Velde.

But on the cobblestones between Amiens and Roubaix, Hinault experienced one of the worst days of his career, spent chasing in thick dust. Ahead of him, Zoetemelk benefited from the help of fellow breakaway riders Thurau, Pollentier, and André Dierickx, all accustomed to riding these same cobblestones in April during the Paris-Roubaix one-day classic. The Badger, victim of a flat tire at kilometer 92,[1] ripped his handsome yellow jersey, now thoroughly dragged over the cobblestones, which a beaming Joop Zoetemelk pulled on at the finish.

By the time the peloton reached the foot of the Alpe, however, the Badger had regained the jersey, having stripped the Dutchman of it once again, this time in the Évian-Morzine-Avoriaz time trial.

Kuiper Flounders

The morning of this key Tour stage, Zoetemelk—who was enjoying an extraordinary season, having triumphed at the Vuelta and, for the third time, at Paris-Nice ahead of Hinault—was in second place, 2:45 behind the Frenchman in yellow. Kuiper, who had signed with Peugeot at the start of the season, along with Bernard Thévenet, had made the Tour his sole objective and was in third place, 14:23 behind. Giovanni Battaglin of team Inoxpran, one of the few Italians to race La Grande Boucle, wore the polka-dot jersey of best climber.

The battle that had gotten off to an early start on the formidable Galibier, swarming with spectators, soon became a war of attrition. Ueli Sutter, team leader of Ti-Raleigh, floundered. He was penalized for receiving illegal pushes and was eliminated when he finished outside the time limit by 7 seconds. Kuiper, accompanied by Michel Laurent, already found himself far behind the leaders, who were watching one another like vanguard soldiers. It was an unsettling coincidence: Kuiper was now faltering on the road to the Alpe during the 17th stage, where he had twice been victorious. Seventeen is an unlucky number for the Italians, like the number 13 for the French, and both of these numbers had been a curse for the Dutchman. Kuiper had abandoned the Tour in 1978, the victim of a crash and broken collarbone during the 17th stage, and also in 1976, after a fall in the 13th stage.

Hinault had control of the race, but the selection everyone had anticipated on the Galibier hadn't materialized. On the descent, about ten riders broke away, led by the Badger's teammate, Lucien Didier of Luxembourg. On the first turns of Alpe d'Huez, Agostinho left his companions behind, crushing his pedals like a winged bull in his distinctive style, sitting on the nose of his saddle. He wore the red jersey of Flandria, which featured another sponsor, Ça-va-seul (It runs on its own). That wasn't obvious to him! Ten years after his Tour debut in 1969, the weather-beaten, stocky Portuguese took a well-deserved victory. He managed to fend off the mob of chasers and crossed the line with practically the same gap between him and the yellow-jersey group as when he had started the climb.

Agostinho's triumph was all the more joyous and satisfying because it consecrated him as a man of the Tour. He was an unfortunate one, certainly, often having been a victim of crashes. He had even gotten injured in the seventh stage of this Tour, hurting a knee after hitting a traffic island. He fought on his bicycle the way an immigrant struggles to gain his place in society.

On the torrid Alpe, the sight of the tenacious Portuguese turning an impressive gear—a 19-tooth and at times even a 17-tooth cog—was reminiscent of his unusual arrival on foot in Divonne at the 1970 Tour. Wearing the blue jersey of Frimatic-Viva, and having been the victim of a crash, he'd carried his bicycle in one hand, a rim and a tire in the other, as elegantly as a cyclocross racer. Will and resilience permeated his character.

Behind him, finishing 2nd on the stage, was the great Robert Alban, who would place 3rd in the 1981 Tour. The Alpe also smiled on Michel Laurent and Jean-René Bernaudeau, the best young rider of this edition, and on Belgian Paul Wellens. It was not so kind to Lucien van Impe, the winner of the previous stage to Les Menuires forty-eight hours earlier. In his 11th Tour, the Belgian was showing signs of wear, arriving in 15th place at 5:56. Mariano Martinez, best climber of the 1978 Tour, also suffered, finishing 17th at 6:41.

Hinault, accompanied by Zoetemelk, dressed in the green jersey, and the Italian Battaglin, adorned in the polka dots of the best climber, limited the gaps. When the Italian attacked less than a kilometer from the finish line, the two favorites did not react.

A few hours later, Battaglin, Davide Boifava's protégé, learned he had tested positive for drugs following the 13th stage to Ballon d'Alsace. He lost two places in the overall standings but kept his status as best climber. Battaglin defended himself by explaining that he had used Zérinol to treat a sore throat.

Zoetemelk's Battle of Honor

The Badger still managed to beat Zoetemelk to the line, catching him after the Dutchman tried a second time to get away, having failed once at the base of the Alpe. "It was a battle between two tired men," wrote Jean-Michel Forest for the now-defunct ACP press agency, "where one man's pride tried to rain a little on the other's exalted parade."

The next day's climb up Alpe d'Huez—the second ascent—would offer Zoetemelk one more chance to best Hinault. The stage boiled down, more or less, to a climbing contest when the gauntlet was dropped at the bottom of the Alpe by Christian Levavasseur, who took off in order to set up Zoetemelk. Van Impe immediately joined him, leaving behind the leaders—Hinault, Zoetemelk, and Battaglin—who were busy navigating the first switchbacks, pinned against the rocks of the alpine wall.

Finally an impatient Zoetemelk risked everything and initiated a break-away, while Hinault stayed glued to the Dutchman's wheel, his yellow jersey unzipped. "It was the last mountain, and I didn't want to leave my terrain without making a mark," said Zoetemelk. "I really like the grade here. So after Bourg d'Oisans, I took off."

Zoetemelk passed Van Impe and attacked again, dropping the Badger and the Belgian as they stood helplessly on their pedals, their gaze fixed on the Dutchman in green who darted off toward a well-deserved victory. All along the winding cauldron of Alpe d'Huez, hysterical cries greeted and encour-aged him: "Yoopie, Yoopie!" His cap turned backward, his hands clench-ing the top of his handlebars, his face contorted, and his shoulders squared, Zoetemelk worked his upper body, with his legs balanced in a steady rhythm that betrayed his sublime effort. He threw all of his energy and all of his heart into this battle of honor: First it was 24 seconds, then 39 seconds with 7 kilometers (4.3 miles) to go, and finally 40 seconds at the finish. It wasn't enough to claim the golden fleece, but it was a brilliant ride nonetheless.

Just behind him, his *directeur sportif*, Jean-Pierre Danguillaume, had coyly maneuvered his Peugeot 403 to shield the Dutchman from the wind. Zoetemelk finished like a cannonball in his 53x14 gear, normally used by sprinters in the final meters of a race.

Having already prevailed on the climb in 1976, the year Alpe d'Huez was reintroduced to the Tour, Zoetemelk once again left a Dutch sig-nature on the decisive stage. In just 14 kilometers (8.7 miles), he erased his negative image as a "wheel sucker," "small-time winner," and "leech." Ever overshadowed by Merckx and Van Impe and often considered un-inspiring, he had finally earned his champion's stripes. He would finish second in the Tour for a fifth time—a true achievement. And Zoetemelk would win the Tour the following year, after Hinault, the early leader, bowed out in Pau with an aching knee.

Agostinho Flats!

Meanwhile, the rest of the peloton struggled to the top. Flanked by Van Impe and Agostinho, the winner the previous evening, who had lost none of his verve, Hinault appeared to be gaining ground on Zoetemelk, cutting his margin at midclimb to just 22 seconds. The Frenchman ascended at his own pace, without panicking, his eyes riveted to the road. He avoided going into oxygen debt by being careful not to exceed a tolerable pace.

Van Impe enjoyed the luxury of dropping Hinault before the summit to claim second place. Agostinho, however, with customary bad luck, flatted 8 kilometers (5 miles) from the finish and wound up fourth. The Belgian champion, Géry Verlinden (Ijsboerke-Gios), was also unfortunate that day, as his second ascent of Alpe d'Huez proved one too many. Still in sixth place overall before the first switchback, he found the prospect so tough and so daunting that he abandoned the climb at the base of the Alpe. The Belgian champion left the race due to "exhaustion, without specific causes," according to a statement by the Tour's medical team.

As for Hinault, in the days following the Alpe, he eventually claimed his second Tour title, 3:07 ahead of Zoetemelk. He kept his momentum going for the remainder of the season, winning the Grand Prix des Nations and the Tour of Lombardy, too. He even became the first Frenchman since Jacques Anquetil in 1966 to earn the celebrated and incomparable Super Prestige Pernod trophy, a veritable world champion's title based on season-long points—a telling competition stupidly abandoned when, in 1988, France introduced a ban on athletic sponsorships by alcohol brands, including Pernod.

CHAPTER SEVEN

1981

The Badger
Denied

FIREWORKS ON THE ALPE?" THAT WAS THE QUESTION POSED BY *L'Équipe* in an eight-column spread after a rest day in Morzine in the Tour's 1981 edition, along with three photos presented as a response. One was of Bernard Hinault, of course, busy at a game of *boules*[1] with his *domestique* Jean-François Rodriguez. On this rest day, Hinault was wearing not resort wear but rather the Miko yellow jersey, as he was well on course to win his third Tour de France.

The second photo showed Robert Alban, solo winner of the previous day's stage to Morzine, perched atop a horse in his racing outfit, waving like a valiant knight. The third was a snapshot of Freddy Maertens, the astonishing Belgian in the Michelin green points jersey, who was making an incredible comeback after three years in the desert.

Maertens had signed with Sunair–Sport 80–Colnago, thanks to Guillaume Driessens, who believed in the veteran's chances. In fact, Maertens would win a total of six stages of the 1981 Tour, including the race's final stage on the Champs-Élysées, as well as the green jersey. The following month, he would take the world championships in Prague with a masterful sprint, beating out Giuseppe Saronni—winner of seven stages at the Giro—as well as Hinault. It was something never before seen in the history of cycling.

Hinault was also returning to the Tour after abandoning the race in Pau the previous year because of knee pain. And so on this 14th day of July, with fans invading the switchbacks of the Alpe early for Bastille Day, *L'Équipe*—like all those covering the Tour—asked, "Yes or no: Is Bernard Hinault capable of an exploit on the climb up Alpe d'Huez?" The first alpine stage from Thonon-les-Bains to Morzine had left plenty of room for doubt.

In fact, Hinault had been content to watch his adversaries. This was not the relentlessly attacking Badger the fans had come to know, but Hinault's tactic seemed quite natural to Jacques Anquetil, who in a commentary for *L'Équipe* observed, "We'll never know if Hinault was holding something back between Thonon-les-Bains and Morzine, but he rode it exactly as he should have." Even so, everyone would be watching Hinault at Alpe d'Huez, where in 1979 he had shown a hint of weakness when Joop Zoetemelk had attacked.

As for Zoetemelk, he was now 35. With a career that spanned more than twelve years, including a Tour title the year before, Zoetemelk was visibly less motivated for this year's battle.

The 1981 Tour, the first of the Mitterrand era and one of change, was also made memorable by the return to center stage of Lucien van Impe, resplendent in a white Boston jersey and curly hair. Van Impe had been the solo winner at Pla d'Adet, where Phil Anderson (Peugeot) had been the first Australian to wear the yellow jersey. Aging riders would leave, and hungry young bucks would waste no time in taking their place. But for the time being, Hinault's teammate Greg LeMond—staying in Paris with Jonathan Boyer and being photographed for *Miroir du Cyclisme* with a beret on his head, a glass of red wine in his hand, and a baguette and a newspaper under his arm—opted not to ride the Tour. At 19, LeMond considered himself too young, as did Laurent Fignon, still an amateur and the dynamo of team US Créteil. They were two serious talents with whom Hinault would soon need to deal on Alpe d'Huez. But not this year.

The Day of Reckoning

The stage from Morzine to L'Alpe d'Huez promised to be deadly—an "old-fashioned stage," declared the esteemed Tour sage Pierre Chany. It was quite long at 230 kilometers (143 miles) and four climbs, including the interminable Madeleine as well as the imposing Glandon, which topped out at almost 2,000 meters (6,562 feet). On this course, worthy of Bastille Day fireworks, Hinault wanted to strike hard from the start. The Badger clearly wanted to win on the Alpe but unfortunately was beaten by a mere 8 seconds—8 historic seconds that would inspire most journalists to write that Hinault faltered that day.

The battle erupted halfway up the slope of the Madeleine, which Hinault decided to conquer without wasting any time. As he crested the summit, the selection was already well under way. Seventeen men were still present at the foot of the Glandon, 70 kilometers (43 miles) from the finish. There Hinault put on another show—but unlike the winged climbers of yesteryear, he did not take off on an epic breakaway. He simply imposed his own pace, a relentless progression, like a steamroller.

Hinault crushed his pedals and eliminated his adversaries one by one. He powered up the climb, relying on his strength, steely will, endurance, and ability to recuperate. The others followed his wheel, among them Van Impe (Boston-Mavic), who enjoyed surging ahead of Hinault at the top of every hill to collect points in the best-climber competition (which he would win, collecting his fifth polka-dot jersey, this one sponsored by Campagnolo). Also present were the tall, lanky Robert Alban (La Redoute–Motobécane), who was no stranger to the Alpe; Zoetemelk (Ti-Raleigh), who was hanging in there; Peter Winnen (Capri Sonne), a name that will come up again; the surprising Fons de Wolf (Vermeer-Thijs-Gios); and the Swede Sven Ake Nilsson (Wickes-Splendor).

The Badger Dropped

On the still snowy Glandon, the Australian Anderson, second in the overall standings, began to fade. By the time he reached L'Alpe d'Huez, he had lost more than 17 minutes.

Up ahead, the race neared the first hairpins that lead to the ski resort overlooking the Romanche valley. Two men shot off to clear the way: Bernard Thévenet's *domestique*, the Frenchman Dominique Arnaud (Puch-Wolber), who was making a courageous comeback in this Tour, and the Belgian Géry Verlinden (Sunair). They were leading Hinault's group by 1:10, benefiting, it seemed, from a certain laxness on the part of the yellow jersey, who was irritated to see his competitors stuck to his wheel rather than leading a chase.

Ten kilometers (6.2 miles) from the summit, at turn 16, Verlinden took off alone. After losing contact, Arnaud followed 26 seconds behind. Hinault was now 53 seconds back, being shadowed by Winnen, Van Impe, Alban, and Zoetemelk. At that moment, Winnen, the small, freckled Dutchman, decided to launch his attack, taking with him Van Impe and Alban. Hinault and Zoetemelk could not counter this sudden acceleration, and a gap was opened. The Badger's eyes narrowed, and his body, like his glance, strained toward a single purpose: to bring back the escapees. Was Hinault feeling the effects of his prodigious efforts on the previous cols? Was he faltering?

Winner of three stages of the Critérium International at the beginning of the season; hero of Paris-Roubaix, that ruthless race he detested but finally embraced at the end of April while wearing the jersey of world champion; unbeatable at Amstel Gold; and absolute dominator of the Dauphiné Libéré—Hinault had made this his season so far. Was he faltering now, on Bastille Day, on the relentless climbs of the Tour?

Faithful to his rhythm and his tactics, Hinault caught up with the three breakaway riders, who in the meantime had passed Arnaud and Verlinden. The Badger was once again at the front of the race, but, as it turned out, not for long. Six kilometers (3.7 miles) from the summit, Winnen went again, this time for good. Alban and Van Impe tried to accelerate, but they soon gave up trying to close the gap. Hinault didn't move.

The battle was joined—not for the overall title but for honor—and it raged on the Alpe, where throngs of scantily clad male and female fans were gathered, simmering in the intensity of the competition and the heat of July. The little Dutch wonder, urged on by ex-sprinter Walter Godefroot, flew toward victory and the white jersey of best young rider of the Tour.

At only 23 years of age, Winnen added his name to the exalted legend of Alpe d'Huez written by Dutch riders. He was not an unknown; he'd recorded an excellent third-place finish at the Tour of Romandie, where he had been the revelation and had even won a stage. Also included among his fledgling *palmarès* had been a second-place finish at the Course de la Paix (Peace Race) the previous year behind a tough group of Soviets. Winnen would triumph on the Alpe again in 1983.

As for Hinault, it was near the town of Huez that he noticeably surrendered after Winnen's attack. The incident became a veritable denouement in the race. "The fact that he suddenly capitulated on the key field of battle, that one so sure of his prowess was forced to endure such humiliation, shocked the entire caravan," wrote Jacques Goddet the next day in *L'Équipe* as part of an editorial titled "A Champion Who Is Also Human."

That evening, Hinault displayed stunning self-confidence and criticized his adversaries for their lack of initiative. "It seems there are riders in this Tour who would be content to finish second or third," he confided to Noël Couëdel of *L'Équipe* in his hotel room. "Well, let them have at it! It's not my problem. As far as I'm concerned, it's fine, just fine. But they are letting everyone down. Me, I'm having fun; I'm fresh and upbeat."

In fact, Hinault had caught Alban and Zoetemelk in his pugnacious style and taken second place in the three-up sprint, only 8 seconds behind Winnen. A few more meters and he would have won the stage! In light of this show of strength, all the talk of faltering did not seem justified.

Maurice Vidal, in *Miroir du Tour*, rebuffed such talk: "If a leader like Hinault does the lion's share of the work along with his teammates for the duration of a difficult stage, and then can't counter all of the late, opportunistic attacks, what is so unusual about it?" Moreover, when the overall standings were calculated at the end of the stage, Hinault had increased his lead over his nearest rivals.

As if to offer a definitive response, Hinault won the mountain stage to Pleynet Les-Sept-Laux the following day, like an ogre hungry for revenge. He went on to win his third Tour—the first to start in Nice—winning five stages in all as well as the most-combative rider competition, sponsored by the chocolate-milk maker Banania. To paraphrase Banania's marketing tagline: *Hinault is A-OK!*

CHAPTER EIGHT

1982

Beat Breu in the
Footsteps of Charly Gaul

IN JULY 1982, THE CYCLING MONTHLY *VÉLO* INTRODUCED A MORE compact format and a new, more modern look, somewhere between the gravity of the newsmagazine *L'Express* and the impudence of the satirical magazine *Pilote*. A cartoon graced the redesigned front page: In a year marked by the first spaceflight of the French astronaut Jean-Loup Chrétien, it depicted Bernard Hinault transformed into Superman. With three Tour de France victories under his belt, the Badger outclassed his competitors more than ever. He was once again the favorite heading into that year's edition of the race.

Bernard Thévenet had called it quits for good at the end of the previous season, but as the old guard retired, a few young riders were beginning to shine. At the start of the season, a certain Laurent Fignon, riding on the same Renault-Elf-Gitane team as Hinault, had distinguished himself by finishing eighth at the Critérium International. At the Giro, which the "boss" had won, the blond *domestique* with granny glasses and proven nerve had worn pink for a day between Cortona and Assisi.

Meanwhile, the Tour de l'Avenir heralded the arrival of an American on Hinault's team, to the delight of Cyrille Guimard, its famed *directeur sportif*, who had an eye for talent. It was Greg LeMond, whose smile and informal way of addressing people in French would soon be famous. LeMond, still only 21, triumphed despite the presence of strong Soviet riders like Sergei

Morosov. LeMond's Tour de l'Avenir performance was a strong follow-up to his remarkable second place against the pros at the world championships the year before, behind the explosive Italian Giuseppe Saronni in Goodwood, England. "Good wood"—solid and resilient, like LeMond himself, who was ushering in a new era of multinationalism for professional cycling.

Second place at the Tour de l'Avenir was taken by Robert Millar, a Scot who didn't hold back once the road slanted upward. People were also talking about a Colombian, Lucho Herrera, already winner of the Clásico RCN.[1] Finally, Thierry Claveyrolat was the real revelation of the race and would soon distinguish himself on the steep slopes of the Tour de France.

The young riders were off, and 1982 looked like it could be a turning point in Hinault's reign. All eyes would be on him at the Tour, where a record 170 riders took the start. The scrutiny would be particularly intense over the twenty-one switchbacks of Alpe d'Huez, where Hinault had often demonstrated a hint of weakness.

Keeping the Beat

The Badger struck hard in this Tour, which started in Basel, Switzerland, for the first time in its history. He took the yellow jersey from the Australian Phil Anderson on Bastille Day in the time trial at Valence d'Agen (won by Gerrie Knetemann), the same place where in 1978 he had led the peloton on a march to protest excessive transfers and early mornings.

After getting over the Pyrénées in yellow, Hinault made it to Orcières-Merlette on the eve of the Alpe stage, still in possession of the golden fleece. He had a comfortable 5:26 lead over his closest rival, veteran Joop Zoetemelk, who was competing in his 12th Tour, and over Anderson, who was in third place at 7:57. It looked like the race was in the bag.

This 16th stage, from Orcières-Merlette (1,840 meters [6,037 feet]) to L'Alpe d'Huez (1,780 meters [5,840 feet]), was the highest of the 1982 Tour. At the start of the race, farmers blocked the course by placing their tractors across the road between Orcières and Pont-du-Fossé. The Tour had also been taken hostage during the 9th stage by Usinor steelworkers, whose employment was in jeopardy; taking advantage of the Tour's media exposure, they stopped the Fontaine-au-Pire time trial, which ended up being canceled. Nothing like this had happened before in the history of the Tour.

This ransom of glory paid out by the Tour took place at a time when people were asking themselves what the future held for this unique event. The directors were talking about a new "open" format to rekindle interest, and the need to highlight "strategic spots" along the route. Debate on the subject had fueled impassioned discussions and prompted Maurice Vidal to write in *Miroir du Cyclisme* that the Tour had become *"une appellation non contrôlée"*—a French product without the kind of standards that ensured the quality of the country's wines.

At the foot of the Alpe, Beat Breu (Cilo-Aufina) attacked. The little Swiss climber, nicknamed the "Flea of St. Gallen" as well as "Pinocchio," was accompanied by Zoetemelk (Coop-Mercier), who hoped to win the stage and had changed bikes at the base of the Alpe. Hill-climbing specialist Robert Alban (La Redoute) went with them. Hinault, wearing the first in his series of yellow headbands, let them go, deciding to climb at his own pace. Twelve kilometers (7.5 miles) from the summit, Breu made his definitive move. His two companions tried to stay with him but soon were just trying to keep his jersey in sight as the blond Swiss sped off into the thin air.

Breu was causing excitement just four days after his victory atop Pla d'Adet in the Pyrénées. More importantly, he had followed up his successes in the difficult stage from Trois Cimes to Lavaredo in the 1981 Giro as well as at the Tour of Switzerland that same year. Everyone agreed that his performances marked the arrival of a super climber, one of a dying breed. Anquetil and Géminiani spoke of him as the successor to Charly Gaul, alluding to his ability to make a move early and sustain his effort. However, Breu would not take the title of best climber that Tour (it would go to Bernard Vallet), nor would he duplicate the legendary exploits of his illustrious predecessors.

But that day on the Alpe, the ex-postman once accustomed to pedaling from mailbox to mailbox put on a marvelous performance. As he crossed the finish line, his hair soaked, Breu could not contain his joy, flashing a liberated, toothy grin. Following his move, about 8 kilometers (5 miles) from the finish, Breu built a 15-second lead over Alban, who was often out of the saddle, manhandling his machine in an effort to close the small gap, inch by inch. Victory was playing out on the heated switchbacks, marking time like sand through an hourglass. Hinault followed 1:20 behind, accompanied by the little climber Raymond Martin; the Dutchman Johan van de Velde (Ti-Raleigh), who would eventually finish the Tour in third place; and the Spaniard Alberto Fernandez (Teka).

Breu versus Alban

Up ahead, between that quartet and Alban, who was chasing Breu, the sea of spectators soon made out Zoetemelk, who had attacked the yellow jersey, and, a little farther down, Bernard Vallet, clutching his bicycle the same way he was trying to hold on to his polka-dot jersey.

The match was still between Alban and Breu, like two boxers only seconds away from the final round. Just as the Frenchman came dangerously close, pedaling with all his might in the hope of snatching victory, the Swiss took off once again. He took the most exciting stage in the Tour barely 16 seconds ahead of Alban, who had finished fourth in the stage the year before. "I wanted to win this stage. And when I think how fast I climbed Alpe d'Huez, I'm even more disappointed," confided Alban at the finish.

Behind the winners, Hinault continued at his own pace and caught his adversaries one by one: first Vallet, then Zoetemelk. He finished fifth behind Breu, Alban, Fernandez, and Martin. Peter Winnen, hero of the Alpe in 1981, finished seventh and reaffirmed his talent by winning the difficult stage to Morzine the next day.

Hinault handily won his fourth Tour, taking the final stage in spectacular fashion on the Champs-Élysées, his second stage victory (the first was in 1979) on the world's most beautiful avenue.

"Old" Zoetemelk finished second for the sixth time and would race another four Tours.[2] Sean Kelly, another veteran, took the green jersey in the points classification for the first time. But 1982 would mark the end of the veterans' reign. The young riders who had made their presence felt at the start of the season were already fanning the kindling of revolt that would burst into flames in the Tours to come.

At Alpe d'Huez, in fact.

CHAPTER NINE

1983

Fignon Makes
His Debut

WHAT COMMOTION! WHAT A REVOLUTION! IN THE MICROCOSM of professional cycling, 1982 was marked by the media frenzy surrounding the announcement of a new "open" format, which would make its tenuous debut in 1983. *Open*: a glorified way of saying that professional races, most importantly the Tour de France, would admit amateurs as well.

Professionals would now face ambitious newcomers from Eastern Europe. Two different worlds, two opposing blocs—were they ready to make a pact and confront one another fair and square? Hinault versus Soukoroutchenko? Such confrontations had heretofore taken place only in the realm of fantasy. The great riders of the Eastern Bloc would never compete against the giants of the road—despite the fact that in 1982, 60 percent of the French public favored the mixed format.[1]

The media debate was based largely on conflicting statements by the two Tour directors: Jacques Goddet, editor of *L'Équipe*, and Félix Lévitan, managing editor of *Parisien Libéré*. On the eve of the 1982 Tour, Goddet voiced the opinion in *L'Équipe* that he would like to see the Tour return to a national team format every four years to encourage the participation of other countries. For his part, Lévitan supported the idea that the Tour embrace the open format to enable all qualified riders to participate beginning in 1983.

Tour organizers were considering such questions of public interest as a result of Bernard Hinault's clear superiority over the peloton. "He is the first representative of a sport to validate good old-fashioned virtues," wrote Philippe Brunel in *Vélo*. "So many traditional values, in fact, that he has acquired a unique aura, judging by the crowds that gather in July along the slopes of Alpe d'Huez."

As it turned out, the 1983 Tour would rediscover the attraction of days gone by due to Hinault's recalcitrant knee, now as famous in cycling history as Cleopatra's nose in Blaise Pascal's *Pensées*. After the Tour of Luxembourg, a bombshell exploded: The Badger was plagued by chronic tendinitis in his right knee caused by bad positioning and his efforts at the Tour of Spain and was withdrawing from competition immediately. With Hinault out of the picture, the Tour would be more open than ever!

The press didn't waste any time, devising headlines such as "'83 Tour: The Great Unknown," "Anything Can Happen," and "Young Riders— *Allez!*" Which young riders? At 22 and now residing in Kortrijk, Belgium, Greg LeMond had just won the Dauphiné Libéré but was giving himself a year to reflect on things before taking the plunge. The same went for Lucho Herrera, who would win at Alpe d'Huez the following year in his very first Tour.

But the Irishman Stephen Roche, the Scot Robert Millar (both with Peugeot), and the Frenchman Laurent Fignon (Renault-Elf-Gitane) all lined up for the start, as did the Spaniard Pedro Delgado (Reynolds), still virtually unknown.

Spain's star was Julian Gorospe (Reynolds), coached by José Miguel Echavarri, a former teammate of Jacques Anquetil and the future *directeur sportif* of a certain Miguel Induráin, the quiet champion of the end of the century. At 23, Gorospe could hold his own against Hinault at the Vuelta.

Ever-Ready Colombians

Also competing in its first Tour was the Colombian team Varta (its sponsor a battery brand). Its participation signaled, if not the advent of the "open" Tour, at least the beginning of globalization, with distant nations represented that had not been involved in the growing pains of the Tour and its early history. Thirty-two Colombian journalists followed the Tour that year. Radio commentators yelled from the passenger seats of motorcycles, their mouths glued to microphones, while others stood at the finish line or in stands reserved for TV journalists. Their loud, rapid-fire commentary, so relentless that it took on the characteristics of a sustained tone, provided something of a sideshow for the European press. Every day, *El Tiempo* and *El Spectator* devoted three pages of coverage to the Tour—more than some French newspapers.

The big gun of the Colombians, Alfonso Flores—a man of small stature with a mustache, winner of the 1980 Tour de l'Avenir and the 1983 Tour of Colombia—abandoned the Tour de France on the Tourmalet, exhausted from the long, flat stages that preceded it.

In this peloton of 140 riders who set off from Fontenay-sous-Bois on an odyssey that would hug the hexagonal contours of France was the first American to compete in the Tour, Jonathan Boyer (Sem Mavic), a friend of LeMond and teammate of the dinosaur Joaquim Agostinho.[2]

This 80th edition took the riders toward the Pyrénées prior to the Alps, giving a Dane the chance to shine: Kim Andersen, the first Viking to wear the yellow jersey, would hold on to it for seven days.

A single stage, Pau–Bagnère de Luchon, crossed this crystalline mountain range that came into existence in the Tertiary geological epoch and included four legendary cols: the Aubisque, the Tourmalet, the Aspin, and the Peyresourde. That was where Millar took his first major victory, while the Frenchman Pascal Simon pulled on his first yellow jersey with the absurd hope of taking it all the way to Paris.

This first showdown in the mountains pushed the young riders to the forefront and distanced the old-timers such as Van Impe and Alban, who finished more than 5 minutes back. Zoetemelk, who had tested positive following the second stage and was penalized 10 minutes, finished 8 minutes back. Sean Kelly was 10 minutes behind.

A Stage without the Yellow Jersey

Unfortunately, Simon fell and fractured his shoulder blade the following day, which would be an enormous handicap and cause him terrible suffering. Fignon, wearing the white jersey of best young rider in the Tour, was displaying formidable form following a stunning time trial at Puy-de-Dôme, taking back 3 minutes from Simon. On the eve of the Alpe d'Huez stage, Simon looked much less like a contender, with a lead of only 40 seconds over the blond Parisian imp.

Behind Simon, the cabinetmaker, and Fignon, the precocious challenger, Kelly was making his presence felt in the overall standings and was dressed in the green jersey, the second he would take to Paris. Delgado, in his first Tour, was fourth, and Angel Arroyo, winner of the previous stage at Puy-de-Dôme, was fifth.

Once again, Alpe d'Huez served as a litmus test for the vulnerability of the older riders and the impudence of the young up-and-comers. The wall of L'Oisans hung over them like a divine judgment that would determine the new chosen one in the absence of old man Hinault. It happened to be the day on which Fignon, in his first year as a pro, pulled out his commander's stripes. The stage started in La Tour du Pin and reached the Alpe via four cols: the Cucheron, the Granier, the Grand Cucheron, and the Glandon. A formidable stage of over 220 kilometers (132 miles), it would not be witnessed by Louison Bobet (who never climbed Alpe d'Huez during his career) or Tullio Campagnolo, the distinguished inventor of legendary bicycle components, who had both passed away earlier that year.

Injured and exhausted, Simon dropped out of the race during this long stage at the summit of the Côte le la Chapelle Blanche. The rest of the stage would be contested in the absence of the yellow jersey: The gods were sending a message before bestowing the golden fleece upon a worthy successor. Word spread quickly through the peloton that the jersey was out. Its absence conferred an even more solemn responsibility on the next to wear it, since the claimants to the throne, notably Fignon and Delgado, would be negotiating the Alpe's twenty-one switchbacks for the first time. It would be a long, slow initiation.

The battle broke out early, well before the terraced hairpins of Alpe d'Huez. The most threatening skirmish began on the descent of the formidable Glandon, the last difficulty of the day before the climb to the ski resort.

Dominique Arnaud, Jean-René Bernaudeau's teammate (Wolber), attacked and took with him the Italian Alfio Vandi, Van Impe's man (Métauromobili), and Raymond Martin (Coop-Mercier), a Zoetemelk loyalist. Twenty kilometers (12.4 miles) from the finish, on the long, flat section leading to Huez, just before the road starts to climb, three more men joined the first three attackers to lead the dance. The first was Bernaudeau, known simply as "JR," who had been extremely active and constantly at the front since the beginning of the stage. He was winner that year of his fourth Midi-Libre. The second was Peter Winnen (Ti-Raleigh), whom Peter Post had signed at the start of the season, and the third was Winnen's teammate, Gérard Veldscholten.

Bernaudeau and Winnen Get Away

Fignon, a white knight without fear, inspired by the combativeness of Pierre Terrail, the valiant lord of Bayard, whose hometown of Pontcharra he had passed on the way, spearheaded the chase, aided by the great Robert Alban.

Just before Bourg d'Oisans, five racers rode away from Fignon and were now positioned between the six breakaway riders and the peloton: Alban, the fierce climber who wanted to take the stage atop the Alpe; Pierre Bazzo (Coop); Marc Madiot (Renault), Fignon's teammate; and two Colombians, Samuel Cabrera and Edgar Corredor, anxious to defend the honor of their country.

Under the oppressive heat, the weakest were exposed as soon as they reached the first switchbacks crowded with spectators and their pedaling and breathing became labored. The mountain took upon itself the selection of a fortunate few while excited fans looked on, like Romans bidding gladiators good riddance as they were thrown to the lions.

At 10 kilometers (6.2 miles) from the summit, near the 17th switchback, Winnen, who had already won atop the Alpe on Bastille Day in 1981, broke away. Accompanying the redheaded Dutchman was the tenacious Bernaudeau, nicknamed "the Vendéen Chouan" after insurrectionary royalists from his native region during the French Revolution. He looked more like a gypsy with his rough complexion and black hair, both highlighted by his orange jersey.

Recovering from a bout of tracheitis, JR had fallen almost 2 minutes behind the favorites by the summit of the Glandon but managed to close the gap on the descent. Determined to shake things up and leading the insurrection at every turn, he, along with Winnen, had built up a 4-minute lead over the Fignon group. He secretly hoped to don the yellow jersey, eating away at the 4:40 deficit between him and Fignon that he had begun with that morning at the start in La Tour du Pin. Behind Winnen and Bernaudeau, the selection was in full swing. Only Alban and Corredor (who would finish third) were still ahead of Fignon, who was pulling off a fabulous climb. All the others, exhausted and weak, had been caught or dropped.

The best young rider of the Tour, wearing the white jersey, was essentially surveying the curly-haired Delgado, whose sense of style compelled him to wear blue-white-and-red gloves and who was accompanied by the fleet veteran Lucien van Impe, wearing a yellow headband and the jersey of champion of Belgium.

At the summit, the Belgian claimed the Poulain-sponsored polka-dot jersey for good, his sixth and last title (matching Federico Bahamontes), snatching it from the Colombian Patrocino Jimenez, the first South American to wear the honor.

Far behind was 37-year-old Joop Zoetemelk, who was struggling more against himself than against the steep slope. At the summit, he had lost over 16 minutes. In the same boat as the day's big losers were Stephen Roche and the Swiss climber Beat Breu, winner at Alpe d'Huez the year before, both finishing more than 9 minutes behind, as well as Millar, who trailed by over 7 minutes.

Two stunning comebacks, largely overlooked by the press, were those of the Spaniard Arroyo and the Irishman Kelly, who both trailed by over 10 minutes on the Glandon but managed to finish only 4:49 and 5:46 behind, respectively. These were two of the race's true exploits—or two cases of a welcome second wind.

In the end, the spirited battle waged by Bernaudeau failed on all fronts. The yellow jersey eluded him in the same moment that the stage did, when he ended up undergeared in the heated sprint against Winnen, with both riders baring their teeth and fixing their sights on the finish line the way a child eyes coveted presents under a Christmas tree.

At the summit, Fignon crossed the line 2:07 behind Winnen. Over 14 kilometers (8.7 miles) and 21 switchbacks, the bespectacled neopro had taken back more than 2:30. He even took the liberty of outsprinting Van Impe and Delgado (in that order) and raising his right fist as a sign of accomplishment that signaled the rise of a new power.

"I turned myself inside out on the climb up Alpe d'Huez to stay with Van Impe and Delgado, who are both better climbers than I am," confided

Fignon. "I gave it everything I had. The thought of wearing the yellow jersey allowed me to transcend myself."

At 23 and in his first Tour, Fignon pulled on the coveted jersey while Hinault, who was vacationing in Autrans and had come to see his friends in La Grande Boucle, looked on. It was practically a passing of authority.

To win at Alpe d'Huez: what a dream. By just a few centimeters, Winnen, the little mailman from the Low Country, had pulled off an impressive repeat victory and had filled with joy the thousands of Batavian fans amassed on the mountainside. The honor and renown of the House of Orange, in that unassailable Dutch fiefdom in the dizzying heights of the Alpe, were saved.

CHAPTER TEN

1984

Hinault Agonistes

Bernard Hinault, absent from the cycling scene for nearly six months due to a knee injury, returned to the peloton in 1984 to captain a team he had assembled himself. In his hospital bed, the Badger had thought long and hard about how to take charge of his season and his affairs. For his physical and technical preparation, he turned to Paul Koechli, one of the best coaches in the field. To handle his business interests, he appointed Philippe Crépel.

Stubborn and seemingly clairvoyant, Hinault was no longer willing to take orders from or heed the advice of the blunt, outspoken, and highly opinionated Cyrille Guimard. He separated himself from the man he had been with from the start of his career to take advantage of an offer extended by the businessman Bernard Tapie, who was just entering the world of sports (much later Tapie would become president of the Olympique de Marseille soccer team and lead it to a historic victory for France in the European Cup). Hinault and Tapie were bound by a three-year contract totaling a stupefying 10 million francs (about $1.14 million at the time, or $2.2 million today). The team would take on the pleasant name of Tapie's chain of health food stores, La Vie Claire. It was revolutionary in structure, in money, and in sheer audacity.

Vélo magazine recognized this momentous event with a cover photo of Tapie dressed in a gray business suit with tie and handkerchief and Hinault, hoisting a glass of champagne, in a blue blazer and a striped sports shirt with open collar. Both were smiling as if in an ad for toothpaste.

Hinault intended to showcase the complete palette of his talents in the La Vie Claire jersey, which featured the geometric shapes and colors of the famous *Composition with Yellow, Blue, and Red* by the Dutch painter Piet Mondrian. He would be going up against Laurent Fignon, winner of the 1983 Tour, as well as the talented young American Greg LeMond, who until now had been absent from the roads of the Tour.

In 1983, LeMond had earned the Super Prestige Pernod award, a veritable world champion's title based on points. The American had earned this distinction by taking the true world championship road race at Altenrhein, by his earlier win of the Dauphiné Libéré (after Pascal Simon tested positive and was disqualified), and by finishing second in both the Tour of Lombardy (behind Sean Kelly) and the Grand Prix des Nations (behind Daniel Gisiger). Consequently, everyone was watching LeMond, who was wearing the same colors as . . . Fignon. Both were ex-teammates of Hinault, and both were now riding for team Renault-Elf-Gitane. It promised to be a year of myriad passions, the settling of scores, and mountaintop duels.

The Colombians would take the Tour start in greater numbers than at the previous year's "open," which if nothing else had opened the door to these riders. They were showing new strength on the flats, which had been their weakness in 1983 during their first appearance at the Tour. The Colombians were led by Lucho Herrera, a man of small stature with an almost juvenile face, who looked even younger without the thin mustache he shaved off for the Tour. Smiling didn't come easily to him, and only rarely did he show his teeth. He answered to the nickname "El Jardinierito" or "Le Jardinier de Fusagasuga" (the little gardener or the gardener from Fusagasuga, his hometown on the high plains of South America). At 23, Herrera, three-time winner of the Colombian Classico RCN race, was embarking on his first Tour as both a winged wonder and a curiosity to watch. Everyone hoped he would put on a masterful performance at Alpe d'Huez, the most beautiful of the mountain stages.

Those in the European professional peloton now knew that in April 1984, LeMond, the world champion, and Fignon, winner of the '83 Tour, had been squarely beaten by Herrera on his home turf at the Classico RCN. Compounding this humiliation had been the victory of Colombian Martin Ramirez a month before the Tour at the Dauphiné Libéré; he had finished ahead of Hinault by 27 seconds and LeMond by 5:07. Now you could smell the gunpowder, and the cauldron of the Alpe was boiling hotter than ever with passion and intrigue.

This 71st edition of the Tour started in Montreuil-Noisy-le-Sec in the *département* of Seine-Saint-Denis, hugging practically the same contours as the previous year's event.

Hinault's Five Attacks

As if to settle any uncertainty about his condition, Hinault struck hard right off the bat, taking the prologue and pulling on the yellow jersey. But Fignon set things right in the Alençon–Le Mans time trial. Wearing a streamlined helmet and hunched over his revolutionary machine with handlebars shaped like airplane wings, Fignon looked like nothing so much as a messenger of the future. He finished like a meteor, 49 seconds faster than Hinault and a staggering 2:08 faster than LeMond. Fignon had scored some points but did not pull on the jersey, which was still on the shoulders of his sympathetic teammate, Vincent Barteau, who would keep it until the foot of the Alps.

Before the Alps, though, came the Pyrénées, where Herrera put on a stunning performance during the stage from Pau to Guzet-Niege (a resort where the South Americans were accustomed to training). Robert Millar would take the stage, but the Colombian took off at the foot of the formidable climb and was able to eat away more than 2 minutes of the Scot's lead in less than 10 kilometers (6 miles).

In Grenoble, on a rest day and the eve of the Alpe d'Huez stage, Barteau was still wearing the yellow jersey, followed in the overall standings by Fignon at 6:29, Hinault at 9:15, and, further down the list, Pedro Delgado at 11:25 and LeMond at 12:53. But most importantly, 2:46 now separated the young Parisian from the Badger, who was going all out to win this Tour, which he—the dominator of the previous years—considered rightfully his own.

So Hinault attacked repeatedly, just as a Winchester rifle fires multiple rounds, on the long climb up the Côte de Laffrey, where Napoleon Bonaparte had made a stop during his return from exile. It was wonderfully symbolic that Hinault should go back on the attack there after a year's absence: Laffrey is an intimidating, historic climb where Joaquim Agostinho and Luis Ocaña dropped King Merckx one day during the

1971 Tour. Five times Hinault drew his gun and attacked, and five times Fignon proudly stayed on his wheel, accompanied by Herrera (Varta) and the champion of Germany, Reimund Dietzen (Teka).

At the summit, the Colombian led, followed by Fignon. Seconds later, the large crowd of spectators who had assembled near the Poulain banner, sponsor of the best-climber award, watched as the racers charged by: Dietzen and Millar (Peugeot) at 21 seconds, Hinault and Beat Breu (Cilo-Aurina) at 31 seconds. Spurred into action, the Franco-Colombian tandem continued its effort on the descent, shocking everyone with its arrogance and nerve. Behind, his authority challenged, Hinault led a heated pursuit with Angel Arroyo (Reynolds), Millar, and Breu.

Over the flat section leading to the foothills of Alpe d'Huez, 20 kilometers (12.4 miles) from the finish, Hinault finally caught Fignon and Herrera. At that point, everyone assumed the riders would watch one another and wait for the twenty-one switchbacks before resuming hostilities. But Hinault, a proud and relentless aggressor, immediately counterattacked and rode alone out in front of Fignon's small group, tiring himself like a rookie just before the big, difficult finale. The peloton looked on in astonishment. Madness! Hinault was thumbing his nose as if at a pack of stray dogs nipping at his trousers: "Go ahead, try to catch me; you'll see whether or not old man Hinault is dead!"

After the finish, Fignon, wearing the jersey of champion of France and as glib and insolent as a schoolboy, uttered a phrase that would make the rounds of the press: "He makes me laugh," he said of Hinault.

Herrera stepped on the gas as soon as the road began to climb. Only Fignon, who was forced to turn on the turbo, managed to stay with him for a bit before dropping back quickly. The Colombian marvel was draped in the handsome blue-red-and-yellow jersey of his national team, his hands atop his handlebars adorned by green gloves. He made his way up the succession of hairpins with a rhythmic, graceful pedaling style, his elbows pointed outward as if the handlebars of his bike were too wide.

Fignon Overtakes the Badger

Herrera was not just climbing; he was gliding along the turns of the Alpe as a considerable crowd applauded him. The Colombian fans expressed their pride and joy in loud ovations, stirred up by the irregular fluttering of a huge flag that cracked like an ensign in the wind. They were celebrating the first flight toward glory of one of their own as if heralding a revolution.

Herrera was the first to pass Hinault. Then Fignon went by without turning back, without so much as a glance. He eclipsed the "old man" with insulting ease. "Insolence is the impudence of talent, the obvious ease with which a champion informs the rest of the world of the distance that separates them," wrote Olivier Dazat.[1] It was a historic ascent, a solemn moment during which Alpe d'Huez consecrated a South American and, above all, was witness to the beginning of Hinault's decline.

Behind the slim Colombian, Hinault was bearing his cross. His face was without emotion, his eyes fixed, his muscles tense, and his shoulders heavy from the weight of years of domination. Fans raised their arms, clenched their fists, and joined hands, calling out when he passed as if offering prayers to the glory of a fallen champion. Even more than his two time trial losses to Fignon in the Tour at Le Mans and La Ruchère, the Alpe crucified him. It was on these same switchbacks that Merckx had faltered in 1977.

Herrera, Fignon, and soon Arroyo, Millar, Acevedo, and LeMond all took their turn, leaving behind the wounded Badger, who had decided, like a soldier, to die rather than give up. The next day, *L'Équipe* paid him tribute in an editorial by its editor, Jacques Goddet, who wrote, "Hinault carried himself like a combatant born of cycling legend. He took off down the road the way a boxer enters the ring, to strike, to destroy, to try and finish alone—yes, alone, in whatever condition, as long as he is still standing."

At the summit, Herrera became one of the most important personalities in Colombia and upon return to his homeland would be greeted as if he had won the Tour. Fignon, who raised his arms in victory, pulled on his second yellow jersey, this time for good. Millar stole the polka-dot jersey away from a broken Jean-René Bernaudeau (55th at 11:49), and Hinault, stopping the clock 2:55 behind Fignon, joined the ranks of the defeated.

This ascent of Alpe d'Huez, led by Herrera like a train out of hell, provoked a number of significant losses. Joop Zoetemelk finished 6:05 back; Simon, the unlucky yellow jersey of the previous year, 8:07 back; Delgado, reputed to be an excellent climber, 9:05 back; and Hennie Kuiper, two-time winner of this very stage, 16:32 back. Among these spectacular losses, Robert Alban's (La Redoute) was perhaps the most notable. The "great stork" had always finished high in the standings atop the Alpe. This time he crossed the line in 32nd place, 8:07 back, suffering the effects of bronchitis.

That year, 1984, when Francesco Moser twice pulverized the world hour record, Hinault, like a great champion, ended the season by taking the Tour of Lombardy, the Grand Prix des Nations, and the Trofeo Angelo Barrachi (with Moser). The Breton had not yet uttered his last word and would still win another Tour—his fifth—as well as a stage. At Alpe d'Huez, in fact.

CHAPTER ELEVEN

1986

The Alpe's Greatest Duel

THE 1985 TOUR FEATURED A MEMORABLE MILESTONE: GREG LeMond took his first Tour stage win at Lac de Vassivière, beating his teammate and race leader Bernard Hinault in the 45-kilometer time trial the day before the race finish on the Champs-Élysées. Hinault claimed his fifth Tour, of course, but that same day he announced to Jean-Paul Brouchon of *Miroir du Cyclisme* that the following year he would serve strictly as LeMond's lieutenant. "I'll stir things up to help Greg win, and I'll have fun doing it," Hinault declared. "That's a promise!"

LeMond's position as future team leader was consecrated in the contract he signed with La Vie Claire team owner Bernard Tapie in 1985, a magnificent $1 million over three years. The deal symbolized not only the hoped-for future of Tapie's team but also the future of professional cycling. LeMond was the first cyclist ever to earn such a sum, and his astonishing salary reset expectations within the peloton. For the first time, cyclists could look forward to parity with the stars of other vaunted pro team sports such as soccer, baseball, and American football. LeMond, the American, brought a new sensibility to the quintessentially European sport of cycling, and his contract announcement would agitate the peloton for many years to come. Moreover, LeMond was, without a doubt, the anointed winner for 1986. Hinault had repeated the announcement several times since the finale of the '85 Tour: "LeMond will be my successor."

Hinault's intentions seemed sincere. At the conclusion of the '85 Tour, in a post-race meeting with the press moderated by the French author and journalist Jacques Chancel, the Badger was asked, "Next year will be your sixth victory?"

"No, no, that's it," he replied.

"What do you mean?" asked a surprised Chancel. "As six-time winner, you'd better Anquetil and Merckx."

Hinault smiled, amused by Chancel's insistence. In a voice tight with emotion, he murmured, "You need to share the experience you've gained. Greg will need me next year."

"That's too easy," retorted Chancel, turning to his numerous guests, happy to put the Badger on the spot. "That way, if he loses, he will have called it ahead of time."

Team boss Tapie, who had been chuckling up to that point, interrupted the flow of the interview and said, tapping his finger, "That's not Hinault's style. If he says at the start that it's Greg who will win, then that means Greg will be leader next year."

Promises, promises.

Curiously, a year later, Hinault's declarations had been forgotten. LeMond, though soundly beaten at the Giro d'Italia in May by Roberto Visentini, showed up at the start of the Tour with one thing on his mind. But for the cycling press, interest lay elsewhere.

LeMond Forgotten

A legendary rivalry was on everyone's minds at the start of the 1986 Tour in the western Parisian suburb of Boulogne-Billancourt, but it was not a competition between Hinault and LeMond. Observers were looking forward to the epic duel that had divided France into two camps, one for Hinault and the other for Le Professeur, Laurent Fignon.

"On my left, Bernard Hinault, wearing the jersey of La Vie Claire, the team he had chosen after his divorce from Cyrille Guimard and team Renault. On my right, Laurent Fignon, wearing the jersey of Système U, the team he had chosen after his departure from Renault, along with . . . Cyrille Guimard." That was how the battle of the titans was announced on the front page of the special issue *Tour de Vélo* in July 1986. There was not a word about LeMond. *Miroir du Cyclisme* ran a similar commentary under the headline "Hinault-Fignon: Legend and Glory." The American was once again forgotten. *Miroir* focused its attention on the French duel, in conjunction with a series of photos titled "Hand-to-Hand," featuring historic sepia photos evoking the battles between Anquetil and Poulidor, Merckx and Thévenet.

Hinault and Fignon? Until then it had been a duel interrupted, suspended—nothing but a dream. Fignon had won the 1984 Tour, handily beating Hinault, who had been recovering from his knee operation. Hinault had won the following year, but Fignon had been absent, recovering from an operation on his Achilles tendon. The rematch that had been highly anticipated since the end of 1984 had not yet materialized, so everyone hoped to see it in 1986. Even the latest addition to the canon of cycling publications, *Cyclisme Internationale*, asked the question on the cover of its fourth issue, which featured a photograph of Hinault in yellow: "On his way to a sixth victory?" Again, not a word about LeMond.

Strangely, everyone—or almost everyone—had forgotten Hinault's public promise at the end of the 1985 Tour to LeMond, who had played the role of perfect teammate: "Next year, I'll be at your service!" A seemingly clairvoyant Maurice Vidal wrote, "Do you really believe that? I still believe Hinault is sincere. Life is based on intentions but sometimes changes course. To such an extent that what will happen between the two racers (and their boss) is just another uncertainty."

What a perfect assessment of reality! It was the terrible year of Chernobyl and the year of French governmental "cohabitation."[1] It was also the year of the difficult cohabitation of Hinault and LeMond within the La Vie Claire team over the course of this explosive Tour, the last for the Badger, who was more determined than ever to show that he was still a force to be reckoned with.

Hinault got things started in the time trial stage at Nantes (61.5 kilometers [38 miles]), affirming himself the stronger of the leaders by finishing 44 seconds faster than runner-up LeMond. Then Hinault wreaked havoc in the first Pyrenean stage from Bayonne to Pau. He broke away with Pedro Delgado (who would win the stage) on the Col de Marie-Blanque, pulling on the yellow jersey later that day with a lead in the overall standings of over 5 minutes to the second-place LeMond, who struggled as soon as things heated up. It was beginning to look as though the Badger had his sixth Tour in the bag.

Fignon's poor form completely changed the face of the Tour. Trailing by 12:43 and running a fever, he abandoned the race in Pau. With the great French rivalry put off, probably forever, everyone now spoke of nothing but Hinault's promise to LeMond in 1985. It was a good way to rekindle interest in a Tour that seemed over before it had really gotten started, thanks to an Hinault who was proving elusive in more ways than one. "Just try to take back 5 minutes from Hinault!" he exulted.

The Badger's Fatal Error

The next day, however, Hinault committed a critical error in a Tour he certainly could have won when he attacked once again, this time alone, on the descent of the Tourmalet. What guts—what panache! But it was a crazy breakaway, considering he had the leader's jersey on his shoulders. This was a move à la Merckx: the yellow jersey, breaking away on his own in the Pyrénées, along the road to Luchon.

Though generally a savvy tactician, the Badger inexplicably attacked a long way from the finish and was caught before the final climb to Superbagnères. At the front, two Americans took the Tour by force as if taking the baton: LeMond, assisted by teammate Andy Hampsten, led the dance. By the end of the day, LeMond was within 40 seconds of Hinault.

All that effort had gotten the Frenchman nowhere in his quest for a sixth victory. In the caravan, everyone wanted to know what Hinault was thinking. He explained his conduct nonchalantly: "If I had succeeded in reaching Superbagnères, I would have won the Tour and everyone would have lavished praise on me. If I failed, I knew that Greg was behind me ready to counterattack and that I was tiring his adversaries. It was sound strategy." Unbelievable: Hinault was claiming to have transformed himself into a super-*domestique* for LeMond.

No one, or almost no one, believed in the promise anymore, especially since Hinault had not hesitated to attack from the beginning of the Tour. Not even in transitional stages like Nîmes-Gap, where once again he had surprised LeMond, who had reprimanded him with angry gestures after catching up in a chase group.

In any event, the Badger lost the yellow jersey the next day during the unprecedented stage in sun and dust from Gap to Col du Granon, with a mountaintop finish at 2,400 meters (7,875 feet). The stage was marked by dramatic setbacks, most notably those of Joël Pellier, who fell victim to hypoglycemia, and Hinault, who suffered from a hematoma on his calf. LeMond thus became the first American to pull on the yellow jersey, which he would wear for the first time in the stage that led to Alpe d'Huez. The route promised to be long and difficult, heated by both sun and passion.

Some didn't accept Hinault's relegation to second fiddle, perceived to be the fault of an opportunistic American who had only found his form in the month of July. Hinault himself may have agreed with this assessment, as he decided to make things difficult for LeMond over the course of this legendary stage.

It would be a decisive stage with regard to overall victory (Hinault was in third place, down only 2:47 on the American), one in which the Swiss Urs Zimmermann (in second place overall, 2:24 behind LeMond) hoped to play a big role. He would be a tough adversary, having already won the Critérium International and the Dauphiné Libéré earlier in the season.

On the descent of the Galibier, Hinault attacked. Only two men were able to follow: the Canadian Steve Bauer (Hinault's teammate) and the Spaniard Pello Ruiz-Cabestany. All along the interminable plunge toward Valloire (almost 20 kilometers [12.4 miles]), Hinault gave it his all—without LeMond, who was stuck farther back. The American began to realize that he could lose the Tour at any moment when he saw the Badger continue his charge up the Col du Télégraphe, before the Croix de Fer and the final climb up Alpe d'Huez.

Dejected, LeMond consulted his *directeur sportif*, Paul Koechli, and finally launched his own attack, a last-chance pursuit race. He devoured the slopes of the Télégraphe with no thought of the risk and was able to catch Hinault on the outskirts of Saint-Jean-de-Maurienne. He had just saved his Tour.

Who could still believe that Hinault had not truly gone for it between the summit of Galibier and the valley leading to the initial slopes of the Croix de Fer? And the main event at Alpe d'Huez was soon to come. Sporting the multicolored combination jersey (a short-lived innovation from the Tour organizers awarded from 1985 to 1989 to the best-placed rider in the combined time, points, climbing, and intermediary sprint classifications), Hinault set the rhythm from the start, ensuring the pace, with LeMond, the fragile and troubled wearer of the yellow jersey, by his side. In the furnace of the Alpe, Hinault's name, shouted by his tens of thousands of rabid supporters, rang in LeMond's ears. Over the deafening roar, LeMond confessed, "I'm afraid of the crowds," and pushed the Badger forward to lead. The sea of fans amassed along the wall of L'Oisans left them only a narrow opening through which to scale the asphyxiating slope, one behind the other.

Meanwhile, their adversaries followed in the distance, with Zimmermann the most dangerous. At more than 3 minutes back, he was chasing in a group that had counterattacked. He would finish third, 5:15 back. Old Joop Zoetemelk would finish 14:21 back, Charly Mottet and Stephen Roche 15 minutes back, and Robert Millar, wearing the polka-dot jersey (which Hinault would take by the end of the Tour), 19 minutes back. Lucho Herrera, who went over the Galibier in the lead, faltered badly, went backward, and finished 26 minutes back!

Amidst the tumult of the Alpe, between the Breton flags fluttering like proud standards, the colors of La Vie Claire painted on the road, and the cries of "Hinault, Hinault" as they passed, Hinault and LeMond, the two leaders, made their way up the climb.

The closely followed duel suddenly ceased, right before the eyes of crazed fans, when the Badger transformed himself into a locomotive, protecting the American to whom he would "hand" his first Tour de France at the top. Not once did Hinault let the American take the lead. Nor did LeMond seek to take it.

A few meters before the finish, LeMond clapped Hinault on the shoulder to thank him. As the Italian journalist Tony Lo Schiavo wrote in *Bici Sport*, "Over the last meters, they joined hands. You would have thought it was a sign of affection. But it wasn't that. In reality, the clasping of hands masked a secret agreement: Hinault promised not to attack LeMond, and the American thanked him by letting him take the stage."

A Two-Headed Eagle

The two racers rolled in unity over the straight section where the road broadens, flanked by security barriers. They exchanged a long look of satisfaction and smiles of relief and mischievousness, congratulating one another with pats on the back like two schoolboys who had pulled off a good prank. Then they crossed the line together—although with Hinault in the lead—each raising a hand in victory.

The next day, the sports daily *L'Équipe* ran the headline "A Two-Headed Eagle" on its front page, followed by an eight-column article. In the presence of the French minister of sport, Christian Bergelin, a delighted Hinault collected prizes for combativeness (sponsored by the bank BNP), best teammate (sponsored by Rocagraf), and best *rouleur*.[2] Above all, he had won his 26th Tour stage, surpassing André Leducq's *palmarès* of 25 stage victories.

Jean Amadou, speaking of Hinault, wrote in *L'Équipe*, "That's the first time I've ever seen a racer smile at the end of this climb. He looked like a kid who had just gotten himself a toy he had been dreaming about. Hinault had already won everything, or almost everything, but what he lacked was Alpe d'Huez. Starting tomorrow, LeMond will be praying that the Breton doesn't decide to give himself one last gift: his sixth Tour."

Their sincere hug and beaming smiles on the podium seemingly ended the war of nerves between the teammates. At least that was what everyone thought. Despite appearances, though, Hinault declared that very evening, just as Amadou had suspected, "The Tour is not over—I'm still racing to win it." It sent a shiver down LeMond's spine. In the end, however, the American would win his first Tour.

"I Could Have Taken 5 Minutes out of Him"

The real story of what had happened on that climb, if it hadn't come to a head on Alpe d'Huez, broke a short time later in the form of shattering declarations. Today they shed light on the battle for that Tour and offer perspective on the duel at the Alpe.

The first to draw was the American, who vented his anger in an interview with the French journalist Henri Haget, declaring, "Hinault is not the man I knew at the start of my career. He's obsessed with winning his sixth Tour, as if he's forgotten that, without me, he never would have won his fifth. I gave him the 1985 Tour. He should remember that, but instead he's created a terrible environment. The worst was the finish at L'Alpe d'Huez, when we crossed the line hand in hand. It was all a big show. I let myself get played like a novice. I had the yellow jersey, and at the foot of the climb, Hinault swore to me that it was all over, that he wouldn't attack me again on the way to Paris. He knew that I could drop him at the first turn, but he asked me to let him lead on the climb to win the stage.

I could have taken 5 minutes out of him by the top. I shouldn't have had any qualms about doing so."[3]

The embittered Badger responded much later, in his memoirs.[4] He wrote, "It wasn't my fault if LeMond didn't understand how I was conducting my race. I did what I did to benefit him, and him alone. I had told him that I would help him, give him a hand in winning the race. At Alpe d'Huez, I could have buried him. I think I could have put a lot of time on him that day, if I had thrown down the gauntlet. At no point was I trying to beat him. After Alpe d'Huez, I only waged a small psychological war to see exactly what he was made of."

The big show had been nothing but a facade. In fact, the two teammates had only pretended to bury the hatchet for the sole purpose of preserving the brand image of team La Vie Claire, by order of the boss, Tapie, who in a later interview with *L'Équipe* remembered, "The first great moment of my career in sports was not my soccer team's victory over Milan but rather Hinault and LeMond at Alpe d'Huez. It wasn't winning that Tour; it was the stage victory. The morning before, they were at each other's throats. I took my plane that evening and, after arriving, spent from two to four o'clock in the morning with them. Hours later, I watched them arrive at the summit of the Alpe together. It was more wonderful than any other experience."[5]

Hinault, who ended his career that year, as he had always said he would, confided later, "I had fun at that Tour!"

What a masterful exit. Imagine Bernard Hinault, who would finish second in the 1986 Tour, 2:45 behind the new American top rider, Greg LeMond, announcing at L'Alpe d'Huez, "Today was my last day of competition." He did so as the grand winner of the world's most prestigious mountain stage. For lack of a more theatrical exit, the Badger climbed the last great col of his career at almost 2,000 meters (6,562 feet).

In retrospect, his conduct was that of a pugnacious former champion, with the victory high atop the Alpe compensating for the absence of a final victory in Paris. That was why everyone—in France, at least—thought the 1986 Tour also belonged to him, in some small way.

CHAPTER TWELVE

1987

Delgado Sets Spain Afire

THE 1987 TOUR WAS ONE OF NO-SHOWS, THE MOST DRAMATIC absence being that of Greg LeMond. He had fallen during the second stage of the Italian spring classic Tirreno-Adriatico, fracturing his left wrist, which forced him out of competition for several weeks. Having recovered from his injury in California, the American champion and symbol of a pro cycling revolution went hunting on his uncle's ranch and was shot in the back when his brother-in-law accidentally discharged his shotgun. LeMond suffered a near-fatal loss of blood, and his injuries were severe. Indeed, upon his return to the Tour in 1989, he would race with thirty-seven shotgun pellets still in his body, some lodged within the lining of his heart. Seven years later, LeMond would retire from competition, announcing, to the great surprise of many doctors, that he was suffering from a neuromuscular disease called mitochondrial myopathy, an announcement he delivered in the middle of a fund-raising telethon! It was a painful confession that made his exploits in the Tour all the more impressive.

Bernard Hinault found himself on the other side of the barriers in 1987, serving as technical adviser to the Société du Tour de France. Lucien van Impe was savoring a well-deserved retirement, complete with the big breakfasts he had earned by winning six climbing titles and as many trophies filled with Chocolat Poulain, the brand that had sponsored the best-climber competition in those days.

Félix Lévitan also would not be following the Tour that year. As co-director of the race, Lévitan had worked in tandem for about forty years with Jacques Goddet, CEO of *L'Équipe*. Lévitan also created the Tour de l'Avenir and a women's Tour de France, the Tour Cycliste Féminin.[1] But the distinguished director of the Société du Tour de France was now being accused of mismanagement. As a result, the 81-year-old Goddet, who had been hoping to retire in order to catch his breath, took the Tour torch for one more year. Lévitan's departure came at a time when Hein Verbruggen, president of the Union Cycliste Internationale (International Cycling Union), intended to revolutionize the cycling calendar.

Change and modernization were gaining a foothold in other areas of cycling as well. More cogs were appearing at the rear of the bike in the race to fill gaps in the racers' gear ratios, and Shimano's index-shifting system was making inroads in the peloton. Conventional toe clips were disappearing, too, as clipless pedals became prevalent. The new shoe-binding system was an innovation facilitated by the pairing of Hinault and Bernard Tapie, a veritable dynamic duo for the Look cycling company, which had set out to make a binding system for cyclists as practical and easy to use as that already found on skis.

No longer able to cling to its cherished past, the Tour started that year from Berlin, where it stayed for the first three stages, paying out cash prizes totaling 3 million deutsche marks—almost 10 million francs, or $1.66 million (nearly $3 million today). As a small consolation for the trouble, on the fourth day the Tour passed through the city of Karlsruhe, where Baron von Drais had introduced the Draisine, predecessor to a number of human-powered vehicles created during the Victorian age and called "velocipedes," precursors of the modern bicycle.

Herrera, Winner of the Vuelta

Who would win this Tour, which was apparently wide open? For the first time in Tour history, a Colombian catapulted to the top of the favorites: Lucho Herrera, cherished son of Fusagasuga, who had just won the Vuelta like a desperado exacting revenge on a conquering Spain. He had enflamed the city of Bogotá, capital of the proud South American country that had once been a colony of New Castile in central Spain and part of the vice-kingdom of New Granada (which had also included Venezuela, Ecuador, and Panama). Other notable pretenders to the title were Pedro Delgado (who had signed with PDM), Stephen Roche (Carrera Jeans), Laurent Fignon (Système U), and Jean-François Bernard (Toshiba–La Vie Claire).

The imposing peloton, 207 strong, would climb the Pyrénées before arriving at the foot of the Alps, albeit without first-time Tour participant Giuseppe Saronni, the classy Italian rider better suited to one-day races, or Sean Kelly, who had suffered a fall on the road to Bordeaux, dislocating his clavicle.

Without a dominant figure and lacking a conductor to lead the band, the yellow jersey changed hands as if in a game of musical chairs. Seven ephemeral princes succeeded one another before the queen stage of Alpe d'Huez: Jelle Nijdam, a Dutchman and prologue specialist; Lech Piasecki, the first Pole to don the tunic, which he did with religious fervor; Erich Mächler, elegant like all Swiss riders, who never lived up to his potential; Charly Mottet, winner of the 1984 Tour de l'Avenir and, symbolically, the stage to Futuroscope; Martial Gayant, the perfect leader for traversing the center of France; Bernard, protagonist of a legendary exploit on the gravelly and asphyxiating road up Mont Ventoux in an extraordinary time trial; and finally Roche.[2]

The Irishman, a lover of classic cars and things mechanical, had gotten away with Delgado in the Villard-de-Lans stage that the Spaniard had won. On the eve of the Alpe d'Huez stage, Roche was first in the overall standings, followed by Mottet (41 seconds), Delgado (1:19), Bernard (1:39), and Herrera (6:47).

The route leading to the plateau of L'Oisans included two first-category challenges before the final assault. The race began in earnest on the descent of the first of those challenges, the Col du Coq. Denis Roux (Peugeot) pushed the pace but was eventually joined by about twenty others. They all attacked the second challenge together, the Côte de Laffrey. At the summit, the Spaniard Federico Echave (BH) took the lead, along with Anselmo Fuerte (BH), Christophe Lavainne (already winner of the stage to Épinal), and Martin Ramirez (Café de Colombia), crossing the finish line at the top of Alpe d'Huez in that order.

On the descent toward Saint-Barthélemy-de-Séchilienne, Echave put his head down and went for it without worrying about the wind—the cyclist's natural enemy—or the long, flat section leading to the Alpe's twenty-one turns. It was there that Van Impe, on his own solo breakaway, had lost the 1977 Tour. However, Echave reached the first switchbacks with a lead of over 4 minutes on his immediate pursuers, Fuerte and Ramirez, and over 8 minutes on the yellow jersey, Roche, who was accompanied by the main favorites.

The long-limbed Spaniard, who was a well-paid (30 million pesetas over two years, equal to approximately $242,000 then, or $430,000 today) and faithful teammate to Fuerte, the leader of the BH team, pulled off a remarkable athletic feat that day. Sitting on the nose of his saddle, his torso leaning forward, he struggled to preserve an advantage that was melting like snow in the sun at every turn. Yet no one caught him, and he crossed the line more than 1.5 minutes ahead of the second-place rider, his compatriot Fuerte, giving Spain two reasons to celebrate. But it wasn't over. Farther back, the race of the great ones had yet to contribute its share of suspense.

Delgado Drops Herrera

From the moment when he reached the first switchback, Herrera attacked. The proud Colombian did not want to repeat the fatal error he had committed on July 14, on the climb toward Luz Ardiden, when he had decided to turn on the turbo just under 4 kilometers (2.5 miles) from the summit. He had waited too long to make his bid for the stage win, which had been claimed by Dag Otto Lauritzen, a Norwegian signed with the American team 7-Eleven-Hoonved.

This time Herrera attacked earlier, leaving Roche, the yellow jersey, and Delgado at the foot of Alpe d'Huez. But the curly-black-haired Delgado, nicknamed "Périco," was heralding a new generation of Spanish *escaladores*—strong on the flats as well as on the climbs, like the future star Miguel Induráin. Straddling his Concorde bicycle, Delgado flew up the switchbacks of the Alpe, dropping Roche. For the price of his stunning effort, he rejoined Herrera at turn number 8, about 5 kilometers (3 miles) from the summit. Périco energetically pushed down and through each pedal stroke, pulling on the handlebar with his forearms. The sound of the crowd carried him. He abandoned Herrera, and with each subsequent turn the Spanish fiesta grew, like a crowd in an arena standing to greet the matador dressed in his suit of lights. Delgado the matador pedaled on, his muscles taut.

But Herrera, steady and incredibly efficient, caught back up to Delgado. The smooth Colombian, wearing a helmet marked "Café de Colombia" and the polka-dot jersey of best climber, was sporting a pair of modern sunglasses that gave him the strange look of a skier turned bicycle tourist. A few kilometers from the summit, he was leading Périco by a handful of seconds, which he held until the finish line. He even passed Fignon, one of the last survivors of the original breakaway launched in pursuit of Echave.

When Echave had reached the first turn with a 6:20 lead over the peloton, Fignon had initiated the counterattack in the Romanche Valley without waiting for his teammate, Mottet (second in the overall standings), who was farther back. It was a strategic error, as far as Tour director Jacques Goddet was concerned; he wrote the next day, "Cruel fate. Fignon surely made this mistake based on the desire to show that he is still a champion. Ironically, it was there that three years earlier, when rival Hinault broke away near the same spot, Fignon had said, 'He makes me laugh.'"

At the foot of the Alpe, Fignon struggled on the first switchbacks. "I had to use my 23-tooth cog for a few hundred meters before shifting back to the 19," he admitted. At the back of the race, Mottet was being left behind for good. Roche, abandoned by his principal rivals, was barely hanging tough when he found providential help in the form of Marino Lejarreta, a respected climbing specialist in all three Grand Tours, and Bernard, wearing the combination jersey of best all-around rider.

At the summit, Périco would finally don the yellow jersey, which no Spaniard had worn since Luis Ocaña had proudly achieved it in 1973, exactly 14 years earlier. Fourteen years had likewise separated Ocaña from his illustrious predecessor, Federico Bahamontes. Delgado's triumph was particularly gratifying because he had abandoned the previous Tour when his mother had died. With the yellow jersey and the top two places on the stage, Spain could dance the fandango high atop the Alpe.

In the overall standings, however, Delgado was only 25 seconds ahead of Roche, a strong, well-rounded rider who had already won the Giro d'Italia under challenging circumstances. The Irishman would deny him the golden fleece for good in the Dijon time trial, the day before the final stage into Paris. Roche would also go on to wear the rainbow jersey a month later in Villach, Austria, pulling off a spectacular triple victory (Giro–Tour–World Championship)—a feat equaled only by Eddy Merckx in 1974.

Delgado would win his Tour the following year, against the backdrop of a doping scandal that nearly provoked a diplomatic crisis between France and Spain.

CHAPTER THIRTEEN

1988

Steven Rooks
Smiles at Last

N 1988, THE ALPE D'HUEZ STAGE TOOK PLACE ON JULY 14—BASTILLE
Day—but it was far from the tricolor fireworks the French had hoped
for. Instead, it was a national fiasco, a kind of Battle of Berezina for
most of the Tour favorites. This deadly, apocalyptic stage took place
during an event marked from the start by the absence or faltering of its
principal leaders.

Stephen Roche, winner of the Giro d'Italia, the Tour, and the world
championships the year before, was suffering from knee problems that
had forced him out of the Vuelta. Roche had moved to a Spanish team
(Fagor, where he had worked to get a position for his friend and trainer,
Patrick Valcke), so his absence was highly disappointing for his sponsors.
The Irishman had undergone surgery on his left knee in November 1987
but had not been able to regain his previous stellar form. In his absence
from the Tour, his teammate Robert Millar became leader of the team.

Greg LeMond, who had won the 1986 Tour after his fratricidal duel with
Bernard Hinault, also had to sit this one out. Victim of a dramatic hunting
accident in 1987, the American was still trying to get back into shape. His
morale low after pulling out of Italy's one-day Milan–San Remo classic in
March, he was looking patiently ahead to better days. They would come
in spectacular fashion in 1989 and 1990. Signed after his divorce from
Bernard Tapie by PDM (the same team Delgado had chosen the previous

year), directed by Jan Giesberts, LeMond yielded his position as team leader for the Tour to a certain Steven Rooks, whose rear wheel would be admired by his competitors on the climb up Alpe d'Huez.

With Roche and LeMond out of commission, observers cast a curious and watchful eye toward Jean-François Bernard (Toshiba), now 26. His nickname, the diminutive "Jeff," was a clear sign of his popularity despite a rather meager *palmarès*. A gifted but inconsistent performer, he had domi-nated the spotlight during the 1985 Tour, when as Hinault's teammate he had become the mascot of Tour television and especially the darling of the French public station Antenne 2.[1] That media exposure would exact a toll later on, the ephemeral glory proving a heavy burden when the results didn't materialize as everyone had hoped.

The man with three first names had pulled off some amazing exploits, including his climb up Mont Ventoux in the 1987 Tour, but he was still fragile. Nevertheless, all of the experts, or at least most of them, were looking to Bernard in 1988. "Show us what you've got, Jeff," read the headline of *Sprint 2000* magazine, which was unveiling a new, more col-orful format to mark the occasion. For its part, *Miroir du Cyclisme* shared with its readers all of the secrets from the medical tests performed in the laboratory on the champion from Nièvre.

Perhaps not surprisingly, in light of all the hype, Bernard was prema-turely being considered Hinault's spiritual son and successor. He had been signed by Toshiba, the successor to Hinault's final team, La Vie Claire, and coached at his request (following his split from Paul Koechli) by the former French amateur team trainer Yves Hézard. But Jeff had had to abandon the Giro after he'd fallen in a tunnel and suffered a hematoma on his hip, just weeks before the Tour.

Everyone was also wondering about Laurent Fignon's form. The be-spectacled Parisian continued to oscillate like a yo-yo between victory and despair. He had won Milan–San Remo in brilliant fashion at the begin-ning of the season after a prolonged absence following the operation on his Achilles tendon in 1985. Less than a month before the Tour, however, he had pulled out of the Dauphiné Libéré, suffering from sinusitis. He therefore arrived at the start of the Tour with little clout, wearing the jersey of Système U and flanked by the rider who would become leader of the team, the feisty Charly Mottet.

In a year marked by presidential elections in France and America, the sports press amused itself by trying to guess the name of the candidate who would ascend the podium in Paris.

Delgado Forgotten

In the end, two names emerged in the prognostications at the start in Pontchâteau-Machecoul in the Loire-Atlantique region: Sean Kelly and Andy Hampsten.

At the grand old age of 33 and wearing the jersey of Kas (a Spanish team), Kelly was the winner of the 1988 Vuelta, his first victory in a Grand Tour, which imbued him with the confidence of a champion heading into La Grande Boucle. But all that was quickly forgotten, as the French mountains will not roll over and play dead for anyone. Although a swift sprinter, he was out of his element as soon as the road sloped upward, despite having won his seventh Paris-Nice that year, a race record. He was a rather staid, traditional Irishman, one of the last riders to persist in the use of toe clips.

The American Andy Hampsten had been impressive at the Giro d'Italia, which he had won after a Dantesque stage contested on the snowy, glacial Gavia Pass. Riding for the U.S. team 7-Eleven, Hampsten had persevered through a blizzard, finishing second on the shortened stage to Erik Breukink. He had then gone on to take the overall victory, the first by an American in the Giro, elevating the hopes of his compatriots beyond all reason for the subsequent Tour.

Almost no one was talking about Pedro Delgado, now back in Spain riding for Reynolds-Banesto after a year in Holland with PDM learning the tricks of the trade. Second to Roche in 1987 and obsessed with the Tour, his raison d'être, the 25-year-old Spaniard focused all of his energies on the event, refusing to race the Vuelta so as to better prepare for the Tour's transalpine stages. That decision was sacrilege as far as the Spanish people were concerned (meanwhile, Spanish fans were becoming acquainted with a new star, Miguel Induráin, riding at Julian Gorospe's side). Just months later, however, they would chant Delgado's name to the point of hysteria and defend him tooth and nail against the systematic attacks leveled against him after a positive drug test.

The Trials of Jean-François Bernard

Before the start of the Alpe stage in Morzine, the Canadian Steve Bauer (Weinmann–La Suisse)[2] was wearing the yellow jersey, which he had defended for four days. In second place, just 11 seconds behind, was little Jérôme Simon (the third of four professional racers in his family, following Pascal and Régis and preceding François). Simon had already won the stage to Strasbourg and was sporting the polka-dot jersey of best climber. Trailing Bauer and Simon in the overall standings were Breukink (43 seconds), Mottet (1:01), and Delgado (1:52).

The 227-kilometer (136-mile) stage—one that Laurent Fignon, suffering from tapeworm, failed to start—would couple the Col de la Madeleine and the Col du Glandon before the final assault on Alpe d'Huez.

From the start of the climb up the Madeleine, Jeff felt that his legs were abandoning him—they just would not turn. He was struggling terribly and was already trailing the leaders by 10 minutes, with the Glandon and the Alpe still to come. This Bastille Day would see him bear a heavy cross. Courageous but on the verge of exhaustion, he labored along with the bigger riders, notably Gilbert Duclos-Lassalle and Guido Bontempi, refusing to abandon the effort. He emerged at the top of the Alpe 22 minutes behind the stage winner, confiding to Jean-Paul Brouchon of *Miroir du Cyclisme*, "I thought about giving up at least fifty times. I thought about a lot of things: about those who will surely say I'm up shit creek; about those who taunted me with unflattering jeers; about Marie-Laure [his wife], who must have been crying when she heard the news on the radio; and about all my problems since the beginning of the season."

Then he confessed, "Too many people were hoping I'd give up. But you don't just drop out of the Tour like that." He would nevertheless abandon the race in the Pyrénées, on the road to Luchon, victim of a urinary infection.

The Alpe Brings Them to Their Knees

On the Madeleine, plenty of other dramas came to a head. Urs Zimmermann, the Swiss who had attacked just a few kilometers earlier, suddenly eased up and then all but collapsed. He would arrive at the summit 20 minutes off the pace. Kelly, the number-one-ranked rider in the world since 1984, and Breukink were also trailing far behind the leaders. Shortly thereafter, it was Mottet's turn to crack: He was 1:05 behind at the foot of the Alpe and more than 8 minutes back at the top. Then Hampsten. Despite his nickname, the "Rabbit," he had been pedaling with Mottet at the base of the climb but finished over 4 minutes off the pace at the top.

"To our knowledge," wrote Pierre Chany the next day in *L'Équipe*, "no stage has ever collectively taken down so many of the acknowledged and overwhelming favorites so suddenly." *Miroir du Cyclisme* proclaimed, "This 14th of July will be recorded in the annals of cycling literature. And it wasn't just the captains and sailors who were lost, but with them virtually all of the certainties we had constructed about modern cycling over nearly 20 years. Then again, how could we have forgotten that, in the mountains, the nature of things is eternal?"

At 1.5 kilometers (just under 1 mile) from the summit of the Glandon, Delgado attacked. Only Rooks, wearing the multicolored leader's jersey of the combination classification, could jump on his wheel before barreling down the other side and finally reaching the first turn of the Alpe, where a stunned crowd was considering this Bastille Day slaughter a general death sentence.

The powerful, determined Spaniard, his sunglasses hanging around his neck, increased his lead and sped toward the yellow jersey, the one he had conquered in 1987 on the very same slopes. The long-limbed Dutchman, who had been his teammate the year before, began to pedal more convincingly, madly encouraged by the thousands of Batavian fans. Coming up from behind, Fabio Parra and Gert-Jan Theunisse put in a monstrous effort, catching the lead duo 3 kilometers (1.9 miles) from the summit. The Colombian, with a boxer's nose and dark complexion, had been the winner the day before in the beautiful city of Morzine at the foot of the mountains of Avoriaz. The bulging-eyed Theunisse wore his blond hair like Dutch soccer star Johann Cruyff and sported a ring in his left ear. Four men were now leading the dance, but not for long.

Rooks, who had been an early-season protagonist, placing in the top five in all the major classics, took off 1.5 kilometers from the finish to claim a much-coveted victory. On this plateau, bringer of good fortune to Dutch riders, 50,000 fans representing the House of Orange chanted Rooks's name. His compatriot and teammate at PDM, Theunisse, garnered second place.

For the first time in Tour history, fans saw two Flying Dutchmen, as tall as basketball players, beat out all the best climbers, including Lucho Herrera, winner of the Dauphiné Libéré a few weeks earlier, but today only fifth and over a minute behind. Rooks, the Buster Keaton of the peloton because he never smiled, and Theunisse, nicknamed the "Wizard of Oss" after the Dutch town where he resided, had worked together like Siamese twins. This inseparable pair would pull off other exploits on these slopes as soon as the following year.

At the summit of Alpe d'Huez, Rooks, who would finish second in the Tour, raised his arms to signal his delight. It was an exception for him to mark a triumph with such a gesture, although the practice is common among other riders. Never before, even on the occasions of his two victories in the classics—the 1983 Liège-Bastogne-Liège and the 1986 Amstel Gold Race—had he manifested such joy. Ah, the magic of the Alpe! And the magic of the Dutch riders on this mountain. In 1988, Joop Zoetemelk had reluctantly retired after an eighteen-year career. But now he could rest easy, knowing that Dutch honor would be upheld. An earlier retirement would have been too soon, as Rooks had abandoned the Tour on the Alpe the year before.

As for Bauer, he had lost his handsome yellow jersey by only 25 seconds.

Delgado Declared Positive

The next day, Pedro Delgado confirmed his stellar form and ambition by winning the time trial at Villard-de-Lans ahead of Bernard, who had suddenly come back to life. Delgado would go on to win his first Tour, fifteen years after Luis Ocaña. But he finished the event under a cloud of suspicion and as the target of accusations that nearly provoked a diplomatic crisis between France and Spain. Six days after Alpe d'Huez and the day after the final stage in the Pyrénées, when the Tour stopped in Bordeaux before making its advance toward the capital, Delgado was accused of doping.

The news broke on television. In *Journal du Tour*, first Jacques Chancel and then Patrick Chêne passed on rumors that the Spaniard had tested positive. Delgado himself learned of the accusation from his teammate Dominique Arnaud. It caused quite a stir, compounded by a press release the next day that confirmed the buzz. But the "Delgado Affair" came to light in a climate of speculation. The analysis revealed the presence of probenecid, a uricosuric drug that also works as a masking agent in athletes. It had been banned by the International Olympic Committee but not at that time by the Union Cycliste Internationale (UCI), the governing body for cycling. Therefore, legally, Delgado had not doped. Still, some had their doubts.

Doctors explained that probenecid could in fact serve to mask the use of anabolic steroids. *Vélo* qualified that year's Tour victory with the headline "Delgado, in Spite of It All." The charged atmosphere was emotionally heightened because the affair threatened the mystique of the yellow jersey, as had been the case with Michel Pollentier in 1979.

Another rider in this Tour was also accused of doping: Gert-Jan Theunisse. He was penalized 10 minutes and fell from 4th to 11th place overall, without much ado.

Three months later, *Vélo*, which had not been easy on Delgado, published an article by Eric Lahmy titled "Doping: Delgado Was Innocent." It declared that probenecid "was not a diuretic, but acted against uric acid, which it significantly neutralized. It had been very hot during the Tour, and Delgado, whose body had a tendency to overproduce uric acid (the concentration of which tends to increase significantly during exertion), had difficulty eliminating it, and was feeling the effects in his legs. His doctor, knowing that it was not banned, had prescribed it."

Alpe d'Huez Has the Last Word

This Tour had begun amidst doubts and uncertainties, as the race itself had been affected by the implementation of new regulations regarding the professional cycling calendar. These changes had been decreed by Hein Verbruggen, boss of the UCI.

Under the new rules, the Tour would need to content itself with a maximum of twenty-one days of racing and above all was not allowed to extend over more than three weekends. The organizers, including a new race director, Jean-François Radiguet, were forced to reduce the event by approximately 1,000 kilometers (621 miles) in order to reach Paris on a Sunday. They also had to devise a "preface," a sort of unofficial prologue presented like a criterium that would nonetheless award the winner, in this case the stocky and powerful Bontempi, the yellow jersey. This Tour, which also inaugurated the VIP start village, would be only 3,281 kilometers (1,965 miles) long—less than 150 kilometers (90 miles) per day—and would be considered one of the easiest.

But the Alpe would have the last word. Never before had so many riders faltered on its slopes: Bernard, Zimmermann, Breukink, Kelly, Mottet, Hampsten—all of them history.

CHAPTER FOURTEEN

1989

Fignon's
Exhausted Attack

"POKER ON THE ALPE?" So RAN *L'ÉQUIPE*'S HEADLINE ON THE morning of Wednesday, July 19, as the Tour was set to leave Briançon and launch an assault on Alpe d'Huez. The issue, which included eight columns on the front page as well as four pages of special coverage, was printed entirely on yellow paper to celebrate seventy years of the golden fleece, the emblem introduced by *L'Équipe*'s predecessor, *L'Auto-Vélo* and worn for the first time in 1919 by Eugène Christophe. On the last page, all twenty-one turns were presented in color. Would this road once again dictate the outcome of the Tour?

When the 1989 Tour had set off from Luxembourg, many had looked forward to a grudge match between Stephen Roche and Pedro Delgado, the past two winners. In 1987, Roche had finished first and Delgado second. But the following year, when Delgado had won, Roche had failed to compete because he had still been recovering from a knee operation. As it turned out, the duel would not take place this year, either. By the time the Tour reached Marseille, to honor the bicentennial of the French Revolution, Roche was already gone. He had dropped out the morning of the 10th stage, at the start from Cauterets—a resort town in the Pyrénées reputed as a place of healing for all illnesses.

As the Tour unfolded, a few keen observers noticed a promising star on the rise: a 24-year-old named Miguel Induráin. The Spanish rider had already won

Paris-Nice and the Critérium International and had finished second in the Tour prologue under sunny skies behind a smiling Thierry Marie, the blond, blue-eyed specialist. Induráin had also won the ninth stage to Cauterets (the town where Roche had dropped out) after making a 90-kilometer (56-mile) breakaway and unfurling a red carpet for his leader, Delgado.

Perhaps it was a sign of things to come. The famous professor Francesco Conconi, chairman of the biochemistry department at the University of Ferrara and the brains behind Francesco Moser's hour record, affirmed prophetically, "There's no telling what his limits are." That was in 1989. Two years later, the reign of the most powerful of Basque champions, as well as the most reserved, would commence.[1]

LeMond's Return

The 1989 Tour quickly turned into a spirited duel between two former winners: Greg LeMond, the 1986 champion, who was at last returning to form after a near-fatal hunting accident, and Laurent Fignon, the haughty Parisian "Professeur" and 1984 winner, who was making a comeback of his own.

That spring, Fignon had been victorious for the second year in a row at the Milan–San Remo classic. This Italophile (to the point of ending his career with Gianni Bugno's Gatorade team a few years later) had also won the Giro, which had instantly propelled him to the status of Tour favorite. As for LeMond, nobody had expected him to have much of a chance at the start of the race. Still recovering from his health problems, he'd had some trouble shopping for a team after an acrimonious departure from PDM, which had wanted to cut his salary by $200,000. He had finally joined the durable Eddy Planckaert (winner of Paris-Roubaix the following year) on the ADR squad—appropriate, perhaps, as ADR was a truck-rental company and LeMond definitely seemed to be renting his ride that year. His fitness at the start of the season had not been good, and he had ridden the Giro primarily in search of form.

Nevertheless, during the stage 4 time trial from Dinar to Rennes, the first serious challenge of this Tour, the American was once again at center stage when he beat out Delgado. Appropriately in the vicinity of the Futuroscope theme park, LeMond emerged as something of an extraterrestrial in his aerodynamic helmet, large sunglasses, forward-sloping frame, disc wheels, and very strange set of handlebars.

Fignon had tried to use similar bars in the Grand Prix Eddy Merckx, only to be booted from the contest by an overzealous judge. Later on, however, he had used the aero bars to win the Grand Prix des Nations. After that, the organizers of the prestigious (but now defunct) Baracchi Trophy, a two-man time trial, had actually insisted that he use the bars to race the event with Thierry Marie; the pair had won.

Following that fourth stage, the LeMond-Fignon duel intensified. LeMond would hang on to the yellow jersey until the 10th stage, when he ceded it to the Parisian during the climb to Superbagnères. But during the 15th stage to Orcières-Merlette—won by Steven Rooks, who had triumphed at Alpe d'Huez the year before—the American wrested it back from Fignon and gained a 40-second lead over his rival. During the next stage to Briançon, LeMond picked up an additional 13 seconds, time that Fignon had lost during the ascent to the Citadelle, which pays tribute to former Tour champions, notably Eddy Merckx, Felice Gimondi, and Bernard Thévenet.

Delgado Desperate, Theunisse Flying

Thus, the American wore the yellow jersey at the start of the 17th stage to L'Alpe d'Huez. LeMond led Fignon by 53 seconds, Charly Mottet by 2:16, and Delgado by 2:48. For LeMond, the Spaniard was still a man to beat.

Delgado was treating every stage like a time trial in a desperate effort to make up for his bungle during the prologue, when he had shown up for the start 2:40 late. Once under way, he had ridden like a madman but had still finished the 8-kilometer (5-mile) test 2:53 down. Courageously, he had managed to narrow the disastrous gap in the Pyrénées. Périco, winner of the Vuelta, was anxious to gild his coat of arms once more after the scandal of "l'Affaire Delgado" the previous year, a wound that a French television show had callously reopened.

This queen stage would once again thrill Dutch fans, who had amassed along the Alpe's hairpin turns, many under enormous parasols or awnings attached to campers. They proudly brandished their blue-white-and-red flags and pushed out their chests to show off T-shirts displaying the faces of Steven Rooks and Gert-Jan Theunisse. From the climb up the Croix de Fer, their man Theunisse was leading the race. With the look of a fragile Viking, clothed in the polka-dot jersey of best climber, he would not disappoint them. The Flying Dutchman, who had opened up a 1:27 lead going up that hill, sprinted down it toward the first of the Alpe's turns and built his lead to 2 minutes over his nearest rivals and 4 minutes over the yellow-jersey group that included all the favorites. Wildly cheered during the long climb to his prize, the Dutchman with the steely gaze thought of all the sufferings he had endured since the start of the season: numerous falls, tenacious sinusitis, and bone fractures in his foot and elbow. He had not even expected to make this Tour, yet on the Alpe he was in the thick of it, climbing its slopes to glory. He was realizing two of his most cherished dreams: to wear the polka-dot jersey and—the ultimate prize—to win atop the Alpe. Because he was superstitious, he also thought of the four-leaf clover tattooed on his right shoulder to ward off bad luck.

At turn 17, trailed by a fleet of support vehicles, Theunisse held a 2:25 lead over the Scotsman Robert Millar (riding for Z, a new team LeMond would join at the end of the year). The Dutchman also led Gianni Bugno, who heralded the grand return of the Italians, by 3 minutes, and the Tour favorites by 4 minutes. The latter group included LeMond, Fignon, Delgado, Marino Lejarreta, Rooks, and Delgado's devoted *domestique*, Abelardo Rondon, who calmly rested his hands atop his bars as he set an infernal pace to protect Delgado and set him up for a final attack planned at 3 kilometers (1.9 miles) from the summit.

Guimard Yells, "Attack!"

LeMond, Fignon, and Delgado knew that the Tour would be decided over this final incline. They watched one another in anticipation of the first sign of fatigue. Meanwhile, under the scrutiny of television cameras that were broadcasting the climb live and in its entirety, they acted like modern-day gallant knights, passing around a water bottle that one had plucked from the hands of a sympathetic fan. It was a remarkable display of chivalry, reminiscent of Coppi and Bartali—those "intimate enemies"—back in the day, sharing a bottle while ascending the Galibier in oppressive heat.

Wheel to wheel, the three ascended relentlessly until 7 kilometers (4.3 miles) from the top, where LeMond began to falter, his shoulders rocking back and forth. It was a sign that Cyrille Guimard, Fignon's *directeur sportif*, recognized: LeMond was out of gas. He threaded his car through the sea of crazed fans and pulled up next to the Parisian. "You've got to go! Now!" he shouted. "Right now!"

Fignon, his face wreathed in sweat, looked over. "I can't do it," he said. "I can't."

Guimard dropped back and waited. The three continued up the Alpe's switchbacks, ticking off the kilometers one by one. And then, at turn 6, just before the hamlet of Huez and only 4 kilometers (2.4 miles) from the summit, Guimard once again pushed his car through the crowds. "Attack!" he cried. "LeMond is cooked. It's now or never!" Fignon, of course, had also noticed LeMond's jerky pedaling, rocking shoulders, and lowered head while he tried to find a good position on his saddle. LeMond was uncomfortable but had silently held on.

Now Fignon made his move, throwing all his aggression and hopes into this painful effort. He wasn't pedaling; he was turning a gear on pure energy. A mere 53 seconds separated him from the American. He had 53 seconds to make up in order to retake the yellow jersey. He held nothing back. At turn 3, 2 kilometers (1.2 miles) from the finish, he had already taken back 52 seconds.

"Suddenly," wrote Philippe Bouvet in *L'Équipe*, "LeMond sat back down in the saddle. He reached for his shift lever. He wavered. The narrow corridor that the fans had yielded was not wide enough; LeMond was all over the place. For 500 meters, it was terrible: The yellow jersey was drowning in the sea of spectators. No car or motorcycle could follow him closely enough to keep the crowd from closing in on him."

Fignon crossed the line with a 26-second lead over LeMond in the overall standings. For the third time in his career, he pulled on the yellow jersey at the top of Alpe d'Huez, his good-luck resort.

Only Delgado was able to catch Fignon, snatching second place from him behind Theunisse, who won the stage. For Theunisse, it was a particularly meaningful triumph. He had come so close the year before, finishing second to Rooks by the width of a tire. Now he had done it! But just a year later, he would become the Alpe's exile. Accused of doping three times in two years, he would be banned from competition for an entire season.[2] Through it all, he proclaimed his innocence and played the part of a martyr, explaining that he had a naturally high level of testosterone that made him test positive.

To purge his pain and keep his muscles in shape, and obsessed with a return to the top in order to prove his innocence, Theunisse took up residence at L'Alpe d'Huez. There, under the stunned eyes of the puzzled natives, he climbed his slope of infatuation three or four times a day, as if he had devised a system of training based on penitence.

The Famous 8 Seconds

At this point in the Tour, Delgado had lost all hope of winning, and LeMond's chances seemed similarly slim. The next day, Fignon, like a true champion, won the Villard-de-Lans stage and increased his lead: 50 seconds ahead of LeMond, with three days to Paris. The race was all but won. But on the last day, in the time trial from Versailles to Paris, LeMond, in front of the American embassy and in the same year as the destruction of the Berlin Wall, robbed Fignon of the yellow jersey in extremis. By 8 seconds! Eight seconds of ecstasy for LeMond and 8 seconds of disgrace and despair for Fignon.

That day, the American used his triathlete clip-on bar, which he had estimated would gain him as much as 20 seconds. Fignon, however, rode his standard bike, sans aero bar, sans helmet, his ponytail flapping in the wind. Why in the world had Guimard not mounted the same bar on Fignon's bike? In Guimard's mind, Fignon had squandered his opportunity to seal his victory on the Alpe, and there was nothing more to be done. "Laurent missed his chance at Alpe d'Huez," Guimard insisted. "He was very strong that day and had the means, I believe, to open up a more significant lead over LeMond." It was an interesting analysis, if not a cruel one. This mistake with technology was not the first: In 1984, Fignon had lost the Giro to Francesco Moser when he hadn't used disc wheels under similar circumstances.

A month later, LeMond became world champion, taking the crown in Chambéry after catching none other than Fignon, who had broken away on the final lap in pursuit of a title he would never win. The American was christened "champion of champions" by *L'Équipe* and, more importantly, "Sportsman of the Year" in the United States by *Sports Illustrated*. He had finally gained recognition on his own.

CHAPTER FIFTEEN

1990

LeMond and Bugno
to the Line

A YEAR AFTER THE DESTRUCTION OF THE BERLIN WALL, THE RUSSIANS invaded Europe. Fortunately, their aggression was limited to the European peloton, to the extent that *Miroir du Cyclisme* (known to be sympathetic to the Communist Party[1]) mixed humor with news when it depicted, on the front page of its March issue, Mikhail Gorbachev as a cyclist with the caption "This is the year of perestroika."

One of the more exciting Eastern arrivals, signed by the Dutch team Panasonic, was the young Viatcheslav Ekimov, nicknamed the "Moser of the Amateurs" because of his talent as a track racer.[2] Alfa Lum signed two other prospects: Djamolidine Abdoujaparov, the formidable sprinter from Uzbekistan who would prove unstoppable at the 1991 Tour, and Dimitri Konyshev, the first Soviet racer to wear a leader's jersey in the Tour and win a stage.[3]

The arrival of riders from the East did seem like a landing of foreign troops. Panasonic, whose presence would be felt strongly at this Tour, was further strengthened by the addition of the East German Olaf Ludwig, the Olympic champion at Seoul in 1988 and the two-time winner of the Course de Paix (1982 and 1986), the East's most famous stage race. This year, he would wear the green jersey into Paris.

Joining PDM were two more East Germans: world amateur champions Uwe Ampler (1983) and Uwe Raab (1986). A Pole by the name of Zenon

Jaskula, who would distinguish himself in the mountains in the 1993 Tour, wore the jersey of Diana–Colnago Animex along with his countryman Lech Piasecki, the first Pole to don the yellow jersey at the Tour.

Panasonic also signed the Dutch "brothers," Gert-Jan Theunisse and Steven Rooks, who were truly inseparable. They had previously left the team owing to personal differences with the director, Peter Post, but after a reconciliation were now back in the fold. They were particularly adept at attacking the Alpe in tandem. Two years earlier, when Rooks had taken the stage, Theunisse had finished 2nd. The next year, it had been Theunisse's turn to win on the plateau and his teammate had finished 7th. But they would not collaborate there during the 1990 Tour because Theunisse was absent, purging his expulsion after testing positive for drug use. He sent Rooks a telegram the day of the stage that read, "You can win this, you ass." But deprived of his twin, Rooks could finish no better than 26th, 5:03 behind Gianni Bugno.

LeMond in Bad Shape

The 1990 Tour, which started from Futuroscope, had a few big surprises in store. The first was the health of Greg LeMond, winner of the previous Tour by only 8 seconds; in spectacular fashion, he would be completely overwhelmed in 1991. Prisoner to the snow at his home in Minnesota during the off-season, he had been unable to train adequately. A viral infection had compounded his problems, leaving him exhausted. As had been the case during his comeback after the hunting accident in 1987, the American was once again struggling desperately to get back to the top.

His struggle began on March 28, the day on which he left the peloton after abandoning the Three Days of De Panne. He was carrying a good 15 extra pounds and suffered a deep depression. In eight starts, he had dropped out of five races. Nothing was working! To add to the distress, he was wearing the world champion's stripes, which made everything that much worse. The press jumped right in, of course, with provocative headlines such as *Miroir*'s "The LeMond Enigma" and *Vélo*'s "The LeMond Mystery" and "LeMond: It's Getting Dire," accompanied by a photo of the champion looking distracted and haggard. Especially telling was *L'Équipe*'s "Has LeMond Lost the Tour?"

LeMond withdrew to a secret location in the United States and began to train rigorously. He was obsessed with one thing: "I will get back on top; I will be a factor at the Tour," which he repeated incessantly while sweating profusely behind a motorcycle ridden by his Mexican *soigneur*, Otto Jacome. LeMond had good company that year under the tent of former champions; Björn Borg was preparing for his big return to competition, and Pelé pulled on his cleats to celebrate his 50th birthday!

LeMond had already experienced some promising signs in the Giro d'Italia and then in the Tour of Switzerland on the San Bernardino pass. For the summer's big event, though, his prospects were unknown.

So it was that at the start of the Tour in Futuroscope, all eyes were on the foreign conqueror as he set off in the prologue on a bicycle equipped with revolutionary bars shaped like the spade on a playing card, with a shift lever at the top, practically under his nose. Always the innovator, LeMond pushed his preoccupation with equipment to embrace yet another strange handlebar, which he used on the flat stages and even at Alpe d'Huez. The ends of the handlebar drops curved in toward one another at about the same level as the fork crown, dropping him into an efficient, aerodynamic crouch that was unlike anything seen in the race before.

In the prologue, everyone's American friend set things straight and erased all doubt: He finished second behind the perennial winner of this type of time trial, Thierry Marie. Second place was not so bad; he was already ahead of all the other favorites, and that was what mattered. Incredibly, LeMond was ready for the big battle.

Of the Tour's other big names, Laurent Fignon, in the distinctive jersey of the home-improvement retailer Castorama (complete with graphics that simulated a craftsman's suspenders), seemed unable to shake his bad luck. After a fall on the road to Nantes, he had suffered pain in his calf and had abandoned in the rain, near the Villers-Bocage feed station before Rouen. Two months earlier, he had dropped out of the Giro after falling in a tunnel. Pedro Delgado, Erik Breukink, and Bugno—winner of Milan–San Remo at the start of the season and, even more importantly, of the Giro—waited in the wings.[4]

Missing from the peloton roll call was Lucho Herrera, who had not been brought back to the Tour because his team had not benefited from the "wild-card" selection granted each year to certain teams that don't qualify for entry based on ranking. Gert-Jan Theunisse was also absent;

suspended for drug use at Flèche Wallonne, he had been banished by *directeurs sportifs* who had launched a protest at the Giro.

Chiappucci Stirs Things Up

Until Alpe d'Huez, the race mainly toured the country, led by Steve Bauer, wearer of the yellow jersey. He was the happy beneficiary of a surprise breakaway during stage 1 when a little devil named Claudio Chiappucci, a revelation on the roads of this Tour, decided to attack near the start. Carrera's climber and king of the mountains at the Giro defied everyone on a flat stage. This indefatigable *provocateur*, a self-described "bionic man," was true to his temperament and succeeded in getting three break-away companions to go with him: the Canadian Bauer, the Dutchman Frans Maassen, and the Frenchman Ronan Pensec, a future favorite of the French public. The four pocketed an 8-minute lead, which they held tight as the race moseyed toward the mountains.

On the eve of Alpe d'Huez, on a formidable climb over narrow roads overlooking Saint-Gervais, Thierry Claveyrolat won the stage at Bettex and pulled on the polka-dot jersey, which he would wear all the way to Paris. Pensec, LeMond's teammate on the Z squad, took the golden fleece on his 27th birthday and held a 50-second lead over Chiappucci in the overall standings. He led LeMond, the Tour's big favorite and his team leader, by 9:52; Erik Breukink by 10:15; and Bugno, Charly Mottet, and Stephen Roche by over 11 minutes.

Those following the Tour couldn't make sense of it all and were look-ing to the climb up the Alpe to serve as supreme judge. For their part, the French put their faith in Pensec: Small in stature with a nasal voice and crew cut, representative of a new generation of racers who were into cars, music, and nice clothes, Pensec seemed made for these times. The 182-kilometer (113-mile) climb to the Alpe would follow its classic route: Col de la Madeleine, Col du Glandon, and then Alpe d'Huez.

Feeling strong after his victory in the Bettex stage, Claveyrolat, nicknamed the "Eagle from Vizille," attacked at the first slopes of the Madeleine. The Spaniard Miguel Induráin, a superb athlete who had won Paris-Nice, joined the Frenchman on the descent and accompanied him to the Glandon before waiting for his team leader, Delgado, who was back in the yellow-jersey group. Meanwhile, farther back, Mottet, winner of the Tour de Romandie, was faltering. The Alpe d'Huez stage had never brought him luck. It was the same for Jean-François Bernard, who, suffering from saddle sores, dropped out of the race.

On the Glandon, when the road began to rise again after a brief descent, Delgado upped his pace, followed by LeMond and Bugno. This important trio caught Induráin, and all four sped off toward Bourg d'Oisans. Over the long, flat section, about 15 kilometers (9.3 miles) in length, Induráin did an extraordinary job opening a gap on yellow jersey Pensec, who was struggling farther back, along with the Mexican Raúl Alcalá (PDM), winner of the time trial stage at Épinal a few days earlier, who was in fifth place, 7 minutes back.

The result? The four riders caught Claveyrolat, and the group now had a 2:30 lead at the foot of Alpe d'Huez, where Induráin—who would win the Tour the next five years running—let his leader take off after having prepared the way for him. Delgado attacked 13 kilometers (8 miles) from the finish, over a long steep section, even before the first numbered turns. He was immediately joined by LeMond and Bugno. Once again, the Tour would be decided on the Alpe's twenty-one switchbacks.

As the stage came down to the final stretch, team Z was playing two sensational cards: the stage win for LeMond and the overall with Pensec. But the belligerent Alpe always holds a surprise or two in store.

Up ahead, LeMond played the role of model teammate and didn't take any pulls, letting Delgado open the gap. From behind, Claveyrolat managed to work his way back up to the lead trio, as did the Colombian Fabio Parra and the Dutchman Breukink, who would clock the fastest time up the climb at 43:19, recorded for the first time in Tour history. At the foot of the Alpe, Breukink was 2:30 behind the leaders. At the summit, he finished third, just 1 second behind the winner.

LeMond's Gamble Pays Off

Delgado began to fade. Three kilometers (1.9 miles) from the summit, he lost contact with Bugno, who had been preparing his attack, furious about a 20-second penalty he'd received for an unauthorized feed the day before. Bugno was followed by LeMond, Breukink, Claveyrolat, and Parra.

Positioned in the middle of the group, the American almost lost control of his bike in the last turn as his hands, aching from a fall, could barely squeeze

101

his brakes. The victory would come down to a sprint, which was uncommon on the Alpe. LeMond and Bugno accelerated furiously toward the line, where Bugno barely nipped LeMond, who was turning too big a gear.

Thirty-eight years after Fausto Coppi, first winner atop this legendary climb, and in the year that marked the 30th anniversary of the Campionissimo's untimely death, Bugno surged as if to pay him homage. Italy exulted as the crazy Italian season continued, following the notable victories of Marco Giovanetti at the Vuelta, Franco Ballerini at Paris-Brussels, and Moreno Argentin at the Tour of Flanders and Flèche Wallonne. Bugno, a somewhat fragile specimen who had undergone music therapy based on Mozart's concerti to treat vertigo, had regained his standing in this Tour.

Meanwhile, back in the pack, the struggling man carrying the weight of the yellow jersey glued his wheel to that of his teammate, Robert Millar, an excellent climber whose long hair swayed to the rhythm of his pedaling. The devoted Scot, Pensec's guardian angel and savior, selflessly towed Pensec to the summit of the plateau. At Pensec's side were Claude Criquielion, clothed in the jersey of champion of Belgium, and Andy Hampsten, the American riding with 7-Eleven, who would win this stage in 1992. They scaled the slope as Francesco Moser and the 1956 Tour winner, Roger Walkowiak, looked on.

At the summit, Pensec had saved his yellow jersey even though he had crossed the finish line a full 48 seconds after Bugno. At the bottom he had been 2:30 behind, so his climb up the Alpe was not so bad. All of France began to dream of yellow, pinning its hopes on this Breton from the same stock as the 1947 winner, Jean Robic. But Pensec's hopes would crumble the next day in the Villard-de-Lans time trial, stamping him with that most damning of labels, "unfulfilled potential." He eventually finished 20th, a dismal 22:54 down.

His teammate LeMond, in the interim, attacked on the road to Saint-Étienne on Bastille Day and on the climb to Luz Ardiden. He took the jersey in the Lac Vassivière time trial, snatching it from Chiappucci, the last holdout from the stage 1 breakaway. Once again, LeMond succeeded wildly after endless initial doubts and won his third Tour. He did it without winning a single stage. What he did not know was that he would never again wear the yellow jersey into Paris. In the roulette game of glory, you don't always win.

A Commissioner in a Helicopter

On the day of the Alpe stage, one rider lost the right to finish the race: Eric Vanderaerden (Buckler), a good classics rider but not a climber, erred in obscurity. On the final climb up the Alpe, he dug deep within himself to make it to the top, finishing in 154th place, more than 32 minutes after Bugno. Little did the Belgian, now placed 133rd overall, know that he was climbing the terrible slope for nothing.

He learned at the finish that he had been disqualified from the Tour for having held on to Maurice Le Guilloux's car on the Glandon. A commissioner who had boarded a helicopter to survey the back of the race had spotted him. Normally this kind of infraction was punished with a fine and a time penalty, but Vanderaerden became the first victim of a new ruling at the Tour, now enforced by aerial surveillance—three years after his exclusion from the Tour of the Mediterranean for the very same offense.

CHAPTER SIXTEEN

1991

The Beginning
of the Indu-reign

SYMMETRICAL ON PAPER, 1991 POSITIONED ITSELF AS A LOPSIDED year of many departures and few arrivals. Some weeks before the start of the Tour, the caravan mourned the loss of the journalist Antoine Blondin in Lyon. A faithful correspondent of La Grande Boucle and a sublime writer, he was a true wordsmith and agile communicator who left behind a stylistic legacy.

It was also the year in which Laurent Fignon would part ways with Cyrille Guimard and the Castorama team, moving to the Italian Gatorade team in 1992. Toshiba, which boasted riders like Tony Rominger and Laurent Jalabert, announced before the start of the Tour that it would discontinue its sponsorship at the end of the year.

A year of departures? There was no better way to quantify it than to note, with a heavy heart, the decrease in the number of French teams. It was no mystery: A number of French riders, twenty-five in all, decamped to foreign squads. Jean-François Bernard, like Fabrice Philipot, would wear the colors of the Spanish team Banesto, becoming Miguel Induráin's teammate and forfeiting his dreams of being team leader. Ronan Pensec, motivated by the yellow jersey he'd worn over several stages the year before, signed with the Spanish team Seur.[1] Gérard Rué joined Gilles Delion at Helvetica, a Swiss team, and Laurent Biondi and Francis Moreau opted for Ton Ton Tapis, a short-lived Belgian team owned by Roger de Vlaeminck and headlined by Stephen Roche, with Laurent Pillon.

At the start of the Tour, 198 riders set off from Lyon, including Fignon, Roche, Luis Herrera (Ryalcao-Postobon), and Pensec, all of whom had made it to the Tour thanks to wild-card selection, their teams not having qualified for inclusion by figuring in the top sixteen teams in cycling's international hit parade. For the first time in several years marked by no-shows, all of the big favorites could be identified in the peloton, though it wasn't easy to recognize them now that helmet use had become mandatory.

This year, three strong contenders would be involved in the showdown: Greg LeMond, who had already won three Tours in five starts; Claudio Chiappucci, the hero of the 1990 Tour, who had also been the spectacular winner of the one-day Milan–San Remo classic at the beginning of the season; and Erik Breukink, who everyone hoped could avoid another notorious *jour sans*.[2]

Also there were Pedro Delgado, still designated leader of Banesto despite the presence of his superbly talented teammate Induráin; Gianni Bugno, who was vying to become the first Italian winner since Felice Gimondi, twenty-six years earlier; Fignon, who had pulled out of the Giro; Luis Herrera, dominant winner of the Dauphiné Libéré, who was eager to make up for his absence in 1990; Charly Mottet, now in the hunt for stage wins instead of the yellow jersey; and Gert-Jan Theunisse, coming back after a yearlong suspension for doping. The 32-year-old Roche was not to be discounted, either, following his success at the Setmana Catalana and the Critérium International, an event he had won for the first time six years earlier.

Roche Misses the Start

The Tour got off to a fast start: LeMond dispelled any doubts about his condition, following his early departure from the Giro in May, by placing third in the prologue behind specialists Thierry Marie and Breukink and above all by attacking in the very first stage, just as Chiappucci had done the previous year. "LeMond Puts on the Pressure," read *L'Équipe*'s headline. He took the yellow jersey in that half-stage, only to lose it later that day.

105

It would definitely be a year of both good and bad departures. Even Roche was part of it: He showed up 7 minutes late for the Lyon team time trial, his teammates long departed, and missed the cutoff mark. Sent home right from the start, on the very first day! In the sixth stage to Le Havre, Thierry Marie set off early on a 234-kilometer (145-mile) solo breakaway, one of the longest in Tour history.

LeMond took back the yellow jersey in the eighth stage, a 73-kilometer (45-mile) time trial from Argentan to Alençon. The winner, however, was Induráin, who left certain favorites far behind: Delgado at 2:05, Luc Leblanc at 2:55, Fignon at 3:39, and Chiappucci at 4:44.

The true start of this Tour, however, took place in the Pyrénées, which came before the cols of the Alps in this year's counterclockwise running. Before that came another significant departure, when Breukink's entire PDM team, decimated by a mysterious illness, packed up and went home.

The 13th stage from Jaca to Val Louron (where the Frenchman Luc Leblanc wrested the yellow jersey from LeMond, who would never wear it again) was the scene of the first real skirmish to shake up the standings. Two men led the dance: Induráin, confirming the talent he had displayed in 1990 while riding in support of Delgado, and Chiappucci, the indefatigable detonator, instigator, and winner of the final explosive effort. LeMond, who faltered badly on the Tourmalet, was now digging deep.

"Jeff" Sets an Infernal Pace

In stage 16, the day before Alpe d'Huez, the American attacked again on the road to Gap in a fit of pride and ended up finishing second. On the same route, Bugno, Chiappucci, and Fignon took advantage of a fourth-category climb to put the pressure on Induráin, who quickly gathered his wits and chased the escapees, limiting the gap.

Once again, you could almost smell the gunpowder emanating from the Alpe; the climb would be the last chance for outsiders to ride away from the long-limbed, quiet Spaniard, who seemed solid and virtually unshakable. As it turned out, the stage would confirm his stranglehold on this Tour, the first of an impressive series that he made look easy.

On the Alpe, the Spaniard kept all of his adversaries in check, thanks to the extraordinary work of Jean-François Bernard. Bernard, who had worked his way back up to the front with his jersey unzipped and a large medallion slapping against his chest, set an infernal pace in order to discourage any potential attack. Induráin followed his wheel with almost disconcerting ease, without even appearing to exert himself, while Bugno, in the Italian national champion's jersey and dark glasses to hide his vulnerability, hung on to this veritable steamroller. Along for the ride was the surprising Leblanc.

Pello Ruiz Cabestany and Thierry Bourguignon, breakaways who had managed to stay away, were caught at the base of the Alpe, where the battle began in earnest. But it would be limited to a futile escape on the initial turns by Bugno, who was quickly caught and fell back into the ranks despite his repeated accelerations. Bugno's move did, however, cause the demise of other favorites. Chiappucci, wearing the jersey of best climber, fell back 40 seconds along with Steven Rooks. Fignon was farther back, limiting the time gaps with the Colombian Alvaro Meija, who would finish fourth in the 1993 Tour. Mottet had already won two stages, yet was always a bit out of his element on this terrain. Theunisse had returned to competition with a bang, winning the Tour of Luxembourg, but wasn't living up to his billing on this climb, which he was ascending as if doing penitence. Mottet and Theunisse were accompanied by LeMond, who was now convinced that he had lost the Tour for good.

Under the circumstances, this climb up Alpe d'Huez was one of the quietest to date, though the intensity of the effort and the Spaniard's prowess added a sublime touch to the beauty of the venue.

About 3 kilometers (1.9 miles) from the summit, Bernard let his leader ride off behind Bugno, the proud Italian, whom Felice Gimondi had come expressly to watch. Leblanc was again in tow. The impassioned crowd opened up the narrowest of corridors for them, their hands reaching for the riders' jerseys. Shortly before the summit, this modern gesture caused Leblanc to fall. He quickly got back on his bike, despite strong pain in his elbow, and was able to catch the lead duo as it wound up for the final sprint. Still shaken, Leblanc had to content himself with third place, while Bugno took the stage for the second straight year.[3] But Bugno did not raise his arms in victory, admitting later that he had not realized he had won. "I had been misinformed and believed there were other guys in front," he said.

Leblanc had pulled off a superb race from the start. He had missed out on a stage victory atop the Alpe because of his fall. As soon as he had crossed the line, he yelled out in anger and pain while Guimard rushed to his side.

This Tour—the last Fignon would race in the colors of Castorama—served as the backdrop for the announcement that Fignon and Guimard would be going their separate ways. Within the team, two camps had already formed: those close to Fignon, who would sign with Bugno's Gatorade squad for the following season, and those who stood behind Leblanc. When a storm broke out at the summit, the *directeur sportif* devoted all his attention to Leblanc. A few meters away, Fignon, drenched like an abandoned dog, found providential comfort: his wife, who handed him a towel. Then he headed off alone to his hotel.

High atop Alpe d'Huez, Induráin had confirmed his immense talent and all but assured himself of final victory. Other Tour triumphs awaited him. It was another departure: the end of one era as a new one began.

CHAPTER SEVENTEEN

1992

Hampsten
Sets His Pace

THE 1992 TOUR STARTED IN SAN SEBASTIAN, SPAIN, IN THE HEART of the Basque country and close to the home of defending champion Miguel Induráin. Before it ended in Paris, this "European" edition of the Tour would pass through six more countries. For the first time since 1910, the Pyrénées were not on the Tour route, making the alpine stages even more critical than usual.

In the 13th stage, the day before the climb up Alpe d'Huez, Claudio Chiappucci took off on a magnificent romp along the road to Sestrières, an alpine village in Italy just a few miles across the French border. He led on the Col des Saisies, where he thought out his scheme, and was still ahead at Cormet de Roselend (a name that evokes the Middle Ages). At the fearsome Col d'Iseran, the apex of the Tour, the diminutive animator was not only still ahead but had virtually donned the yellow jersey as leader on the road. He was also the first to arrive atop Mont Cenis before reaching Sestrières, where the legendary Fausto Coppi had won in 1952. When Chiappucci crossed the finish line, he had completed a heroic 223-kilometer (139-mile) breakaway, 126 kilometers (78 miles) of which were solo.

The day before his win at Sestrières in 1952, the long-legged Campionissimo had also taken the Alpe d'Huez stage, the first of the climb's long history. Imagine the hysteria of the Italians had Chiappucci pulled off a similar exploit at the summit of the Alpe, the most prestigious of mountain stages. "Chiappa," who deserved to win up there, inspired the cartoonist Pellos to depict him as a pirate brandishing a saber, always ready for assault. Everyone hoped for an attack on the Alpe, though his exhaustion after his magnificent ride to Sestrières made the prospect improbable, if not impossible.

But on the road to Alpe d'Huez, Claudio "la Grinta" ("gritty" or "courageous") swore to himself that he would cross the line ahead of Induráin, the serene leader who never seemed to exert himself. Through a powerful ride of his own, Induráin had pulled on the yellow jersey at Sestrières, somewhat eclipsing Chiappucci's distinction as dominator of the day.

Bugno Plays His Hand

Behind the new king of France was Claudio the dauphin, 1:42 back, followed by world champion Gianni Bugno at 4:20. Bugno had based his entire season on the Tour, even skipping the Giro d'Italia to conserve his energy, which had invited a lot of negative press against his unpatriotic decision. He had been betting everything on the Alpe d'Huez stage to revitalize his *palmarès*. By now, he knew he could not make up his deficit. Still, Bugno could benefit from the kind of indulgence that was granted to riders of his stature if he could win at L'Alpe d'Huez for the third year in a row.

Thanks to Bugno, the race for the stage got under way early on the prestigious Col du Galibier. He was accompanied by his Gatorade teammate Laurent Fignon. They appeared to be off to a good start, but Induráin, an excellent descender, soon set things right at the base of the hill, catching the leaders. They had yet to face the Croix de Fer, which would give them a panoramic view of the countryside, followed by the glorious twenty-one switchbacks along the Alpe's summit road.

At that point, Greg LeMond was already losing ground to the tune of more than 10 minutes, accompanied by his loyal teammate Gilbert Duclos-Lassalle. The previous day, on slopes invaded by thousands of crazed fans, LeMond had reached the resort of Sestrières almost 50 minutes behind Chiappucci. Now he stopped near the feed station at San-Jean-de-Maurienne, exhausted. Since the beginning of the Tour, LeMond had been unable to recover from one stage to the next. At San-Jean-de-Maurienne, he abandoned the race. The following year, he would once again pull out of La Grande Boucle, a race he had been able to win three times at the last minute, like Zorro jumping out of a hiding place.

Another rider 50 minutes behind Chiappucci was in agony after his own effort the day before: the French champion Luc Leblanc. He was languishing, accompanied by Armand de Las Cuevas, Induráin's young French teammate. Leblanc, whose victory at the French national championship had strained his relationship with teammate Gérard Rué when he had bridged up to Rué before taking the title, now looked like a novice who had been dropped at the beginning of a race. The tricolor French champion's jersey, which he had intended to honor to the limit of his abilities, weighed on him heavily. Courageous and proud, the young man from the French region of Limousin struggled toward the summit. The year before, he had made a remarkable climb up this very slope, keeping pace with Induráin and Chiappucci. Now he was barely ahead of the sag wagon. He would not even make it to the finish within the time limit.

The fast pace of the Tour had surely taken its toll on both LeMond and Leblanc. Yet only a few months before, the American had won the Tour DuPont and had been seriously thinking about an hour record attempt. As for Leblanc, he had only lost the Dauphiné Libéré on the final day of the race, after having worn the leader's jersey, and had compensated by taking the Midi-Libre just days before the Tour. Their inexplicably poor form held some mystery and cast a dark shadow on the magic of the Alpe.

Other big names fell as well. Steven Rooks, a veteran of this stage who had won it in 1988, fell more than 11 minutes behind. Stephen Roche, who would emerge from the fog a few days later at La Bourboule, was over 12 minutes back. Fignon, despite his stage victory at Mulhouse, was exhausted from his efforts on the Galibier and reached the summit 28 minutes behind the winner.

But the most spectacular casualty of the day was Bugno. Already in trouble through the first turns of the Croix de Fer, he yo-yoed while trying to stay with Induráin's group. Up ahead, LeMond's teammate Éric Boyer attacked, followed by four racers: the Spaniard Jesus Montoya (Amaya), the Italian Franco Vona (GB-MG), the Belgian Jan Nevens (Lotto), and the American Andy Hampsten (Motorola).

Chiappucci Attacks, Hampsten Wins

At the foot of Alpe d'Huez, the five breakaways held a 3:50 lead over Induráin and Chiappucci's group, which Bugno had managed to rejoin after a prodigious descent. It was there, on the slopes that the legendary Fausto Coppi had once made his own, that Chiappucci, in the jersey of best climber, blew the race apart the day after his sensational entry into the temple of the greats.

Induráin, wearing the yellow jersey and a pair of yellow-framed sunglasses, immediately jumped on the Italian's wheel without giving him an inch. Richard Virenque, the young Frenchman and hero of Pau (where he had donned the golden tunic), and Pascal Lino (who would take the yellow jersey the next day) hung on, joined by Gert-Jan Theunisse. But the pace set by the possessed Italian, who alternated between sitting and standing on his pedals, caused things to come apart for good.

Meanwhile, up ahead, Hampsten left his breakaway companions and took off alone toward a well-deserved victory, clearing a passage between two human walls of spectators who were dangerously closing in on him before opening their clutches at the last possible moment.

"I rode it with a simple tactic, and not a very smart one," Hampsten later recalled in an interview with syklingensverden.com. "I just set the pace on the bottom of the climb and started applying pressure halfway up. My opponents knew I was strong that day, and I was a sitting duck if I showed any weakness. But after two hours of being in a breakaway, I knew I had a great chance.

"Usually climbers like to see their rivals ahead of them like deer in the crosshairs of a rifle," Hampsten continued. "But by riding confidently at the front I knew they would doubt their strength in the second half of the climb. In '89, I did the climb wanting to win but with food poisoning. I was in the lead group at the bottom of the climb and finished 87th. I went as hard as I ever have to just get to the finish. So in '92 when I was in a good break and my legs were flowing, I made sure I suffered as much as I did three years before, and I was sure to win."

The little Rabbit (as Hinault had nicknamed him) exulted when he crossed the line, sending kisses to the sky on this blessed day. "Alpe d'Huez was my best win!" he exclaimed. Hampsten was the first American

L'Alpe d'Huez

Start of the 21
switchbacks
to the summit

Alpe d'Huez Winners

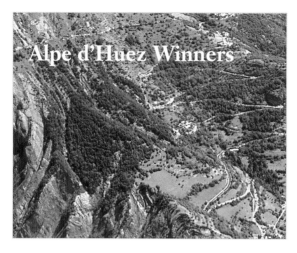

1952

FAUSTO COPPI (I)
10th stage, 266km,
start in Lausanne.
Winning margin: 1:20 over
J. Robic.
Tour 52: **Coppi 1st**
over S. Ockers (at 28:17).

1976

JOOP ZOETEMELK (NL)
9th stage, 258km,
start in Divonne-les-Bains.
Winning margin: 0:03 over
L. Van Impe.
Tour 76: **Zoetemelk 2nd,**
4:14 behind L. Van Impe.

1977

HENNIE KUIPER (NL)
17th stage, 185km,
start in Chamonix.
Winning margin: 0:41 over
B. Thévenet.
Tour 77: **Kuiper 2nd,**
0:48 behind B. Thévenet.

1978

HENNIE KUIPER* (NL)
16th stage, 240km,
start in St. Etienne.
Winning margin: 0:08 over
B. Hinault.
Tour 78: **Kuiper abandoned** on
stage 17; winner B. Hinault.

1979

JOAQUIM AGOSTINHO (P)
17th stage, 167km,
start in Menuires.
Winning margin: 1:57 over
R. Alban.
Tour 79: **Agostinho 3rd,**
26:53 behind B. Hinault.

1979

JOOP ZOETEMELK (NL)
18th stage, 119km,
start in L'Alpe d'Huez.
Winning margin: 0:40 over
L. Van Impe.
Tour 79: **Zoetemelk 2nd,**
13:07 behind B. Hinault.

1981

PETER WINNEN (NL)
17th stage, 230km,
start in Morzine.
Winning margin: 0:08 over
B. Hinault.
Tour 81: **Winnen 5th,**
20:26 behind B. Hinault.

** M. Pollentier, winner of the stage by 0:38 over Kuiper, was banned from the race for attempted
doping fraud.*

1982

BEAT BREU (SWI)
16th stage, 123km,
start in Orcières-Merlette.
Winning margin: 0:16 over
R. Alban.
Tour 82: **Breu 6th,**
13:21 behind B. Hinault.

1983

PETER WINNEN (NL)
17th stage, 223km,
start in La Tour du Pin.
Winning margin: s.t. as
J.R. Bernaudeau.
Tour 83: **Winnen 3rd,**
4:09 behind L. Fignon.

1984

LUIS HERRERA (COL)
16th stage, 151km,
start in Grenoble.
Winning margin: 0:49 over
L. Fignon.
Tour 84: **Herrera 27th,**
58:30 behind L. Fignon.

1986

BERNARD HINAULT (F)
17th stage, 163km,
start in Briançon.
Winning margin: s.t. as
G. LeMond.
Tour 86: **Hinault 2nd,**
3:10 behind G. LeMond.

1987

FEDERICO ECHAVE (SP)
18th stage, 201km,
start in Villard de Lans.
Winning margin: 1:32 over
A. Fuerte.
Tour 87: **Echave 12th,**
31:06 behind S. Roche.

1988

STEVEN ROOKS (NL)
12th stage, 227km,
start in Morzine.
Winning margin: 0:17 over
G.-J. Theunisse.
Tour 88: **Rooks 2nd,**
7:13 behind P. Delgado.

1989

GERT-JAN THEUNISSE (NL)
16th stage, 165km,
start in Briançon.
Winning margin: 1:09 over
P. Delgado.
Tour 89: **Theunisse 4th,**
7:30 behind G. LeMond.

1990

GIANNI BUGNO (I)
10th stage, 182km,
start in St. Gervais.
Winning margin: s.t. as
G. LeMond.
Tour 90: **Bugno 7th,**
9:39 behind G. LeMond.

1991

GIANNI BUGNO (I)
16th stage, 125km,
start in Gap.
Winning margin: 0:01 over
M. Induráin.
Tour 91: **Bugno 2nd,**
3:36 behind M. Induráin.

1992

ANDY HAMPSTEN (USA)
14th stage, 186km,
start in Sestrières.
Winning margin: 1:17 over
F. Vona.
Tour 92: **Hampsten 4th,**
13:40 behind M. Induráin.

1994

ROBERTO CONTI (I)
16th stage, 224km,
start in Valréas.
Winning margin: 2:02 over
H. Buenahora.
Tour 94: **Conti 6th,**
12:29 behind M. Induráin.

1995

MARCO PANTANI (I)
10th stage, 162.5km,
start in Aime La Plagne.
Winning margin: 1:24 over
M. Induráin.
Tour 95: **Pantani 13th,**
26:20 behind M. Induráin.

1997

1999

2001

MARCO PANTANI (I)
13th stage, 203.5km,
start in St. Etienne.
Winning margin: 0:47 over
J. Ullrich.
Tour 97: **Pantani 3rd,**
14:03 behind J. Ullrich.

GIUSEPPE GUERINI (I)
10th stage, 220.5km,
start in Sestrières.
Winning margin: 0:21 over
P. Tonkov.
Tour 99: **Guerini 22nd,**
39:29 behind L. Armstrong.

LANCE ARMSTRONG (USA)
10th stage, 209km,
start in Aix-les-Bains.
Winning margin: 1:59 over
J. Ullrich.
Tour 01: **Armstrong 1st** over
J. Ullrich (at 6:44).

2003

2004

2006

IBAN MAYO (SP)
8th stage, 219km,
start in Sallanches.
Winning margin: 1:45 over
A. Vinokourov.
Tour 03: **Mayo 6th,**
7:06 behind L. Armstrong.

LANCE ARMSTRONG (USA)
16th stage, 15.5km TT,
start in Bourg d'Oisans.
Winning margin: 1:01 over
J. Ullrich.
Tour 04: **Armstrong 1st** over
A. Kloden (at 6:19).

FRÄNK SCHLECK (LUX)
15th stage, 187km,
start in Gap.
Winning margin: 0:11 over
D. Cunego.
Tour 06: **Schleck 10th,**
16:43 behind O. Pereiro.

RIGHT *It was Georges Rajon, a local innkeeper, who made the race up the Alpe a historic part of the Tour. He's pictured here (left) with five-time Tour winner Jacques Anquetil, who never contested a Tour stage on the Alpe.*

BELOW *Fausto Coppi made up a 5:04 deficit to win the Tour's first ascent of the Alpe and recapture the yellow jersey. To recuperate, he chose a quiet room at the rear of the Hotel Christina and spent most of the next morning, a rest day, in bed.*

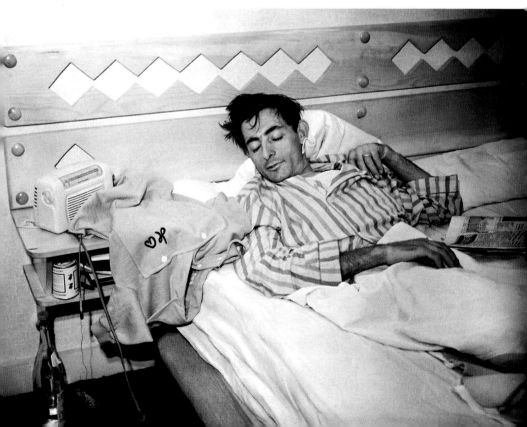

The Tour's return to the Alpe in 1976 saw victory by the durable Joop Zoetemelk and the start of a love affair between the mountain and the Tour's Dutch fans. Zoetemelk won again in 1979, the year the Alpe was climbed twice. He's shown here in 1986, when, though resplendent in the world champion's jersey, he finished 14:21 behind Bernard Hinault and Greg LeMond.

LEFT *Hennie Kuiper continued Holland's domination on the Alpe. In 1977, he won the stage by 41 seconds and finished the Tour in second place overall. In 1978, though again victorious on the Alpe, he abandoned the race on stage 17.*

BELOW *Another Dutch victory! In 1981, Peter Winnen attacked alone with 6 kilometers to go and held a winning margin of 8 seconds over Bernard Hinault. Two years later he repeated the feat in a wheel-to-wheel duel with Jean-René Bernaudeau.*

ABOVE *You might expect the Swiss to take naturally to the Alpe's high climbs, but in fact the diminutive Beat Breu has been his country's sole winner, prevailing in 1982 with a spectacular solo attack 12 kilometers from the summit.*

RIGHT *The Colombians arrived in force in 1984, led by Luis Herrera, "El Jardinierito." The Little Gardener collected the roses atop the Alpe with a memorable ride that left Laurent Fignon and Bernard Hinault gasping in his wake.*

ABOVE *Betrayed by his teammate's promises to help him win, Greg LeMond fought a desperate battle against Bernard Hinault to claim his first Tour title. Leading Hinault by 2:47 overall, LeMond feared for his life on the Alpe and elected to let Hinault lead the climb. Though they finished atop the Alpe hand in hand, the Badger's repeated attacks caused a bitter rift that has never healed.*

TOP RIGHT *In 1988 Steven Rooks had it all: the polka-dot jersey of the king of the mountains, the combination jersey of the best overall rider, and victory on the Alpe, returning the French mountain to Dutch hands.*

BOTTOM RIGHT *Gert-Jan Theunisse scored another victory for the House of Orange in 1989, breaking away to win solo by 1:09 over Pedro Delgado. Sadly, he would be banned from competition the following year, a result of three doping violations in twenty-four months.*

TOP LEFT *Gianni Bugno scored consecutive victories, though barely; his winning margins over Greg LeMond in 1990 and Miguel Induráin in 1991 totaled 1 second. Wearing the Italian national champion's jersey, he led Induráin to the top of the Alpe in the first year of the Spaniard's five-year reign over the Tour.*

ABOVE *Marco Pantani, here on his way to a solo victory over Jan Ullrich by 47 seconds in 1997, claimed an even greater winning margin of 1:24 over Miguel Induráin in 1995. A gifted climber, Pantani also recorded the three fastest ascents of the Alpe, with a best time of 36:50 in 1995.*

BOTTOM LEFT *In 1992, Andy Hampsten became the first American to score a victory on the Alpe, putting a spectacular 1:17 on his breakaway companions to finish all alone in one of the greatest rides of his career.*

LEFT *In 2001, Lance Armstrong feigned weakness on the slopes of the Glandon, then surged to victory on the Alpe over a despairing Jan Ullrich, who could not respond to Armstrong's attack at the foot of the mountain. The moment was immortalized by the Texan's famous look over his shoulder.*

ABOVE *In an explosive stage marked by repeated attacks by the favorites, Iban Mayo broke away to claim his first stage victory in the Tour in 2003, with a winning margin of 1:45 over Alexander Vinokourov.*

ABOVE *Lance Armstrong's second win on the Alpe came amid the pursuit of his record-breaking sixth Tour victory. History was also made on the Alpe in 2004: It was the first time the climb was run as a time trial. Armstrong won it going away, with a 1:01 margin over Jan Ullrich.*

LEFT *In the most contentious Tour in years, Fränk Schleck's Alpe win in 2006 was ultimately overshadowed by the alleged doping violation of the race's overall winner, Floyd Landis.*

to win the Alpe d'Huez stage, the Tour de Romandie, and the Giro (1988). "I wouldn't trade this victory for a world championship," he exclaimed, speaking into a cluster of microphones thrust before his boyish face, a white baseball cap on his head. Indeed, Hampsten had touched paradise!

The next to cross the line was Vona, his jersey almost entirely unzipped, who replicated his second-place finish the day before in Sestrières. Boyer followed a short time later, then Nevens.

Induráin-Chiappucci: A Matter of Pride

Then it was Chiappucci and Induráin, neck and neck. The Italian proudly led; the Spaniard sat on his wheel, looking as relaxed as a cycling tourist. The crowd acknowledged the two great ones, the survivors of this exhausting day.

A few kilometers before the summit, Induráin took the lead position out of pride, in order to emphasize his dominance on this prestigious terrain. But just before the finish, the Italian surged past the Spaniard, who was assured of winning his third Tour. It would be Induráin's second grand tour victory of the year; he had also taken the Giro in a dominating performance during which he had worn the pink leader's jersey for twenty of the twenty-two stages. In the Alpe d'Huez pressroom, the correspondents spelled his name somewhat differently for the headlines that day: "Indu-reign."

As for Bugno, he climbed the slope slowly and painfully, confirming with every turn of the pedals that this season had eluded him, while unhappy Italian fans unjustly booed him. He crossed the line more than 9 minutes off the pace, in 26th place. That evening, the presence of his young son, Messin, comforted him. Little did Bugno know that come August in Benidorm, where Induráin sometimes vacationed, he would again win the world championships—ahead of the Spaniard!

The End of LeMond?

Everyone wondered whether LeMond's terrible collapse before Alpe d'Huez proclaimed the end of the American champion. In fact, LeMond would never again lead an important race. A few weeks later, the American confided to Claude Droussent of *L'Équipe*, "Duclos-Lassalle and I, we

113

dropped out at the feed zone. We were behind by 30 minutes, and we knew we would never make the time cut, not with the Croix de Fer and the Alpe still to climb. I had nothing left. I can't even say that my lungs were on fire or that my legs ached terribly. No, I wasn't hurting. I just didn't have any energy left. It plays with your mind—it's terrible." LeMond stopped racing in 1994, despite himself, suffering from mitochondrial myopathy.

CHAPTER EIGHTEEN

1994

Pantani
Sets a Record

TAKE COURAGE, INDURÁIN; IT WILL BE A TOUR OF SUFFERING." So read the front page of the Italian cycling magazine *Bicisport* at the close of the Giro, under a nice photo of Induráin in yellow and visibly feeling the effort. A premonitory vision, but one that would apply not to Induráin so much as to his rivals.

Would the upcoming Tour really prove murderous and inhuman? Would it resemble the Tour of 1952? As it turned out, the comparison was not far-fetched, given the oppressive heat and long succession of mountain stages that would take their toll on the riders. It was a Tour that left everyone in a daze, full of heroic feats and abandonment by the stars, many of whom dropped like flies. "I've never seen anything like it over eleven Tours de France," confided Gérard Nicolet, one of the Tour doctors. The cause? Suffocating heat that prevented racers from recovering.

This daunting Tour began in the northern city of Lille. Chris Boardman, holder of the hour record, covered the 7.2-kilometer (4.5-mile) prologue at an unheard-of speed exceeding 55 kilometers per hour (34 miles per hour) and donned the yellow jersey for a brief spell. At the conclusion of the first stage in Armentières, the Tour claimed its first casualties, including Laurent Jalabert and Wilfried Nelissen, the Belgian champion, who tumbled to the ground when an inattentive policeman stepped into their path to take a photo.

After several days in England, the Tour crossed the Channel again, this time to Cherbourg, France. During the sixth stage, Greg LeMond became another prominent victim. The 33-year-old simply could not tackle the hills and dropped out, despite his high hopes for returning to the top with his new team, Gan.

In the ninth stage, a 64-kilometer (40-mile) time trial from Périgueux to Bergerac, Induráin took the yellow jersey by using a colossal gear (55x12) that propelled him forward almost 10 meters with each pedal revolution. His performance atoned for his sole defeat in this discipline, suffered a month earlier at the Giro in Fallonica, a small city facing the island of Elba on the Mediterranean coast, famous for its seafood dishes. On that occasion, the Russian Evgeni Berzin had set off like a missile over the 44-kilometer (27-mile) course, beating Induráin by 2:34. Coincidentally, the Swiss legend Hugo Koblet had once upset Fausto Coppi, the Induráin of his day, on that same circuit.

Chiappucci, Rominger, and Bugno—Out!

During stage 11 in the Pyrénées (won by a resilient Luc Leblanc, who edged out Induráin), Claudio Chiappucci got sick on the Lourdes-Hautacam climb, then dropped out. Chris Boardman pulled out as well. Even Tony Rominger, the Swiss who had won the Vuelta for the third successive year, taking six stages and wearing the leader's jersey from the first day to the last, came to a stop on the long, straight road leading to Albi in stage 13. His star would shine again, but in the firmament of the hour record, at the Bordeaux-Lac velodrome on November 5, engraving with gold lettering an hour record of 55.291 kilometers (34.356 miles)—a mark better than Induráin's.

Gianni Bugno, who had been trying to find himself and was suffering from depression, also bowed out after the 13th stage.[1] Little did he know, in his distress, that he would emerge from obscurity at the beginning of the 1995 season by taking the Tour Méditerranée in splendid fashion, including the Marseille stage, high atop the ascent toward the basilica of Nôtre-Dame-de-la-Garde.

During the Tour's only flat stage—the 14th, from Castres to Montpellier—eighteen racers withdrew and thus avoided the fearsome Ventoux, Alpe d'Huez, and the arrival atop Val-Thorens, just four days from Paris. They included Lance Armstrong, the world champion who was participating in only his second Tour; Jacky Durand, the champion of France; Steve Bauer, who excelled on long, flat courses; and two previous winners at Alpe d'Huez, Steven Rooks and Gert-Jan Theunisse.

Following the 15th stage, which included the Ventoux, the peloton traveled to Valréas for the start of the stage to Alpe d'Huez. The caravan returned with immense joy to the climb up the Alpe, which had been omitted from the race in 1993 in favor of an ascent toward Isola 2000, an injustice that fortunately was committed only that one year.[2]

Induráin was still in the yellow jersey and held a 7:56 lead over Richard Virenque, a French fan favorite with soap-opera good looks who was wearing the polka-dot jersey of best climber, which he would keep all the way to Paris. For Induráin—"Miguelón" to his legions of Spanish fans, "Big Mig" to his fans everywhere else—it was in the bag. This Spaniard was a steamroller, solid as steel.

Induráin Takes Charge

Once again, Alpe d'Huez would offer the competition one last shot at redemption. True, they might not upset Induráin (you can't move a mountain, after all), but at least they could gain a few seconds on one another.

The French contingent was particularly strong, especially Festina teammates Virenque and Leblanc, who was affectionately called "Lucho" after his marriage to a woman named Maria. From the start of the mountain stages, these two had shown remarkable form and audacity. In the 12th stage, Virenque had staged an interminable 100-kilometer (62-mile) breakaway before arriving first at the summit of Luz Ardiden. (Their aggressive spirit would carry over some weeks later to the world road championship, on Sicilian roads dominated by the temples of Agrigento, where Leblanc would don the rainbow jersey fourteen years after the last French winner, Bernard Hinault. Adding to the joy of the French team, piloted by Bernard Thévenet, Virenque would finish third.)

Induráin's fans had gathered at Luz Ardiden, a resort in the Pyrénées, to exult. Excited by the sun and alcohol, they brandished the green-white-and-red standard—the Ikurina, flag of the Basque country. They nonetheless applauded the surprising exploit of the man from the Var region of France. But could "Ri-chaaard," who was surrounded by adoring groupies, hang on to second place in this extraordinary Tour? Many were also putting their money on Leblanc, who was in fourth place at 8:35.

"Pantani Will Hurt You"

As the great battle loomed, many also put their hope in Marco Pantani, barely 24 and in sixth place at 11:55, the great revelation of this Tour. He was an exceptional climber with incredible acceleration, even on the steepest grades. *Bicisport* had warned Induráin, "Pantani will hurt you on the hills." Dubbed "Elefantino" ("little elephant," in honor of his protruding ears) by the Italian press, Pantani had already put on a show in the Dolomites during the preceding Giro, in which he had finished second behind Berzin.

The race heated up right from the start, on the hill of the priory at Aleyrac. Fourteen second-tier racers formed a cosmopolitan breakaway: Angel Carmago and Hernan Buenahora (Kelme), Thierry Gouvenou (Gan), Thierry Marie (Castorama), Ronan Pensec (Novemail), Jörg Müller (Mapei-Glas), Bruno Cenghialta and Giorgio Furlan (Gewiss)—the latter coming off victories in Tirreno-Adriatico, Milan–San Remo, and the Critérium International—Alberto Elli (GB-MG), Roberto Conti (Lampre), Udo Bölts (Telekom), Roberto Torres (Festina), and Giancarlo Perini and Antonio Santoromita (ZG). The fugitives, who built up a 10-minute lead, were soon reduced to a dozen (Gouvenou and Furlan were dropped on Col d'Ornan, before the descent on Bourg d'Oisans) and still had a comfortable lead of 8:50 on the peloton when they reached the foot of the Alpe.

At that moment, Conti, the highest placed of this group in the overall standings (11th at 17:55 behind Induráin), decided to attack. He had climbed the twenty-one switchbacks three times (1990, 1991, and 1992) and each time had collapsed within the first 3 kilometers—the most formidable—before the village of La Garde. This time, the native of Italy's Romagna region shook his bad luck; his star must have been shining overhead, as it had the previous day on Mont Ventoux, where he had finished fourth. *Vai, Roberto!*

"I said to myself, 'I'll try my luck by going right from the start,'" Conti related afterward to *Il Giornale*. "Those first 3 kilometers on Alpe d'Huez,

I had already climbed them three times, and each time I was dying. I swore to myself that if I won up there, I'd go home right away."

Winner of the best young rider jersey at the 1987 Giro, Conti, a good climber, had always preferred the role of *gregario* to that of leader. For the first time in his career, after giving nine years of loyal service to others, he finally took a victory of his own—at Alpe d'Huez, no less. Like Coppi! Crazy with joy, Conti raised his hands at the finish line and dedicated this sublime moment to a young boy in his hometown who was suffering from leukemia. Contrary to his vow to quit if he won the stage, Conti would go on to finish the Tour in sixth place.

Behind him, however, a battle raged. Pantani shifted into a small gear at the base of the Alpe. He did not simply slip away from the group of the favorites; he launched. He surged, taking off in his own style, spinning a gear for all it was worth. Every turn of the pedals widened the gap. Leblanc glued himself to Pantani's wheel for a few meters but then decided to let him go. Had the Frenchman kept up that pace, his heart in overdrive, he would have exploded before the summit. But how in the hell could Pantani ride away from everyone like that?

By now, Pantani had captivated all eyes and thrown off all the stopwatches. At the bridge of Romanche, before turn 21, he was trailing the leaders by 8:50. Over the final 14 kilometers (8.7 miles), he picked up almost 4 minutes on Conti and even passed some of the breakaways (Torres, Carmago, and Pensec, who threw up his arms in a gesture of helplessness as Pantani passed). Pantani's stunning climb was one of the fastest on record, besting Induráin's by 2:15.

Had Pantani made his move earlier (he finished 8th), he might have won the stage. Throughout the Tour, he had relied on his climbing abilities to gain ground on the leaders. Consider this: Following the 11th stage to Hautacam, the first in the Pyrénées, Pantani was 26th overall, 15:03 behind Induráin. In Paris, he finished 3rd, 7:19 behind the Spanish king. In ten stages, he cut his deficit in half. This climber from another era, who promised legendary feats in Tours to come, made his gains in the mountains. And this was his first Tour, though he had already finished 2nd at the Giro, taking the stages to Merano and Aprica. At the Tour, as had been the case at the Giro, he might have won the event outright if not for the time trials, his weakness. The legendary Gino Bartali called him an *arrampicatore*, a winged climber, not to be confused with a common climber, or *scalatore*. As Gino the Pious affirmed, Pantani was in a class of his own.

Virenque's Challenge

But Pantani did not escape unchallenged. Virenque chased on his own after the climber from Cesenatico, a port town on the Adriatic coast. Over the mythical hairpins, these two conquerors of the peaks were suddenly engaged in a duel. Virenque had by then dropped Induráin and was focusing on Pantani. The crowd was thrilled and urged Virenque on as he rocked his bicycle from one side to the other, entirely focused on the intensity of his effort.

He could no longer win the Tour. But at that moment, the Alpe became, once again, "one of those places that pulls the spirit from its lethargy," as Maurice Barrès expressed so well in his novel *La Colline inspirée* (The sacred hill). "Famous or unknown, forgotten or as yet unborn, such places draw us, and make us accept, unconsciously, a superior set of rules to those that normally govern our lives."

Virenque's lead over the Spaniard grew to 1:22. In that moment, he became a national hero of the July romance. This d'Artagnan from La Londe with the boyish face was the knight Ivanhoe, his polka-dot armor opened to reveal a generous heart. He galloped in his assault of the Alpe to defend the Gauls, who still hoped to see a Frenchman wearing the yellow jersey on the royal throne. "Virenque takes giant steps," read a witty headline in *L'Équipe* the next day.[3]

In the end, though, Virenque's gains were modest. As Induráin approached the summit, he was done playing games and went into overdrive. Only Leblanc and Vladimir Poulnikov (who was then 5th overall) were able to stay with him. Virenque, who failed to catch Pantani and finished 11th, conceded almost his entire lead to Induráin, who finished just 35 seconds behind the Frenchman.

Before this tortuous Tour reached Paris, it claimed another prominent victim: Armand de Las Cuevas, who had been fourth in the overall standings at the summit of the Alpe, only to quit a few days later, suffering from bronchitis. As for Virenque, he would never get any closer to the Spaniard and, after a poor showing in the time trial at Avoriaz, slipped to fifth place in the final standings, just behind his countryman Leblanc.

Piotr Ugrumov, till then a virtual unknown, made his presence felt over the last four days and captured second place.

This 1994 Tour, like that of 1952, would go down as one of the toughest in a momentous year for cycling, marked by the stunning suicide in May of the Spanish legend Luis Ocaña and by a host of high-profile retirements at the end of the season, including those of Sean Kelly, Charly Mottet, Pedro Delgado, Raúl Alcalá, Thierry Claveyrolat, Phil Anderson, Moreno Argentin, Éric Caritoux, Marc Madiot, and Franco Chioccioli. Laurent Fignon had retired twelve months earlier. Also notable was the sad end, in early 1994, of the celebrated *Miroir du Cyclisme* cycling magazine, whose appeal had been waning for some time.

Seemingly oblivious to these human travails was the unflappable Induráin, who sailed to his fourth straight Tour victory. Bernard Pratviel, of *La Dépêche du Midi*, wrote, "Miguel was a raging bull." True, but he was fully in control of his immense talent. He had also justified his astronomical monthly salary of 1,230,000 francs ($228,216)—higher, even, than LeMond's record-breaking deal, signed during his tenure with Bernard Tapie.

CHAPTER NINETEEN

1995

Pantani and Induráin:
The Face-Off

"INDURÁIN POISED TO MAKE HISTORY." SO RAN *L'ÉQUIPE*'S FRONT-PAGE headline in big, black letters over a beautiful photo of the Navarrese rider engaged in his discipline of choice: the time trial. Wearing an aerodynamic helmet adorned with the Banesto logo, he seemed to jump from the page in search of a fifth consecutive Tour title, a first in the race's history. The Tour was Big Mig's turf, his source of happiness, his reason to ride.

Induráin's powerful thighs, steely gaze, and aero bars with crablike bar-end brake levers made him look like a creature from a science fiction book, ready to sink his tentacles into his adversaries. His image dominated the ones below it depicting the Tour's three five-time winners, whose smaller pictures already positioned them at a lesser level. Famously blond Jacques Anquetil was pictured sitting on his green Helyett bicycle. Bernard Hinault was shown with his hands in the drops of his handlebars, his biceps flexed. And Eddy Merckx was astride his orange Molteni team bike in his favorite position: hands atop the levers and elbows spread out—a movement accentuated by the forward-and-back motion of his shoulders in step with his pedaling motion in a style no one could forget.

Among the contenders intent on deposing the Spanish monarchy established in 1991 were two Frenchmen, as likable as they were talented and darlings of the French public. The first was Laurent Jalabert (team ONCE), half greyhound, half bulldog, and survivor of that terrible crash in the final sprint in Armentières the year before. He was coming off a strong early season. The second was the baby-faced Richard Virenque (Festina), who suffered each July from a mysterious illness that covered his chest with red spots and gave him a terrible itch that made him want to attack as soon as the road rose upward. They headed a French delegation that numbered only thirty-three and did not include Luc Leblanc (who was undergoing surgery for pain in his left leg).

Jalabert had become the third-ranked cyclist in the world (behind Tony Rominger and Induráin) after winning a succession of races: Milan–San Remo (in front of Maurizio Fondriest of Lampre-Panaria), Flèche Wallonne (again ahead of Fondriest), Paris-Nice, the Critérium International, and the Volta a Catalunya (in anticipation of the Vuelta in September, which he would win ahead of Abraham Olano). Jalabert had established himself as a feisty racer, willing to risk everything in order to advance in the overall standings.

As for Virenque, he bet everything on the mountains, but he had improved dramatically in time trials, which had been his weakness. The 1995 Tour, which started in Brittany, suited him, with numerous mountain-top finishes—including Alpe d'Huez, of course, but also La Plagne and Guzet-Niege.

The French public was eager to see these two animators mount an attack. Not since Hinault a decade earlier had a native won the Tour, and fans were growing restless. *L'Équipe* encouraged the pair with a long article in an early-July issue titled "It's Your Turn, Frenchmen!"

There were a few foreigners in the mix who likewise aspired to topple Induráin. Among the most threatening were Rominger (Mapei-GB), the Swiss voyager and winner of the Giro; Pavel Tonkov (Lampre-Panaria), the Russian who must have used a hidden fuel-injection engine to claim the Tour of Switzerland; Evgeni Berzin (Gewiss-Ballan), the young Russian star who had placed second in the Giro after having won it the previous year; and Alex Zülle (ONCE), another Swiss racer whose climbing prowess had earned him Induráin's respect.

The Return of Pantani

Eusebio Unzue, Induráin's *directeur sportif*, added these names to the list of rebels: Chris Boardman (Gan), always the favorite in time trials; Bjarne

Riis (Gewiss-Ballan), a Dane with an assassin's smile; and Marco Pantani (Carrera Jeans–Tassoni), the Italian who would be christened the "Pirate" the following year on account of his new buccaneer look (goatee, bandanna, and earring). And he was a pirate of the passes, a big-gear terror between 1,000 and 2,000 meters (3,300 and 6,500 feet).

The prodigious climber from Cesenatico dreamed of Alpe d'Huez. The year before, Roberto Conti (Lampre) had beaten him to the Alpe (though Pantani had set the fastest time). But this time, Pantani vowed that he would win atop the Fortress of L'Oisans. "Pantani will take revenge at Alpe d'Huez," he predicted darkly. He knew the key was to time his move well so as not to be overtaken by some joker at the last moment.

Pantani had only recently recovered from a terrible accident that had almost cost him his life. On May 1, a few days before the start of the Tour of Switzerland, Pantani had been hit by a small car, a Fiat Punto, near Santarcangelo. Suffering from a concussion and a serious knee injury, he reluctantly had to forgo the Giro, his primary objective for that season. "Pantani, we will recover," encouraged the cycling magazine *Bicisport*, featuring a striking photo of Pantani bleeding from the side of his head. His fans firmly believed that the Tour would serve as his springboard to get back to form. And it went without saying: on Alpe d'Huez.

During the seventh stage, on the road to Liège, Induráin flexed his muscles and showed that he had no intention of abdicating. Wearing a retro-style helmet and with a determined look on his face, Induráin surprised everyone by breaking away from his adversaries during the climb up Mont Theux, steep terrain for which most observers thought he was ill-suited. Only Johan Bruyneel (ONCE) stayed on the Spaniard's wheel and managed to nip him at the line (Bruyneel would become, a few years later, Lance Armstrong's *directeur sportif*). Although Bruyneel temporarily claimed the yellow jersey from Riis, Induráin was the real winner. He gained nearly a minute on his main rivals for the yellow jersey and vaulted from 10th place to 2nd, just 31 seconds behind Bruyneel.

Induráin Scores a Knockout

The next day, in the 54-kilometer (33.6-mile) individual time trial, Induráin prevailed and took the yellow jersey. Finishing just 12 seconds behind was Riis. Two days earlier, in Charleroi, the 31-year-old outspoken

Dane had donned the yellow jersey for the first time in his career. Though he was a talented racer, no one suspected then that he would be the one to deny the Spaniard a record sixth victory a year later. Nor was it widely suspected that he was using erythropoietin (EPO), as he would later confess, or that using it was a common practice among riders in the peloton. That revelation would await the Festina scandal of 1998.

The ninth stage and first in the mountains started in Le Grand Bornand, where a number of Tour winners had been forced to wage their wars in the rain: Eddy Merckx, Bernard Thévenet, Lucien Aimar, Joop Zoetemelk, Jan Janssen, Bernard Hinault, and Roger Pingeon. At the foot of the long final ascent to La Plagne, Induráin responded to Zülle, who had attacked early and led for almost 100 kilometers (62 miles), looking for his first stage win. On this climb, where one expects to see only featherweights and mountain goats prevail, it was the great Spaniard who took off, his cap turned forward like Merckx (hear, hear!), gaining precious seconds on his rivals with every pedal stroke. Although he finished 2:02 behind Zülle, Induráin strengthened his hold on the yellow jersey and gained more than 2 minutes on Tonkov and Pantani, more than 4 minutes on Virenque, and more than 5 minutes on Jalabert.

The day before the formidable climb of the Alpe, Induráin went to bed with the yellow jersey safely in his possession. Behind him were Zülle (2:27), Riis (5:58), Rominger (6:35), Ivan Gotti of Gewiss (6:54), and Jalabert (8:14). In 11th place was Pantani (14:02), and in 13th was Virenque (14:20).

As the 10th stage to L'Alpe d'Huez got under way, Induráin was expected to shine, perhaps even register his first non–time trial stage victory of this Tour. A notable nonstarter was the Italian sprinting superstar Mario Cipollini, who had won two stages. An early casualty of the stage was Jacky Durand, who fell during the interminable descent down the Madeleine. He lay spread out on the road for some time before he picked himself up and dropped out of the race.

On the hill of the Croix de Fer, thirteen racers parted company with a group that included Induráin and favorites Pantani, Zülle, Riis, Rominger, and Tonkov. Among the breakaways was Jalabert, who was having an excellent Tour. Also in this group were Virenque, who wore the polka-dot jersey although he was suffering from bronchitis, and Gotti, the revelation of this Tour, who would later confirm his talents as a climber, especially in the 1997 Giro. When the breakaways reached the summit of the Croix de Fer, they had built up their lead over Induráin and his group to 1:25. By the time they reached the foot of Alpe d'Huez, they had added another 50 seconds to their lead. Then another race began.

After the Romanche bridge, on the first long incline, Alberto Elli (Technogym), one of the escapees, attacked and splintered the group as the crowd roared its approval. His former companions in the breakaway, meanwhile, were staggering, affected by the scorching sun and asphyxiated by Elli's pace, which proved too fast. They were also quickly losing their lead over the yellow jersey and his companions, including Pantani. The Italian climber was behaving like a Tibetan monk who feels he must lead the way up the sacred mountain and illuminate a path for others to follow.

Pantani Lives Up to His Prediction

Pantani loved to play the game of every man for himself. He took off about 12 kilometers (7.5 miles) from the summit, before the hamlet of La Garde, on a murderous incline. He looked back frequently to assess his lead and, once satisfied, stood on his pedals and accelerated with shocking ease. He then sat back down on his saddle and held a steady tempo. He repeated this pattern as he scaled the climb, overwhelming the other riders. He seemed to glide above the asphalt, generating power with every pedal stroke. The angel with a devil tattooed on his shoulder (the emblem of his favorite soccer team, Milan AC), Elefantino electrified the crowd, slicing a path as they stepped aside to let him pass.

Pantani passed the scattered breakaway riders, who now seemed riveted to the road, petrified by the intensity of their efforts, one by one. He passed Jalabert in green, Virenque in red and white, and Gotti; they all tried in vain to stick to his wheel. They fixed their stares on this mischievous, elusive imp but were unable to match his cadence. Berzin enjoyed a particularly good view of Pantani's climb; the Russian had bowed out at the feed zone in Sainte-Marie-de-Cuines and was now trailing the Italian in the Gewiss car. Pantani was about to make good on his prediction, and his fans voiced their approval.

Induráin, who had also overtaken the breakaways scattered along the ascent, engaged his turbo engine farther back, about 8 kilometers (5 miles) from the summit. He was followed by two wheel-suckers: the bespectacled Zülle, who looked like a young student, and Riis, a future winner of the Tour. For the duration of the route, Pantani and Induráin engaged in a long-distance duel. It would prove a virtual tie, since the distance between them remained the same.

Pantani embraced the sky as he crossed the finish line. For the first time, he had inscribed his name on a Tour stage exactly as he had hoped. Pantani was not only back in the peloton, he was the new king of this mountain.

Induráin and Zülle finished 1:24 behind, just ahead of Riis. Jalabert finished seventh, at 2:36, showing enormous progress in the mountains. Two days later, on Bastille Day, he put on a performance to remember, staging a 198-kilometer (123-mile) breakaway, arriving first in Mende. He would finish the Tour a strong fourth. As for Virenque, he crossed the line just behind his compatriot, at 2:50. He would finish the Tour in ninth place.

Four days after the Alpe d'Huez stage, Pantani slew the competition on the misty ascent to Guzet-Niege. He jumped twenty-seven places in the overall standings, climbing to 7th. Though he would slip to 13th in the final standings, his performance inspired *L'Équipe* to write the headline "Pantani—He Astonishes Us."

Little did Pantani know that he would soon land back in a hospital bed. That October, as he was descending from Pino Torinese in Milano-Torino, just 8 kilometers (5 miles) from the finish line, a reckless driver in a white Nissan SUV, heading the wrong way, ran him over. Once again, the spry Italian dodged death.

Armstrong Points to the Sky

Fabio Casartelli (Motorola), the road champion at the Barcelona Olympic Games, finished the Alpe d'Huez stage 20:53 behind Pantani. Six days later, Casartelli suffered a deadly fall while descending the Portet d'Aspet at kilometer 34 (mile 21) of stage 15, from Saint Girons to Cauterets. Casartelli was just 25 and left behind a young wife and son. Racing in the Tour was the fulfillment of a childhood dream. His death plunged the Tour into mourning.

The next day, to honor the young Italian, the Motorola team was allowed to cross the finish line just ahead of all the other teams. Only cycling offers such a strong show of solidarity in a time of immense distress. The riders wash away their sweat with tears and honor a fallen brother with profound dignity. Lance Armstrong, Casartelli's friend as well as teammate, took stage 18 to Limoges. As he approached the finish line, the American raised his eyes to the sky, his index fingers pointing skyward. Casartelli had given him the strength to break away from the pack, he said, this time without the consent of the peloton. Only a few months later, Armstrong, who was likewise marked by destiny, announced that he was suffering from testicular cancer, an illness he would confront with exemplary courage.

This dramatic Tour fell for the fifth consecutive time to Miguel Induráin. "The Greatest," ran the headline of *Vélo*. That was probably an overstatement when one considers all of the glorious Tour champions over the years. But in 1995, it was certainly true.

CHAPTER TWENTY

1997

The Pirate,
Alone at the Helm

INDURÁIN'S FOLLY" READ *L'ÉQUIPE*'S HEADLINE IN OCTOBER[1] IN enormous black letters over a photograph of the five-time Tour champion in his winter workout suit. The Spanish cham pion had dared to hint at the close of the 1996 season that he was ready to retire.

Induráin had competed halfheartedly in the Vuelta that year, only to drop out in the 13th stage on the climb to Cangas de Onis. For the first time in six years, he had failed to win the Tour,[2] which had gone to Bjarne Riis. The "old-timer" was apparently washed up at the advanced age of 32. He began to question himself, even as lucrative offers poured in to induce him to continue his racing career. Quitting prematurely was the alleged folly.

Banesto offered Induráin a lifetime position after his racing career if he would go on for just one more season. ONCE dangled a contract worth 20 million francs ($3.4 million then, or $4.35 million today) if he would join Alex Zülle and Laurent Jalabert for at least one year. But Induráin, in agreement with his wife, Marisa, declined. On January 2, 1997, in Pamplona, he announced that he was retiring. "It was extremely difficult for me to reach this decision because I'm fine physically, and I think that I could still get in condition to win a sixth Tour de France," Induráin declared. "But to be at the highest level demands a lot from you, and with each year that passes, it becomes more and more difficult to attain. I believe I made the best decision for myself and my family."

From that moment, an enormous question hung over the 1997 season: Who would win the Tour? The list of contenders was long, and the peloton was in need of a new boss.

The "Little Frenchmen" Take Advantage

While awaiting the installation of a new king to fill the vacant throne, the regency took full advantage in the form of lesser-known French riders, who joyfully applied themselves. Emmanuel Magnien (Festina) won the Tour Méditerranée; Philippe Gaumont (Cofidis) took Ghent-Wevelgem, thirty-three years after Jacques Anquetil's victory; and Laurent Jalabert added Paris-Nice to his accomplishments. Jalabert also triumphed at Flèche Wallonne (in front of Luc Leblanc) and barely lost Liège-Bastogne-Liège to Michele Bartoli (MG-Technogym). Meanwhile, Frédéric Guesdon (La Française des Jeux) surprised Eddy Planckaert and Andre Tchmil (Lotto-Mobistar) on the track at the Roubaix velodrome, and Frédéric Moncassin (Gan) barely lost the Tour of Flanders to Rölf Sorensen (Rabobank). "Ah! These little Frenchmen," exclaimed an enthusiastic Roger Couderc, the popular French television sportscaster.

The Tour was getting closer. Everyone was dreaming of it, especially a Frenchman now somewhat long in the tooth, one of which was causing him great pain. Richard Virenque, surprising dominator of the Grand Prix d'Ouverture that February, had undergone a wisdom-tooth operation and still had disquietingly poor fitness just days before the start of the Tour in Rouen. (Rouen, of course, was the birthplace of Jacques Anquetil, whose death ten years earlier was being commemorated with the start.) Virenque had dropped out of the Classique des Alpes and called it quits at the Dauphiné Libéré on the Izoard.

Yet the true heir apparent for the race, second to Riis the year before, was not French at all. He was a 23-year-old German named Jan Ullrich. He wore a ring in his left ear and hailed from the former East Germany, where he had been schooled since childhood in the methods of his trainer, Peter Becker. Ullrich turned big gears with amazing ease. He was coming into his own on the powerful Telekom team—though its leader, Riis, had been strangely unimpressive after placing second in the Grand Prix of Frankfurt. Nonetheless, Ullrich now had his sights on the Tour.

Born under a Bad Sign

The 1997 Tour would turn out to be a duel between a Frenchman and a German, both of whom would be kept honest, especially on Alpe d'Huez, by an exceptional climber, Marco Pantani (Mercatone Uno), who was emerging from a long period of doubt. The bald man with elephant ears and a goatee also wore an earring in his left ear. His emaciated face and tortured stare reflected a string of misfortunes.

Pantani, Claudio Chiappucci's apprentice, had been the best young rider at the 1994 and 1995 Tours. The future had been his. Unfortunately, he had been deprived of participation in the 1996 Tour by a stupid accident at Milano-Torino in October 1995 that had nearly cost him his life. He had collided at full speed on a descent with a car that was going the wrong way. His tibia and fibula shattered, he was bedridden for nine months. Many racers in his position would have given up, but Pantani clung to destiny. He returned to competition in August 1996.

At the start of the 1997 season, Pantani was once again a contender, finishing fifth at Flèche Wallonne, third at the Tour of the Basque Country, and eighth at Liège-Bastogne-Liège. He had hoped to shine at the Giro, but at the start of the eighth day, a black cat strayed onto his path, causing a group crash. What misfortune! Pantani reinjured his thigh and dropped out.

The Pirate, who seemed to come from another planet as soon as the road slanted upward, vowed to reveal his return to form at the Tour—at Alpe d'Huez, of course, where he had won in 1995. Without Induráin, this Tour would be wide open.

Falls, Falls, Falls . . .

From the start, this hotly contested Tour produced significant casualties. The Uzbekistani racer Djamolidine Abdoujaparov, a three-time winner of the green jersey (1991, 1993, and 1994), tested positive for bromantin and glenbuterol in the second stage. Abdou, the king of amphetamines and growth hormones, would never again race in the Tour.

But mostly this Tour was plagued by falls in the early going, produced by the peloton's fast pace as it streaked toward the mountains. On the third day, Tony Rominger (Cofidis) quit after fracturing his clavicle. On the fifth day, Alex Zülle dropped out after taking a tumble. The next day, Evgeni Berzin bowed out with an injured shoulder. Numerous leaders in the early stages lost precious minutes on account of these repeated falls. Among the most perturbed were Leblanc (who fell on the same shoulder he had injured at the Giro), Pantani, Ivan Gotti, and Riis.

Their nerves frayed, the racers were on edge. Tom Steels was expelled from the Tour after the sixth stage when, in full sprint, he threw his water bottle at Moncassin at the finish in Marennes. The German sprinter Eric Zabel knocked down Damien Nazon with a blow to the shoulder. A vexed Nicolas Jalabert, Laurent's younger brother, delivered an uppercut to the Australian sprinter Robbie McEwen.

Cédric Vasseur (Gan) donned the yellow jersey after the fifth stage to La Châtre, following a solo breakaway over the last 147 kilometers (91 miles). Twenty-seven years earlier, his father, Alain, a teammate of Luis Ocaña, had pulled off a similar exploit: Wearing the Bic jersey, he had staged a marathon breakaway of 172 kilometers (107 miles) on the road to Felsburg, Germany. But unlike his son, he had not pulled on the golden fleece.

To the delight of French fans, the younger Vasseur still wore the jersey in the eighth stage, during the descent toward Pau, the first encounter with the Pyrénées. But in the next stage, from Pau to Loudenvielle, Festina celebrated Bastille Day in a big way. Laurent Brochard, the Frenchman who would go on to win the world road championship later that year in San Sebastian, Spain, finished just ahead of teammate Virenque. Vasseur still clung to the yellow jersey, but his lead over Ullrich had dwindled to a mere 13 seconds.

Ullrich Takes Charge

The next day, in the stage from Luchon to the summit of Arcalis, in the tiny principality of Andorra, Ullrich set things straight and fulfilled his ambition. He broke away 9.5 kilometers (5.9 miles) from the finish, suddenly upping his pace. He mashed his pedals, remaining in the saddle, and dropped his helpless adversaries. He had already shown himself to be an excellent *rouleur* in the previous Tour, when he had edged out Induráin in the time trial to Saint-Émilion (averaging over 50 kilometers [31 miles] an hour). Now the versatile German had dominated a mountain stage, thanks in large part to his youthful ardor and his ability to use his dorsal muscles to generate colossal power.

Just behind Ullrich, at 1:08, were two of his top rivals: Pantani, who still had something to prove, and Virenque, who wore the polka-dot jersey. The big loser that day was Riis, who finished 3:23 back. Laurent Jalabert finished 18:59 back, and Leblanc, whose thigh ached, finished more than 43 minutes behind.

During stage 12, the 55.5-kilometer (34.5-mile) Saint-Étienne time trial, Ullrich consolidated his hold on the yellow jersey. "He's the New Boss," read *L'Équipe*'s bold headline,[3] and with good reason, as the Alpe d'Huez stage approached. In the overall standings, Virenque, who had finished a surprising second in the time trial, held second place (5:42), the resilient Spaniard Abraham Olano was third (8:00), Riis was fourth (8:01), Pantani was fifth (9:11), and Fernando Escartin was sixth (11:09).

At last the crucial Alpe stage was at hand! In an interesting twist, the organizers had reduced this classic stage solely to the 13.8-kilometer (11.7-mile) climb. Before the traditional twenty-one switchbacks, there was not a single major challenge. Curiously, Pantani ordered his teammates to set a blistering pace well before the final ascent so as to splinter the peloton. His assault was ambitious, and 350,000 admiring fans lining the route voiced their admiration as one of the most memorable climbs in Tour history unfolded.

Just before turn 21, Pascal Hervé pushed himself to lead the dance as Virenque got on his wheel, poised for an ambush. The man from Var seemed to be in optimal form, ready to assert himself over the final stretch. Meanwhile, behind him, a number of stars were already struggling, notably Laurent Dufaux (Festina), Oscar Camenzind (Mapei), Olano (Banesto), and Michael Boogerd (Rabobank).

Like a Motorcycle

Ahead, a battle exploded. Ullrich, the yellow jersey, set the pace. Firmly seated, his elbows projecting at right angles from his torso, he showed his adversaries who was boss. Virenque struggled to stay on his wheel. Also keeping pace were Pantani, Riis, Francesco Casagrande, and Escartin. The rest of the peloton was lagging and increasingly stretched out. The German was putting on a show. He was drawing closer to a Tour victory, his great ambition. Yes, he really was the boss. Who could challenge him?

Turn 20: Pantani had thrown away his cap and now rose out of the saddle. From behind, he jumped to the left side of the road and accelerated. Ullrich's rhythm seemed impossibly infernal, yet the Pirate caught up to the German! Pantani, still out of the saddle and with his hands in the drops, devoured the climb. Virenque tried to keep pace, determined not to crack. A bomb had exploded.

The casualties were numerous, including Escartin and Casagrande, who were dropped. The stragglers formed small groups and continued their tedious ascent. Meanwhile, up front, Pantani was thoroughly enjoying himself. He leaned his head and torso forward, dancing about. Only three riders were still on his wheel: Ullrich, Virenque, and Riis.

Pantani periodically accelerated, matching his rhythm to a small gear. Just after La Garde, still on the lower section of the Alpe, Riis cracked, unable to maintain the pace at 28 kilometers (17.4 miles) an hour. Pantani took notice. He was the leader of the orchestra, the interpreter of the symphony of L'Oisans. He decided to increase the tempo even more. He made his second attack before Ribot. Only Ullrich managed to keep up. Virenque eventually recaught Ullrich's wheel but began to lag again at the next turn. It was too much for him. Yet the wearer of the polka-dot jersey continued to fight. His tank was not completely empty, and he wisely chose to proceed at his own pace.

Pantani could now hear nothing but the music of the adoring crowd. Forgotten were his bronchitis at the start of the Tour and his recent streak of bad luck and subpar performances.

Ullrich somehow managed to stay just behind Pantani. The irked Italian landed a final blow, still 10 kilometers (6.2 miles) from the summit. This time, the yellow jersey succumbed. A gap opened, and the Italian's path to victory was now clear. A virtuoso had heated up the Alpe, evoking the memory of the great Campionissimo. "One man, alone at the helm," read the headline of the Italian journal *Corriere dello Sport*, echoing the words of the radio announcers who had once broadcast Coppi's breakaway.

At Pantani's approach, the thick ranks of fans lining the Alpe from base to peak stepped back slightly to open a narrow corridor. They were dumbfounded and awed. They all wondered how the Italian had gotten there so fast. "Let Marco through," they yelled. A fan dressed as an American Indian ran alongside the Italian, yelling *"Vai, Marco, vai!"* ("Go, Marco, go!"). This bizarre character rattled Pantani and nearly made him lose his balance. The irritated racer sprinted away, like a king intent on avoiding the riffraff. Pantani owned the Alpe; it called him. Here he could shed all his troubles and rise from the ashes. As he crossed the line, he let out a powerful shriek, a cry of deliverance.

"Only You, Pantani," read the headline of *La Gazzetta dello Sport* the next day. "Pantani's Cry," recapped *Tuttosport*. Ullrich finished second, 47 seconds behind. Virenque came in third at 1:27. Casagrande, the revelation of this Tour, came in fourth at 2:27, a second ahead of the fading Riis.

Once again, Alpe d'Huez had rendered its verdict, selecting the Tour's top three finishers, though not in the same order. Pantani, who had pulverized the record for the ascent, setting a new time of 37:35, won again at Morzine two days later and finished the Tour in 3rd place. Virenque, who had won in Courchevel, gave it all he had on the road to Montbéliard in the 18th stage, briefly threatening Ullrich before settling for 2nd. The German ultimately prevailed and enjoyed a richly deserved victory, positioning himself as the potential champion over the next decade. Unfortunately for him, however, his own struggles and the arrival of Lance Armstrong would upset the expected order.

CHAPTER TWENTY-ONE

1999

Armstrong: Return of the Miracle Man

ALPE D'HUEZ WAS SPARED THE GREAT EARTHQUAKE THAT ROCKED the cycling world at the 1998 Tour. Absent from the route that year, it did not witness the police raids on hotel rooms or the protests by the cyclists, nor did it host the overzealous journalists who sought to pile on the evidence linking the sport to its scourge: doping. The purge that year culminated in the expulsion of the entire Festina team, including its leader, the prominent French climber Richard Virenque.

The 1999 Tour, which would return to the Alpe, was supposed to project a more positive image. Indeed, Lance Armstrong, a cancer survivor, was poised to make a sensational return to the peloton. But by the start of the race, high hopes had given way to major disappointments. Absent were Jan Ullrich (torn knee cartilage), Laurent Jalabert (who chose to race in Spain instead), Marco Pantani, the defending champion of the Alpe (ousted from the Giro a few months before), and Bjarne Riis (suffering from a broken elbow and hand incurred at the Tour of Switzerland).

Moreover, it was increasingly apparent that the wounds of 1998 had not healed. The entire TVM team was banned for its role in the drug scandal of the previous edition. And despite opposition from the organizers, a discredited Virenque took advantage of a loophole in UCI regulations to be eligible for this Tour. *L'Équipe* denounced his presence[1] as well as that of Manolo Saiz, ONCE's *directeur sportif*.

The very day of the prologue, Dr. Pierre Dumas, former chief doctor of the Tour, who had assisted a stricken Tom Simpson before he had died on the Ventoux in 1967 with an abundance of amphetamines in his system, offered a painful reminder that drug use is a long and enduring vice within the peloton. Describing the drug culture of his day, he told the journalist Philippe Brunel, "Hygiene was a concern. Often, [the racers] passed along the same syringe without even washing their hands. It didn't even bother them to shoot up in front of me. Many suffered from an inflammation of the perineum, what we called the third testicle."[2]

The racers saw themselves as marked men. They worried that authorities would raid their rooms or homes, as had happened to Pavel Tonkov, Mario Cipollini, and Ivan Gotti a few months earlier during the Giro, per order of a judge in Ferrara, Italy, who was overseeing a probe into drug abuse in professional cycling. Racers were also fearful of investigative journalists. *Der Spiegel*, a German newsmagazine, had accused Telekom's medical staff of administering drugs to its members, and Danish television had pointed a finger at Riis. None of these developments boded well for the future of cycling.

Christophe Basson, a racer with La Française des Jeux, further peeved the peloton. From the start of the Tour, he would make numerous anti-doping declarations in a daily newspaper column. This white knight was on a crusade. He was in the right, of course, but he went clumsily about his mission. For the racers, this Tour was not supposed to be a high-profile trial, not after the ordeal of the previous year. But "Bobosse" was piling it on. He became the dog that disrupts a game of skittles.[3] Demoralized and shunned, he would pull out of the Tour in stage 12, at Saint-Galmier, famous for its mineral water. A few months later, he left professional cycling. Of course, the drug allegations did not disappear with him.

Speed and More Speed

Although the 1999 Tour did not ultimately offer the clean break from the past that many had hoped for, Armstrong's return was nonetheless an uplifting story. He had missed the last two Tours as he had recovered from testicular cancer as well as from the removal of lung and brain tumors. The press and public were intrigued by his stirring story, made all the more dramatic by the fact that the resurrected Armstrong was a stronger racer than ever. He had always been a good *rouleur*, but the weight he had lost and the spinning technique he had developed transformed him into a great climber as well.

Armstrong wasted no time underscoring his remarkable transformation. At the prologue in Puy-de-Fou, he wore the blue U.S. Postal jersey with the number 181, a streamlined helmet, and aerodynamic sunglasses. He covered the 6.8 kilometers (4.2 miles) in 8:02, an average of 50.7 kilometers (31.5 miles) per hour. A comeback indeed! For the first time, he donned the yellow jersey. The victory confirmed his arrival as a top competitor and marked the start of a reign that would last seven years.

It was not only Armstrong pushing the speed limit. The 1999 edition was notable for its blistering pace throughout. Mario Cipollini's winning speed in the fourth stage from Laval to Blois was 50.35 kilometers (31.3 miles) per hour, an absolute record. This Tour would also establish a record average speed of over 40 kilometers (24.9 miles) an hour.

Armstrong's Show of Force

As an athlete who had beaten death itself, Armstrong was greeted warmly upon his return to the public eye. Yet his stony persona also projected an air of coolness. Square-jawed and solid as a rock, Armstrong maintained his distance. What was most striking about him, perhaps, was his supreme self-confidence and unshakable serenity. He exuded a tranquil but irrepressible force. Evidently, Armstrong had retrieved an unflagging inner strength from his journey through the misery of oncology.

And now he was ready to prove himself. He won the eighth stage and his second time trial, a 56.5-kilometer (35.1-mile) loop around Metz, reclaiming the yellow jersey. But the next stage, the first foray into the mountains, from Grand-Bornan in Savoy to Sestrières, Italy, was his first true test. It was also, some said, the peloton's first test to see if it could resist the temptation to use drugs. "We're going to see if things have changed," mused Philippe Bouvet in *L'Équipe*.

Armstrong traversed the Galibier, devoured the Montgenèvre, and reached the foot of Sestrières in the lead. His pursuers, now few in number, were astonished, as were the television viewers who watched the hallucinatory spectacle. Armstrong was alone in the mountains under a glacial rain, his legs bare, wearing a yellow jersey and a cap. He had taken the bull by the horns. He was in the drops of his handlebars, just like Eric Zabel and Cipollini—who had dropped out some time before—at the finish of a stage.[4] Armstrong stood on his pedals, his favorite position, and moved his legs at incredible speed. He was sprinting! No one had ever seen such agility or such a fluid style.

An excited Armstrong devoured each gradient and insolently dominated each incline on the mountain, casting aside the dark years for good. One can only imagine what he had gone through between October 1996, when he had announced that he had cancer, and February 1998, when he had returned to competition at the Ruta del Sol: the exhaustion; the chemotherapy; the loss of hair; his thinning body; and the doubts, fears, and disorientation. At last, Armstrong taunted death on the slopes of Sestrières, finishing first. And he took his revenge on death as well, the day before Alpe d'Huez, which promised to be another spectacle.

After the finish in the Italian ski resort, racers and journalists marveled at Armstrong's dominant performance. The overall standings stood as follows: The American led Abraham Olano (ONCE) by 6:03, Christophe Moreau (Festina) by 7:44, Alex Zülle (Banesto) by 7:47, Laurent Dufaux (Saeco-Cannondale) by 8:07, and Virenque (Polti) by 10:02.

From Sestrières to Alpe d'Huez on Bastille Day would be no cakewalk, not with Mont Cenis and the very difficult Croix de Fer preceding the Alpe, and especially since no French rider had yet won a stage. Armstrong was again expected to shine, drawing extra motivation from the presence of Jim Ochowicz, his first *directeur sportif* at Motorola. Ochowicz had been at Armstrong's side from the start of his cycling career, after his stint as a triathlete, and had also been there when Fabio Casartelli had met his death at a turn on Portet d'Aspet in 1995.

The national holiday and return to France after the Tour's brief incursion into Italy, where Virenque took back the polka-dot jersey, inspired two French *rouleurs*, Stéphan Heulot (La Française des Jeux) and Thierry Bourguignon (Big Mat), an indefatigable attacker. They broke away along the sinuous descent of Mont Cenis, 150 kilometers (93 miles) from the finish, and by the foot of the Croix de Fer had built up a lead of 11:20. For both riders, it was imperative that they hold their advantage up the long climb to have any hope of getting to the valley of L'Oisans and reaching the summit of the Alpe as victors.

But as the pair began the climb, they slowed considerably. Their lead shrank to 6:05. By the time they reached the foot of the Alpe, it was down

139

to 4:17. It wasn't enough, especially because they were no longer working together. Heulot, encouraged by the crowd, pressed on alone, while Bourguignon preferred to climb at his own pace. Meanwhile, the peloton was approaching, thanks in large part to the American Tyler Hamilton, who was dictating the pace on behalf of his teammate Armstrong.

At this point, everyone was expecting another show of force from the Texan Armstrong. Instead, he was content to easily follow and control the race, despite a malfunction in his rear derailleur that prevented him from using his 19-tooth sprocket. He had to pass directly from the 17-tooth cog to either the 21 or 23, pedaling either "too hard" or "too easy," as he said later. In any event, he would also confide that he felt no inclination to overdo it and possibly invite further drug allegations.

Zülle, on the wheel of his *domestique* Manuel Beltran, overtook Heulot 3.5 kilometers (2.2 miles) from the finish. The Swiss star, like most of the former Festina riders, had paid for his sins of 1998. Fourth in the overall standings, he had a shot at the podium. He knew that Olano (second overall) and Christophe Moreau (third) were foundering behind him. Zülle was looking to become dauphin to Armstrong and was playing a similar card.

Nine riders followed Beltran's wheel: Zülle, of course; Giuseppe Guerini (Telekom); Pavel Tonkov (Mapei); Fernando Escartin (Kelme); Virenque (Polti); Dufaux; Kurt Van De Wouwer (Lotto); Carlos Contreras (Kelme); and, naturally, Armstrong.

The initial attack by Heulot and Bourguignon, two valiant workhorses, proved futile, though it had been beautiful and courageous. They deserved to settle the dispute for victory between themselves after having led the race for 140 kilometers (87 miles), but it was not to be.[5]

Guerini in the Picture

A few minutes from the finish line, the favorites were eyeing each other to see who would make a move. But Guerini did not leave them much time for reflection as he launched his attack, his jersey unzipped, skier's sunglasses covering his eyes. In his disjointed pedaling style, he quickly opened a significant gap, and in his delight to be in the unlikely position of leading the favorites, he rushed toward the finish, 2.8 kilometers (1.7 miles) farther up the road. The crowd cheered him on, swallowing him in their extended arms.

On his left, an overzealous fan suddenly stepped into the narrow passage to take a photograph of the oncoming racer. Unbelievable! Guerini saw him and went to pass him on the left. The befuddled fan hesitated, not knowing which way to go, then in a panic lurched at the last instant, slamming right into Guerini from the side. The Italian fell, stopped in his tracks, his feet releasing from the pedals. Guerini did not waste any time dwelling on his misfortune. He grabbed his bike, set it on its wheels, and jumped back on, driven by the instinct to win. His human obstacle tried in vain to help him while the crowd screamed in anger, but Guerini could hear nothing, having already sped away.

Retake command he did. Ullrich's humble teammate, who had twice finished the Giro in third place (1997 and 1998), now inscribed his name in the annals of Alpe d'Huez as a winner. Twenty-one seconds later, Tonkov arrived, followed 4 seconds later by the group of favorites, including Armstrong, who finished fifth. Just in time!

Although Armstrong had not dominated the stage, he had increased his overall lead over Olano to 7:42. As it turned out, the American would wear the yellow jersey all the way to Paris. He even completed a sweep of the time trials when he won the 19th stage at Futuroscope the day before his triumphant arrival on the Champs-Élysées.

Armstrong: "I Don't Take Anything"

But Armstrong could not avoid persistent allegations of drug use. In a post-race interview on the podium in L'Alpe d'Huez, the television producer Gérard Holz put the question directly to Armstrong: "Lance, people are asking questions about you. Following your illness, did you take certain products?" The big boss's answer: "Absolutely not." Armstrong had already declared during a press conference, "I've come a long way to get back on top. I beat my cancer. I live in France, in Nice, and I train here, where the antidoping campaign is intense. Do you think I'd be crazy enough to take banned products?"

La Dépêche du Midi published a supportive interview with Dr. Michel Marty, chief of oncology at Hospital Saint Louis in Paris. "I don't know of any doping products associated with chemotherapy," Marty said. "What's more, his last treatment was sixteen months ago. There's no way it could be affecting his performance now. We are overreacting here; there's so much suspicion surrounding cycling that when a cancer survivor wins we automatically assume it must be due to the drugs he used in his treatment."[6]

Curiously, Armstrong revealed in 2001 that he had in fact consulted with the controversial Italian professor Michele Ferrari, who was known to have administered the illegal drug EPO to numerous cycling champions. But, the American insisted, "I have never talked about EPO with [Ferrari], nor have I ever used it." The disastrous 1998 Tour had nonetheless sown the seeds of suspicion, and the Festina scandal cast a long shadow over Armstrong's remarkable comeback.

That was a pity, for Armstrong's story is as beautiful as a fairy tale. In 1992, at the age of 21, the American began his professional career with Motorola. He entered his first Tour the following year and won the 8th stage to Verdun before pulling out following the 11th stage to Isola 2000, an alpine ski resort. In 1994, he won the world championship in Oslo and entered his second Tour, dropping out in the 15th stage just before Mont Ventoux (he was then 33rd in the overall standings, 26:03 behind Induráin). In 1995, he won the stage to Limoges and finished his first Tour in 36th place, 88 minutes behind Induráin. Armstrong started the 1996 Tour but called it quits during the 6th stage, on the road to Aix-les-Bains during a torrential downpour, his throat on fire. He was in 51st place at that point, 5:03 behind yellow jersey Heulot.

Up to that point, Armstrong had enjoyed a respectable, if unremarkable, cycling career. In four tries between 1993 and 1996, he had completed the Tour only once. But then came cancer, recovery, an amazing comeback, and historic exploits. Armstrong courageously endured his years of darkness, which he later credited with transforming his life and cycling career. He returned in 1999, starting the Tour for the fifth time. He not only completed the race for the second time, he utterly dominated it, registering the first of his record seven straight victories.

To return to the top, Armstrong had trained extremely hard, using fixed gears and small chainrings to improve his spinning and adapt to the insanely high heart rates typical of the best climbers. Even before his illness, he had demonstrated power, winning the Classica San Sebastian in 1995 and the Flèche Wallonne in 1996. But now, twenty pounds lighter, he showed that he was also a great climber, able to spin his legs at a prodigious cadence. Incredibly, he could now emulate Induráin in time trials and Pantani on climbs. At 28, Armstrong had earned his nickname: "Miracle Man."

142

CHAPTER TWENTY-TWO

2001

The Look

As the 2001 Tour approached, the peloton feared new drug-related incriminations. Just a few weeks before the start of the Tour, the Giro had experienced yet another "blitz," a raid by the authorities. On the rest day in San Remo, some 400 Italian police officers invaded the racers' hotel rooms. Like the 1998 Tour, the 2001 Giro staggered on. But nearly every team came under suspicion, and many top riders found themselves facing legal charges. Dario Frigo, for one, confessed to having practiced blood doping. Ivan Gotti reportedly hid his illegal substances in his father-in-law's camper.

Marco Pantani, who was again implicated in the Giro drug scandal, became—like Richard Virenque in 1999—the Tour's persona non grata.[1] Pantani denounced what he called an injustice, but he was not the only big name absent from the race. For various reasons, Alex Zülle, Mario Cipollini, Laurent Dufaux, Pavel Tonkov, Richard Virenque, and Fernando Escartin were among those who stayed home.

Adding to the tensions, the Tour was barely under way when the journalist David Walsh of London's *Sunday Times* published explosive new charges fingering the champion himself, Lance Armstrong, who was seeking his third straight Tour victory. In a highly detailed article, Walsh presented a number of troubling allegations linking Armstrong to drugs, focusing on the racer's association with the controversial Italian doctor Michele Ferrari, whom the American himself had praised for his integrity.

Walsh asserted that Armstrong had visited the doctor on numerous occasions over the years, and even listed the dates and locations of their encounters. Walsh also quoted a former Motorola racer who asserted that EPO had been widely used by the team when Armstrong had been a member. The source also cited a few other troubling affairs, including the case of Lance's former teammate Kevin Livingston, who had experienced strange variations in his red-blood-cell count.

Walsh's charges hit a nerve and reawakened interest in a curious incident from July 2000, when a French television crew recovered a bag that a teammate of Armstrong had thrown into a wastebasket. It was found to contain a number of products, including Actovegin, a medicine based on calf plasma that is purported to improve oxygen transport as a sort of muscle combustible, and therefore to enhance performance.[2]

Armstrong's battles were now no longer confined to the road; they extended into the arena of public opinion as well. Many assumed that he must be on drugs to dominate the competition the way he did. But the American would continue to assert his innocence. Strengthening his case, the Tour incorporated a new test that year, designed to detect the presence of EPO.

The Armstrong-Ullrich Duel

In this Tour that included fifty-one Frenchmen, Armstrong was again the odds-on favorite to claim a third straight title. For the first time in his career, he ranked number one in the UCI rankings. He had demonstrated mastery both in time trials and in the mountains, even under glacial rain. He had spent hours in the saddle to maintain his form and had ridden many of the Tour's toughest stages far in advance. He knew the profiles of the upcoming climbs by heart.

The U.S. Postal team had also been strengthened for Armstrong's benefit. The 30-year-old leader himself had recruited a climber second only to Pantani, the Spaniard Roberto Héras (formerly with Kelme). Armstrong plucked José Luis Rubiera from the same team and persuaded the Colombian Victor Hugo Peña to join as well. Armstrong was determined to add the Tour to his season's *palmarès*, which already included the Tour of Switzerland and overwhelming dominance in that race's hilly time trial between Sion and Crans-Montana.

Jan Ullrich was the only previous winner (1997) besides Armstrong in the race, and the German was naturally considered the American's top rival. The 27-year-old Ullrich again wore the jersey of German national champion, as he had in 1997. He had also raced the Giro, finishing 52nd, an hour and a half behind Gilberto Simoni. But for Ullrich, the Giro was merely a warm-up exercise for the Tour as he tried to shed a few kilos and get into fighting shape.

Ullrich arrived at the Tour extremely motivated and determined not to finish second for the fourth time.[3] He also had a strong team behind him, having convinced Telekom to add some climbers to the roster who would cater to his needs. Assigned to assist Ullrich were Giuseppe Guerini, Andreas Klöden, Alexander Vinokourov, and Livingston, recruited from Armstrong's team. However, Telekom's sprinter, Eric Zabel, was displeased at losing the services of Gian Matteo Fagnini and the robust Rolf Aldag.

Ullrich was a true superstar, a powerful cycling machine, although his questionable training habits left some room for doubt. The calm, fit Armstrong, in contrast, was ready to play his cards. The 2001 Tour was shaping up to be the clash of the titans that everyone had wanted since 1993, when the German had become the amateur world champion and the American his professional counterpart.

The Pontarlier Trap

Surprisingly, the much-anticipated duel almost failed to materialize. Early in the contest, both favorites suddenly found themselves far behind in the general standings. The intense struggle between U.S. Postal and Telekom had inadvertently opened the door for other teams to make their mark before the mountain stages. And in the eighth stage, before the Alps and the Pyrénées, both favorites fell into a trap.

The 222-kilometer (138-mile) route began in Colmar. At kilometer 5 (mile 3), Belgian Ludo Dierckxsens (Lampre) launched an attack. He was soon followed by thirteen more riders, and with 60 kilometers (37.3 miles) to go, they built up a huge lead of 32:10 over the peloton.[4] Erik Dekker (Rabobank) eventually won the stage in Pontarlier, finishing 35:34 ahead of the principal favorites, Armstrong and Ullrich. The Australian Stuart O'Grady (Crédit Agricole) emerged with the yellow jersey and a 35-

minute lead in the general classification over Armstrong (24th overall) and Ullrich (27th overall).

As a result of the breakaway, several participants wound up with surprisingly strong positions in the overall standings, notably François Simon (Bonjour) in second place and the Kazakh Andreï Kivilev (Cofidis) in fourth. Kivilev, who would die tragically in a race accident two years later,[5] would have been even higher in the standings had he not lost 18 minutes in the fourth stage through a tactical error.

Two days later, on the eve of the Alpe d'Huez stage, sprinter O'Grady still had the yellow jersey and a considerable advantage over the two favorites. Laurent Jalabert, in 11th place, was enjoying a magnificent Tour, having already won two stages with solo breakaways. The one to Colmar, on Bastille Day, had evoked his triumph at Mende six years earlier. "Jaja," as his fans called him, even threatened Patrice Halgand for the polka-dot jersey. Also ahead of Armstrong and Ullrich were the dangerous Joseba Beloki (ONCE) in 14th place and Christophe Moreau (17th), who had won both the Dauphiné Libéré and the prologue of this Tour, finishing 4 seconds ahead of Armstrong.

If It Hadn't Been for Television

Three racers jumped ahead at the start of the Alpe stage: Eladio Jiménez (iBanesto), Antonio Tauler (Kelme), and Laurent Roux (Jean Delatour). They quickly built up their lead. On the Madeleine, Tauler faded, but the opportunistic Roux, followed by Jiménez, reached the summit with an 8:50 lead over the peloton. On the Glandon, Roux distanced the Spaniard and rode the climb alone. At the summit, Roux still held a 5:50 lead over the peloton, led by Jalabert.

On the slopes of the Glandon, in the middle of the pack beside Sylvain Chavanel (Bonjour), Armstrong was grimacing. Johan Bruyneel, his *directeur sportif*, reached on his cell phone by television commentators, offered an instant analysis: "Lance doesn't seem well. He's anxious for this stage to end." Meanwhile, up ahead, Ullrich dictated the pace, following the wheels of four teammates: Klöden, Livingston, Vinokourov, and Jens Heppner.

As it turned out, the American was merely feigning discomfort for the cameras. Why? Because he was staying out of the wind and saving his strength for an attack up Alpe d'Huez. "That was my plan," he revealed later. "We were not in a position to set our own pace; our riders were either too sick or too weak." Indeed, only Rubiera was at his side; the other teammates were missing in action. Peña and Steffen Kjaergaard had fallen, Viatcheslav Ekimov and George Hincapie were lagging far behind, and Tyler Hamilton had a stomachache.

At the foot of the Alpe, Roux was still out front with a 6-minute lead over Armstrong. The American got on the wheel of teammate Rubiera, who attacked the mountain with all he had. They began to pull away, followed by Ullrich and Kivilev. The other riders were already in trouble. Suddenly Armstrong took charge. He stood on his pedals and looked back over his shoulder to size up Ullrich.

It was a do-or-die moment for Ullrich. Surprised, he seemed almost to pout, knowing full well that he could not follow an attack. Ullrich didn't even try to go with the attack. He lowered his head, hunched his shoulders like a wounded bull, and remained glued to the hillside where, until that moment, he had been feeling good.

The American, his jersey unzipped, gave a command performance on his blue Trek, rolling out a minuscule gear (39x23). He spun at a very high cadence, between 85 and 90 rpm. From time to time he stood on his pedals to relax his muscles. Once reseated, he resumed his unrestrained pedaling. He seemed to pedal with ease, relishing the steep grade before the admiring and astonished eyes of his fans, including his friend the actor Robin Williams.

At Huez, Armstrong caught Roux and took the lead at last. His masterful performance was reminiscent of his heroic climb to Sestrières in 1999, during a rainstorm, and his ascent to Hautacam in 2000. In the end, he covered the Alpe's twenty-one switchbacks in 38:01, just 26 seconds shy of Pantani's 1997 record.

Although Armstrong still trailed by some 20 minutes in the overall standings, he had demoralized his chief rival and effectively killed the suspense of the event. No other racer, not even the great Eddy Merckx, had displayed such arrogance. To recall anything similar, one had to think back to the 1996 Tour, when Bjarne Riis, who had consistently declared that he was the strongest rider, had calmly drifted back to size up his principal rivals (Induráin, Virenque, Dufaux, and Leblanc), before launching a third attack that left them in the dust. That had been at the peak of the EPO era.

Boos for Armstrong

Both applause and disapproving whistles greeted Armstrong at the finish line.[6] The crowd at L'Alpe d'Huez, as skeptical as it was admiring, was focused on a fundamental question: Was Armstrong really the great champion of the new century, or did he simply have access to a yet-unknown pharmacopoeia? It was rather unjust to be suspicious of him at that point. The American, after all, had always claimed to be clean, and no firm evidence had indicated otherwise.

Ullrich finished 2nd, back 1:59. He had lost over 8 seconds per kilometer behind Armstrong, "the motorcycle." Beloki was 3rd. A grimacing Simon, hunched over his bicycle, finished 29th, 10:20 off the pace. But he succeeded in his bid to take over the yellow jersey that he would wear until the climb up Pla d'Adet, where Armstrong would finally take it away. The Frenchman thus atoned for his older brother Pascal, who had bowed out of the 1983 Tour during this same stage while wearing the yellow jersey, suffering from a fractured shoulder blade. François's heroic performance ranked with other memorable exploits by this family dynasty: In 1982, Pascal had taken the stage from Orcières to Merlette; in 1985, Régis had been the winner in Pau; and in 1988, Jérôme had won in Strasbourg.

The next day, Armstrong won the 32-kilometer (19.9-mile) time trial at Chamrousse. The day after that, in stage 12, he finished behind the Colombian Félix Cárdenas (Kelme) at the summit of the Plateau de Bonsacre, closing to within 10 minutes of the yellow jersey. But most importantly, Armstrong had widened his lead over Ullrich to more than 4 minutes. The German had attacked at the base of the climb, but Armstrong had been on his tail the whole way, once again denying him a backward glance of his own. Two kilometers (1.2 miles) from the finish, the American once again gave his rival a fiery stare, just as he had on Alpe d'Huez.

In the Pyrénées the next day, the American dominated the stage to Saint-Lary-Soulan, at last taking the yellow jersey from Simon. Armstrong would wear it all the way to Paris for his third straight victory. He also became the first racer since Fausto Coppi to win the Alpe stage and the Tour in the same year. Ullrich finished second, followed by Beloki. For only the second time in history, the top three finishers of the previous Tour repeated in the same order. Curiously, they had also finished on the Alpe in the same sequence.

CHAPTER TWENTY-THREE

2003

Armstrong
Battles Bad Luck

W AS IT A WARNING SIGN? WHEN LANCE ARMSTRONG AND HIS
U.S. Postal team gathered in Paris to participate in the opening
ceremonies of the 2003 Tour, the centennial edition that would give the
American a chance at a record-tying fifth victory, a bird of ill omen re-
lieved itself on Armstrong's manager, Johan Bruyneel.

For Armstrong, it seemed like a premonition that making history
would not be easy. He instantly thought back to his fall in the Dauphiné
Libéré just a few weeks earlier—on Friday the 13th, no less. He had just
started the stage from Morzine to Chambéry, charging down a descent at
Tanninges, when his wheel caught in a sewer grate, slamming him to the
ground. Fortunately, he only injured his elbow, though he felt somewhat
embarrassed by the rip in his shorts that exposed both buttocks.

That misfortune did not stop Armstrong from winning the race (his
second in a row, and his second in all). But it did raise troubling questions.
"My accident in the Dauphiné was not normal," he complained afterward.
"Nobody had ever seen anything like that before. The brakes were glued
to the fork. Why? No mechanic would do that!"[1]

Had someone been out to get Armstrong, or was he just a victim of
bad luck? And how did that bode for his chances to win a fifth straight
Tour, something only Miguel Induráin had done? True, the American
was yet again the odds-on favorite, but his nemesis, Jan Ullrich—the

only other Tour winner in the 2003 lineup—was back after missing the previous edition.

A host of young pretenders was also eagerly waiting in the wings, including the American Tyler Hamilton; the Spaniards Iban Mayo, Aitor González, and Joseba Beloki; and the Italians Ivan Basso and Gilberto Simoni. As it turned out, the 2003 Tour would indeed offer the defending champion his toughest challenge in years as he overcame one near-disaster after another.

This circuit was nonetheless supposed to be a festive celebration marking a century of Tours. In 1903, sixty crazy racers (or "energy generators," in the words of Henri Desgrange, *patron* at *L'Auto*, the organizing newspaper) embarked on the greatest cycling adventure ever undertaken. They gathered at the hotel Au Réveil Matin at Montgeron, just outside Paris, to start the first of six stages. Maurice Garin, a naturalized Italian, won the inaugural contest, which helped to revive the concept of a road race, long overshadowed by the more popular cycling sport of track racing.

Although Americans were the strongest racers on wooden and cinder velodrome tracks, no Yankee took part in the original Tour. Nevertheless, the race carried a soupçon of American flavor. One of the French riders, Hyppolite Aucouturier, wore the colors of the American Bicycle Company (ABC), a consortium of the most prominent American brands that dominated the market at the beginning of the twentieth century. Aucouturier took two stages and might well have won the event had it not been for the food poisoning he suffered on the first day.

To commemorate the original running, Tour organizers started the first stage of the 2003 race in Montgeron and based the itinerary on the original circuit. Many of the stages thus ended in major cities, notably Lyon, Marseille, Toulouse, Bordeaux, and Nantes. But of course this exceptional event could not deprive itself of its mountain temple, Alpe d'Huez, which would once again consecrate with yellow the eventual winner in Paris.

L'Équipe, the successor to *L'Auto* and organizing sponsor of the Tour, published a special edition dated July 5, 2003. It was printed entirely on yellow paper, as *L'Auto* had been in its time, which had inspired the yellow jersey, introduced in 1919.[2] "One Hundred Years—It's Monumental," ran the headline over a photomontage showing Garin and Armstrong side by side and featuring the original paper from July 1, 1903, as a backdrop. The Frenchman, sporting a mustache and wearing a long-sleeved jersey, straddled a bicycle marked "La Française Diamant," while the American conqueror, wearing a helmet like a knight's, bestrode a blue Trek. There they were: one ancient hero and one modern, united in the same quest.

"The first time I heard anyone talk about the Tour was in the mid-1980s, when I was still a triathlete," Armstrong recalled. "I'd swum and run with my high school, and I rode with a local club. Those guys hardly talked about anything but the Tour de France. They knew all the names, places, racers, results. They talked about racing strategies—it was a real passion for them. They followed it as if it passed right by their doorstep. They were the ones who got me familiar with the Tour. But it didn't really sink in until Greg LeMond won it in 1986. It was a new thing in America."[3]

Armstrong's Fall

The 6.5-kilometer (4-mile) prologue took place at the foot of the Eiffel Tower (which had just marked its 114th anniversary) in an extraordinary celebration of sport. The route followed some of the most beautiful thoroughfares of Paris and passed numerous landmarks, including the Place du Trocadéro, the Place de la Concorde, the Pont d'Alma, and the Palaces des Invalides. The Australian Bradley McGee (FDJeux.com) won, finishing 8 centimeters (3 inches) ahead of the unfortunate Scotsman David Millar (Cofidis), who had dropped his chain. For the first time, Armstrong made a poor initial showing, finishing a distant seventh.

In truth, Armstrong was still suffering from back pains as a result of his fall in the Dauphiné Libéré. In addition, his right ankle was sore, due to new shoes he had broken in just a few days earlier. Finally, he had contracted a gastric disorder from his children. It did seem as though misfortune were stalking the Texan when, during the first stage to Meaux, he fell 450 meters (a little less than 500 yards) from the finish line. Armstrong and ten others went down in a terrific tumble provoked unintentionally by the Spaniard José Enrique Gutierrez (Kelme–Costa Blanca). To cross the line, Armstrong had to borrow the bike of his *domestique* José Luis Rubiera, known as "Chechu." The American complained of pain in his right shoulder and suffered from a hematoma on his right hip. Fortunately, his ailments appeared manageable.

Still, the accident was an uncomfortably close call. "It was real carnage," Armstrong commented when he learned that his compatriot Hamilton

(CSC), the winner of Liège-Bastogne-Liège and the Tour de Romandie and a serious contender for the yellow jersey, had broken his collarbone. But Hamilton astonished people with his willpower as he staggered to the finish line, completing the stage that Alessandro Petacchi (Fassa Bortolo), the speedster the Italians called "Ale-jet," had won in a sprint.

Armstrong's first sigh of relief came after the finish of the fourth stage, a team time trial covering 69 kilometers (42.9 miles) around Saint Dizier. For the first time, U.S. Postal won this difficult event, averaging 52.37 kilometers (32.5 miles) per hour. The victory propelled young Victor Hugo Peña into the yellow jersey, the first Colombian in history to wear this magical emblem that had eluded Lucho Herrera, Fabio Parra, Alfonso Florez, and Santiago Botero.

Armstrong rose to second place overall, just 1 second behind his teammate. As the Alps loomed, the yellow jersey was well within his grasp. "Everyone is thinking ahead to Alpe d'Huez," the American revealed to *L'Équipe* in his daily interview. "Myself included."

The first mountain stage, from Lyon to Morzine-Avoriaz, quickly established an initial hierarchy. Richard Virenque (Quick Step–Davitamon) put on a surprising show of force, breaking away for the last 189.5 kilometers (117.8 miles) and taking the stage as he had three years earlier. Meanwhile, Armstrong, Ullrich, Hamilton, and Beloki all finished together, more than 4 minutes behind, as they saved themselves for the Alpe. That left the Frenchman, eleven years after his promising debut in the Tour, with the yellow jersey and a 2:37 lead over Armstrong, who was in second place. Virenque also wore the polka-dot jersey, which he hoped to take to Paris for the sixth time.

Manzano's Revelations

Overshadowed by Virenque's one-man show was the strange and frightening collapse of Jesus Manzano (Kelme–Costa Blanca). When Virenque broke away from the peloton on the first climb, Manzano was at his side. A few kilometers later, however, the Spaniard suddenly didn't feel well and collapsed. Tour officials feared for the racer's life, but fortunately he recovered. In retrospect, however, the mysterious episode should have raised a red flag. Several days before the start of the Tour, Dr. Michel Audran, a doping specialist, had sounded a cry of alarm. "Blood transfusions are still undetectable," he'd warned, "and easier to practice than they were 15 years ago in terms of withdrawing and preserving blood. They can offer an alternative to taking EPO."

Less than a year later, on March 23, 2004, Manzano admitted that he had done just that the morning of the stage to Morzine. In a candid interview conducted by the Spanish newspaper *AS*, Manzano revealed that "his team practiced self-transfusions for the Tour de France" and that his collapse the previous year had, in fact, been caused by the practice and exacerbated by drug use. He confessed:

> That morning I was injected with 50 milliliters [1.7 ounces] of a substance I had never taken before. I called my girlfriend and told her, "Mark my words, today I'm going to do well, from what I gather." Midway through the stage, there was a breakaway and I suddenly felt a hunger attack, as if the change of pace had done me in. It was very bizarre. My hands fell asleep. Three kilometers [1.9 miles] later, I felt the need to vomit. I was feverish and broke into a cold sweat. I was trembling. Virenque took one look at me, then left me behind. I continued for 500 meters and don't remember anything after that. I had the impression that if I fell, that would be the end. My tongue felt bloated, and I could no longer breathe. I wanted someone to drill a hole in my throat. I had a bloated stomach and I could not urinate.

Manzano's revelations would provoke yet another scandal and schism in the world of professional cycling. They triggered the Puerto investigation in Spain that would ultimately implicate a host of top racers, including Ivan Basso, Oscar Sevilla, Francisco Mancebo, Joseba Beloki, Jörg Jaksche, Santiago Botero, Roberto Héras, Tyler Hamilton, Alejandro Valverde, and even Jan Ullrich, who chose to retire as a result.

But for now, the centennial Tour continued without the specter of another drug scandal. The day after Virenque's stunning triumph, all eyes were focused on the great showdown of the Tour: the queen stage from Sallanches to L'Alpe d'Huez. The 219-kilometer (136-mile) course included ascents up the Télégraphe and Galibier before the final climb up the Alpe.

Two favorites couldn't take the pace on the very first climbs: Gilberto Simoni (Saeco), the recent winner of the Giro, and Santiago Botero, Telekom's new leader, who had been recruited from Kelme at the start of the season. At the summit of the Galibier, the Italian Stefano Garzelli (Caldirola-So.Di) passed into the lead, pocketing the Henri Desgrange prime, awarded every year to the first racer who reaches the highest point of the Tour. On the descent, to everyone's surprise, the Spaniard Mikel Astarloza (AG2R Prévoyance) and the Frenchman Didier Rous (Brioches La Boulangère) attacked. Tensions grew in the Vallée de la Maurienne as Astarloza and Rous built up a lead of 2:10 before they started up Alpe d'Huez.

Beloki and Hamilton Draw Their Weapons

Armstrong led a chase group that included the principal favorites. As they reached the foot of the Alpe, the mounting pressure finally caused an explosion. Manuel Beltran, the only new member of Armstrong's team, immediately set a blistering pace. He had been recruited for just this kind of work, but he stepped on the gas too soon and too completely. He was soon in the red and had to drop back while Rubiera took over. "He's new to our team," Armstrong told the press that evening, "and probably has not yet learned how we do things. We wanted to establish a sustainable tempo, but that was supersonic."

Virenque, meanwhile, was paying for his heroic performance the previous day. He was dropped, but the satisfaction of climbing the Alpe in yellow on Bastille Day was enough for him. Ullrich, the big favorite, was losing ground. Suddenly, 10.5 kilometers (6.5 miles) from the summit, Beloki attacked. Armstrong's *domestique* Héras was unable to respond, leaving Armstrong to fend for himself. "Go ahead, Lance, go!" yelled U.S. Postal team director Johan Bruyneel into the team radio. Armstrong, hearing Bruyneel's instructions in his earphone, stood on his pedals and attempted to catch the streaking Spaniard, but the American's choppy style gave the impression that this was not to be his day. Beloki built up a 30-second lead on the American as he overtook the breakaways Astarloza and Rous. Armstrong nevertheless managed to get on Beloki's wheel 3 kilometers (1.9 miles) later.

Then Iban Mayo (Euskaltel), winner of the Tour du pays Basque that year, who had finished second at Liège-Bastogne-Liège and in two stages of the Dauphiné Libéré, likewise attacked in a bid to claim his first Tour stage victory. Armstrong did not react, preferring to keep a steady pace and let the Spaniard go.

Next it was Hamilton's turn to fire a shot or two. But wrapped in bandages like a mummy to immobilize his fractured collarbone and with just one good arm, how could he possibly use his handlebars for leverage? His mechanic had put three layers of tape on his handlebars and brake levers so that Hamilton's fingers would be well cushioned and not aggravate his fractured clavicle. The mechanic had also reduced the air pressure in Hamilton's tires to dampen road shock. And Hamilton was no stranger to pain. "I learned to suffer extreme cold when I was a downhill skier," Hamilton later told *L'Équipe*. "I skied in the coldest spot in North America. Sometimes in the afternoon, after sitting long minutes on the lift, I was frozen stiff." Now, to everyone's astonishment, Hamilton attacked.

Once again, Armstrong did not panic over this move by his former *domestique*. Though his face showed visible strain as he was being attacked on all sides, he kept up a steady pace. Beloki took the offensive again—and again. Six times he threw everything he had at them, and five times Hamilton fired back. Each time Armstrong was able to dodge the bullets and avoid cracking. He pulled himself back to the frontrunners each time, to the cheers of half a million fans who had taken over the Alpe. Taking it all in was the recently retired Laurent Jalabert, now a commentator on French television.

Who else would dare attack Armstrong at this point? From nowhere, a ghost appeared: Alexander Vinokourov. With Botero out of contention, Telekom's hopes rested with "Vino," the calm Kazakh, who put in a Herculean effort to try to get away, taking full advantage of his powerful build. Vino had won Paris-Nice earlier in the year (as well as in 2002) and had dedicated his victory in the fifth stage to his friend and countryman Andreï Kivilev, who had suffered a fatal crash in stage 2 in Saint Chamond, near Saint-Étienne. Now he took off in pursuit of Mayo.

At the summit, the Basque racer won the stage ahead of Vinokourov (1:45 back) and Armstrong (2:12 back), who managed to finish ahead of Beloki and Hamilton. Armstrong's time up the final ascent, 38:01, was 3:19 slower than his winning pace two years earlier, but he had limited the damage, pulling on his first yellow jersey of the centennial Tour. The headline in *L'Équipe* above eight columns of type on the front page read:

"In Yellow and Against Everyone." The real news was that, for the first time, Armstrong's adversaries had had the nerve to attack him.

Armstrong Heads Off-Road

In the overall standings, the Texan now led Beloki by 40 seconds, Mayo by 1:10, and Vinokourov by 1:17. Also in contention were Hamilton (in sixth place, 1:52 back) and Ullrich (in eighth place, 2:10 behind). Eusebio Unzue, Mayo's *directeur sportif*, remarked, "Armstrong has descended to the world of mortals." But neither Armstrong nor the world of mere mortals had seen anything yet.

During the following stage, Armstrong got the scare of his life—at least as a cyclist—on the descent of the Col de la Rochette, 4 kilometers (2.5 miles) from the finish in Gap. Vinokourov was on the attack, sailing toward victory, and Beloki was close behind, followed by Armstrong. On a boiling-hot day, the riders streaked down a twisting road slick with melted tar. As the Spaniard rounded a curve, his rear wheel slid and the tubular tire came unglued, sending the bike lurching to the left, then immediately to the right as Beloki struggled in vain to regain his balance. He slammed to the ground, suffering a fractured femur, hand, and elbow. He screamed in pain as Manolo Saiz, his *directeur sportif*, held him in his arms. Second overall, he would leave the Tour in tears, abandoning the race and his hopes for victory.

Armstrong was a bit luckier. Tailing Beloki, he barely avoided a fall himself. Armstrong instinctively veered to his left, plunging into a field bordering the road. Suddenly he was transformed into a mountain biker. He deftly streaked down the grassy slope that met the road as it curved back around, dismounted to run the last few meters of the slope and jump over a ditch, his bike in hand, then got back on his bike to join the chase group. It was an exceptional demonstration of sangfroid. Even then, he was not out of the woods.

A few days later, in stage 12, a 47-kilometer (29-mile) individual time trial from Gaillac to Cap'Découverte, Armstrong faltered and finished second, 1:36 behind Ullrich. The resurgent German not only celebrated the birth of his daughter Sarah-Maria that day, he also closed to within 34 seconds of the yellow jersey. The proud Ullrich had not won a Tour in five years, not since Armstrong had returned to the peloton. But now, for all the talk of rising stars, this Tour was increasingly shaping up as a rematch of their 2001 duel. The German had switched teams from Telekom to Bianchi, clearly benefiting from the Italian training methods, which were more focused than those he had followed as a young racer in former East Germany.

The next day was stage 13 from Toulouse to Ax-3 Domaines, the first foray into the Pyrénées. Once again, Armstrong flirted with disaster. He struggled up the Col de Pailhères in suffocating heat and once again ceded precious seconds to Ullrich. The German now trailed Armstrong in the overall standings by a mere 15 seconds. And Vinokourov, in third place, was only 1:01 behind.

In stage 14 to Loudenvielle, won by Simoni, it was Vino's turn to gain ground. Mounting an attack up the Peyresourde, the final ascent, the ambitious Kazakh picked up 43 seconds, moving to within 18 seconds of Armstrong, who was hanging on to the yellow jersey he had donned at Alpe d'Huez by mere threads.

The drama played out the next day in the Pyrénées. About 10 kilometers (6.2 miles) from the summit of Luz Ardiden, in the heat of battle, Armstrong went to the front with Mayo and Ullrich on his wheel. Cutting the turns close, he caught his brake lever on a fan's souvenir musette bag and fell to the ground. He took Mayo down with him, while Ullrich avoided a fall. Then, as Armstrong darted off to rejoin the leaders with the help of his teammate Rubiera, his right foot came out of the pedal when his chain slipped, causing him to lose his balance once again and to regain it only after his crotch had slammed against the top bar of his bike.

It was the turning point. Fed up and desperate, Armstrong summoned all his strength and left his rivals behind, passing them one by one on his way to the end of the 13.4-kilometer (8.3-mile) climb (nearly identical to the Alpe). At the summit, Armstrong triumphed and consolidated the lead he had taken at Alpe d'Huez, distancing himself from his rivals: Ullrich, in second place and now 1:17 behind, and Vino, in third, now 2:45 behind.

At 31 years of age, Armstrong took his fifth straight Tour (1999–2003). As far as L'Équipe was concerned, the American had made history. Over the next two years, we would see that he was anything but in decline, as many had thought, but rather on his way to victory in two more Tours, in 2004 and 2005.

CHAPTER TWENTY-FOUR

2004

Six-Shooter:
Armstrong Aims at the Record

L'ÉQUIPE'S HEADLINE PRECEDED EIGHT COLUMNS ON THE FRONT page: "Armstrong Aims for the Moon." Across the center of the page was a picture of the American in the yellow jersey, sunglasses on his forehead, and a chain around his neck with a small cross attached that was apparently swaying from side to side as he pedaled. God save Armstrong!

With this cliché as backdrop, the paper's premise was nonetheless germane: Could Armstrong succeed in his insane quest for six Tour victories? It was a record that had eluded four other giants whose portraits surrounded his: Jacques Anq uetil, Eddy Merckx, Bernard Hinault, and Miguel Induráin.

That was the big question of this tumultuous 2004 season. It began with sorrow and anger as the peloton mourned the passing of one of its great climbers, Marco Pantani, who had died from an overdose of cocaine on Valentine's Day. His peers had affectionately dubbed this scrappy Italian "the Pirate" because of his trademark bandanna, earring, and goatee. Also known as "Elefantino" ("little elephant") on account of his protruding ears, he was the only rider Armstrong feared when he attacked in the mountains. Indeed, Pantani never fooled around once he had made up his mind to attack. Though he suffered numerous falls that left him bedridden for months, he erased them by leaving an indelible imprint on the legendary climbs of the Dolomites, the Ventoux, and Alpe d'Huez.

And no one will forget his Giro-Tour double in 1998, the year he became only the sixth Italian to win La Grande Boucle and the first since Felice Gimondi in 1965.[1]

A fragile champion, Pantani never got over his exile from the 1999 Giro after the stage to Madonna di Campiglio. He was proudly wearing the pink jersey, just two days away from his second straight victory in Milan, when he learned that test results showed an excessively high hematocrit level (red-blood-cell count). The racer vigorously protested his innocence and even suggested that he was the victim of a conspiracy. But he was sent home in disgrace, like a cheater.

Though he would win two stages at the 2000 Tour, he struggled with depression from then on, forsaken by Christina Jonsson, his fiancée, and dulled by his excesses. He ended his life in a room at the hotel Le Rose, in Rimini, near his villa in Cesenatico, on the Adriatic coast. From his window, he could look out and contemplate the romantic spot where he had first kissed Christina. He died of sorrow, of an overdose, of doping.

Next to the photo of Armstrong in yellow, *L'Équipe* ran an editorial entitled "Let's Never Forget Pantani," written by the editor-in-chief, Claude Droussens. It put the season back into its sad context: "It is important that we not forget the somber events in cycling over the past few months. . . . Six years after the trauma of the Festina Affair, cycling is no doubt much less healthy than its executives would care to admit. Marco Pantani died at 34 years of age from an overdose of cocaine at the end of winter. Was it doping-related? It's likely. Marco Pantani is dead. We should promise ourselves never to forget that, if only to ensure that he did not die in vain."

Armstrong's Secret

To pay homage to Pantani, Tour organizers decided to christen the 16th and queen stage "In Memory of Marco Pantani." On that day, close to a million fans were expected to gather at Alpe d'Huez to watch the climax of the Tour, following its meanderings in the Pyrénées and the Alps, just four days before its arrival in Paris. For the first time, organizers had decided to have the riders climb Alpe d'Huez as an uphill time trial.

The stage promised to be extraordinary, both because the riders would climb the twenty-one switchbacks against the clock and because of

Armstrong's crazy bid for a sixth Tour, which had already sparked a media frenzy. *Vélo* magazine's first issue included a centerfold portrait of the entire U.S. Postal–Berry Floor team in their winter training outfits, with the caption "Far from the excitement of their first races and any distractions, Lance Armstrong and his 'Tour de France' team prepare themselves under the California sun."

And how exactly was the American to win his sixth Tour? His *directeur sportif*, Johan Bruyneel, partially lifted the veil of secrecy. "This team only exists for the Tour. Everything we do all season long is in preparation for that event. We know how to build a true Tour team. We don't just randomly pluck nine racers in June to race three weeks in July. No, we start thinking about the Tour in December. And we pick only racers who fit in. I don't care how good they are, if I'm not 100 percent sure that they will sacrifice themselves for the team's goal, I'm not interested. They have to suppress any personal ambition. If they can't, we're not the team for them."

For this new season, Armstrong had employed the Portuguese José "Ace" Azevedo (formerly with ONCE) to replace Roberto Héras, who had sprouted wings and flown off to a new team, Liberty Seguros. Its director, Manolo Saiz, had promised Héras that he would be the designated leader.

Similar migrations threatened to upset the order of things and possibly hamper Armstrong's bid. Tyler Hamilton, coming off an impressive fourth-place finish at the previous Tour despite his debilitating injury, quit CSC to wear the Phonak jersey. With the help of the Spanish climber Oscar Sevilla (formerly with Kelme), Hamilton hoped to contend for the top spot. Ivan Basso (formerly with Fassa Bortolo), seventh at the last Tour, joined CSC. Joseba Beloki (formerly with ONCE), who had lost his shot the previous year following his crash, signed with the French team Brioche La Boulangère, bringing along his brother Gorka and his friend Unaï Yus.

For his part, Jan Ullrich left Bianchi and rejoined his favorite team, Telekom, now renamed T-Mobile. There he would benefit from an all-star cast as he sought his second Tour victory in seven years and his first over the elusive American. His diverse teammates included the Kazakh Alexander Vinokourov, the Colombian Santiago Botero, the Australian Cadel Evans, and the Italian Paolo Savoldelli. Ullrich had assembled so many strong riders that Armstrong mused, "To win the Tour, you need a team with a leader and eight guys who are devoted to him. Will Botero and Vino be willing to work for Ullrich from the start of the season?" As if to cast doubts on his own chances, the American added, "I am not the Tour favorite. Besides, this winter I went out a lot, and I ate a lot of donuts!"

But for *Vélo* magazine, at least, Armstrong was the favorite. And as its editors saw it, his biggest threat once again was Ullrich, the only other Tour winner in the lineup and runner-up five times, all but one of those times to Armstrong. Ullrich, recently crowned Germany's top athlete, had apparently buckled down to take what might be his last shot at his American nemesis. Each month, from the start of the season, the magazine provided status updates on the two principal protagonists. The German's winter training in Baleares had been somewhat disrupted when he had come down with the flu, but he had since refined his form in Tuscany, accompanied by his small family and teammate Tobias Steinhauser.

The first encounter in the Lance and Jan Show 2004 took place in early March in Spain, during the Vuelta Ciclista a Murcia. There, in the stage 2 time trial, won by José Ivan Gutierrez, Armstrong drew first blood. He covered the 21 kilometers (13 miles) in 26:08, a minute ahead of his rival. Was that a sign of things to come?

The two adversaries would not meet again until the Tour, but their paths were very different. Ullrich displayed poor form at the Flèche Wallonne, which he abandoned after 90 kilometers (56 miles). He also pulled out of Liège-Bastogne-Liège and the Amstel Gold Race (all three events were won by the Italian Davide Rebellin, an unprecedented feat). Ullrich, overweight—as was his unfortunate habit leading up to the Tour—retreated to his home in Switzerland to accelerate his preparation for the July event. He engaged in multiple sessions with his personal trainer Rudy Pevenage and his physiotherapist Birgit Krohme.

Ventoux Hustle

Armstrong rode the Critérium International and was disappointed not to win the overall with a better performance in the 8.3-kilometer (5.2-mile) individual time trial, where he finished third. He won the Tour of Georgia in the United States, then followed that with a win in the Dauphiné Libéré, where the Bedoin–Mont Ventoux time trial would provide an excellent test and training for the Alpe d'Huez time trial at the Tour. But he struggled on that course and finished fifth, 1:57 behind the winner, Iban Mayo (Euskaltel), and also behind three other Tour rivals: Hamilton (Phonak), the winner of the Tour de Romandie, Sevilla (Phonak), and Juan Miguel Mercado (Quick Step–Davitamon).

But could it be that the wily American had deliberately hidden his form on the slopes of Mont Ventoux, just three weeks before the start of the Tour? Ullrich thought so. "I'm not going to fall for that trick. Lance showed above all at Ventoux that he's a great actor. It's impossible to imagine that someone of his talent and experience could barely make it up the Ventoux. I think he's done a good job preparing, suppressing his competitive instinct at strategic moments in his approach to the Tour."

Armstrong was indeed focused and determined, and he studied the climb up Alpe d'Huez with unusual intensity. In the weeks leading to the Tour, he took on the twenty-one switchbacks at least ten times in order to commit every meter of this legendary ascent to memory. As usual, he assigned a great deal of importance to the slightest details. The British magazine *Procycling* eagerly reported the latest Armstrong anecdote. Allegedly, he had sent his watch back to manufacturer Nike when he'd discovered that it weighed 40 grams (1.4 ounces) more than his set limit! Was there any doubt that Armstrong was ready for this Tour?

Ullrich, too, had apparently returned to top form. Barely ten days before the start of the Tour, he won the final time trial at the Tour of Switzerland in brilliant fashion, taking the event by a single second. But critics still suspected that the German was not in optimal shape. Like Armstrong, he was keeping his true form something of a mystery. Only the Tour would reveal the fullness of their respective fitness levels.

The Tour began that year in Liège, Belgium. It began without Vinokourov, who had fallen a few weeks earlier at the Tour of Switzerland. Joseba Beloki was also out after splitting with his French team, Brioche La Boulangère. For Armstrong in particular, they represented two dangerous competitors who were now out of the way.

From day one, the 6.1-kilometer (3.8-mile) prologue, the American dispelled any doubts about his form: He finished second, 2 seconds behind the Swiss rocket Fabian Cancellara (Fassa Bortolo), a specialist in that discipline.

And his rivals? They were off to a rather poor start. Ullrich finished a disappointing 16th in the prologue, 17 seconds behind Cancellara.

Hamilton, though experienced in time trials, wound up 18th, 18 seconds back. Mayo, who was not making progress as an all-around rider, finished 26th, 21 seconds in arrears. But in the same year that an astonishing Greek national soccer team came out of nowhere to beat the heavily favored Portuguese by a score of 1-0 in the European Cup final, who could say that no great surprises were in store at this Tour?

The first shocker came as early as the third stage, between Waterloo and Wasquehal. Mayo lost any chance at overall victory when he fell while the race covered a section of cobblestones after Armstrong's team had stepped on the gas to charge over the dusty, rough roads at full speed. Mayo lost 3:53 on the stage and was now 4:23 behind in the overall standings. Armstrong was smiling. He smiled again the next day at the end of the 64.5-kilometer (40-mile) team time trial between Cambrai and Arras in northern France, which he and his team won with an average speed of 53.7 kilometers (33.4 miles) per hour in the rain—Armstrong's friend.

The result could have been disastrous for Armstrong's remaining challengers (Hamilton and his men lost by 1:07, and Ullrich and team by 1:19), but they benefited from a new regulation that mitigated time lost in team time trials. In effect, Hamilton lost only 20 seconds and Ullrich only 40. It wasn't fair to Armstrong, but he had taken the yellow jersey after only four days of racing.

Would he try to keep it, compelling his teammates to work to defend the gold mantle and wear themselves out before the mountains? No, Armstrong preferred to lose it the next day to a big 184-kilometer (114.3-mile) breakaway free of any Tour contenders, one that reached Chartres with a lead of 12:33. Stuart O'Grady (Cofidis) took the stage, but the big winner was the French national champion, Thomas Voeckler (Brioche La Boulangère), the new yellow jersey at 25 years of age, with a 9:35 lead over Armstrong, who slipped to sixth place overall. Armstrong was smiling again; his plan had worked perfectly.

When a Bike Is Too Light

After a rare visit to the Massif Central, the mountainous region in central France, the Tour reached Castelsarrasin for the start of stage 12, which would take the race into the Pyrénées. Armstrong was still sixth overall, 9:35 back—exactly where he'd been in the standings at the end of the fifth stage. Now that the Pyrénées had arrived, he was ready to finish off his rivals. He attacked on the final ascent toward La Mongie, where he gave the stage victory to Basso, the only rider capable of following him. Mayo came in 1:03 later, Ullrich 2:30, Héras 2:57, and Hamilton 3:27. The Tour was practically decided, but Voeckler still had the yellow jersey.

Armstrong took over again the next day, which featured a half-dozen tough climbs before a fearsome finish at Plateau de Beille; once again, only Basso could keep up. The American shaved Voeckler's lead to just 22 seconds. Ullrich trailed by 2:42, Héras was foundering at 21:35, and Hamilton dropped out due to back pain. Armstrong no longer had any true rivals. He had the Tour in the bag with the Alps still to come.

In the 15th and first alpine stage, Valréas to Villard-de-Lans, Armstrong pounded in the final nail. He took the stage (with Basso finishing 2nd once again) and finally pulled on the yellow jersey for good the day before the Alpe d'Huez time trial, which Armstrong said "excited" him. At that point, Basso was 2nd in the overall standings (1:25 back), followed by the German Andreas Klöden (3rd at 3:22); the Spaniard Francisco Mancebo (4th at 5:39); and Ullrich, who was supposed to be the American's main rival, 5th at 6:54.

The riders were now at the foot of the Alpe, where Armstrong would face his only true challenger: the clock. "And Now, Alpe d'Huez, the Grand Finale," read the front page of the *Dauphiné Libéré*, the region's daily newspaper, featuring a huge photograph of the twenty-one switchbacks being overrun by cars, campers, and innumerable tents of the nearly one million fans.

"Guillotine at the Alpe?" asked the paper on a following page. Was Armstrong going to kill them all? He had chosen his weapon, opting for his usual Trek rather than the special bike that he had ordered at the start of the season. But to shave off a few ounces, he removed the integrated shift and brake levers from the left side of his handlebar and installed a traditional friction shift lever on the left side of the bike's downtube to engage either the 53- or 39-tooth chainrings. He didn't change the integrated configuration on the right side, which he would use to engage the ten rear cogs, ranging from 13 to 23 teeth.

Before the start of the time trial, however, the judges weighed Armstrong's bicycle and found it too light. The minimum limit was 6.8 kilos, or 15 pounds; Armstrong's bike floated onto the scales at 6.69 kilos, or

14.75 pounds. The U.S. Postal wrench swung into action to make up the difference. Returned to the scales, the bike was still 0.06 kilo (2.1 ounces) below the minimum. The panicked mechanic scrambled as Armstrong's start time approached. He mounted a heart rate monitor on the handlebars. It took four inspections before the jury gave the green light: 6.88.

Armstrong got on the starting ramp. On his chest, nothing but a heart rate strap. On his head, nothing but a pair of sunglasses. In his right ear, the indispensable earbud that connected him via two-way radio to Bruyneel. No helmet. No special clothing. Ready . . . Armstrong was off!

In the car following him were his fiancée, the singer Sheryl Crow, and friend Robin Williams, the actor. Thousands of fans lined the road waiting for Armstrong to pass. U.S. Postal jerseys popped up everywhere in the crowds, and banners hailed the champion. He alternated between pedaling in the saddle and standing. When he stood on his pedals, his motion was spectacular: fluid, powerful, commanding. His eyes were fixed on the road, and his attention was entirely focused on the turns that ticked away in their famous countdown: 21, 20, 19, 18. . . . After 9.5 kilometers (5.9 miles), at the village of Huez en Oisans, Armstrong already had a 40-second lead on Ullrich; 1:07 on Klöden; and 1:15 on Basso, his dauphin.

Although Ullrich had already lost the Tour, this was perhaps his last chance to exact revenge on the American, who had taunted him on this very slope three years earlier. The German, sporting a curious look with braided hair flattened on his head, had opted for a bladed front wheel and clip-on aero bars. Ullrich was climbing the Alpe with his hands on those aerodynamic extensions, a position generally employed to go faster on flat terrain. He had made a mistake, confusing the Fortress of L'Oisans with a Bavarian autobahn. He pushed, strained, grimaced, and struggled, putting everything he had into the deadly switchbacks.

Motorcycle Cops Tail Armstrong

Armstrong took hold of Alpe d'Huez the way one seduces a lover: with little talk and great passion! His drawn face bore witness to all the work he had done to woo this lover. He gave it everything. He had courted the mountain that spring, when snow had still blocked his way, to better understand this object of his fascination. Ten times he had lavished affection on it, caressed it, made it his.

He plunged through the crowd. From a distance, one could only see a yellow spot that slowly progressed through a sea of humanity amid fanatical cries and wild gestures. Well behind the racer, Tour director Jean-Marie Leblanc followed in his car, praying that Armstrong would emerge unscathed. The Tour boss had good reason to fear the worst. In 1975, when a dominant Eddy Merckx had set out to win a record sixth tour, daring to challenge Anquetil's historic mark, a reckless fan had punched the Belgian in the stomach as he'd made his way up the Puy-de-Dôme.

The authorities were doing everything in their power to protect the American champion. A plainclothes police officer, riding a motorcycle with a secret service agent on the back, opened a path for Armstrong. Behind him, another agent followed in a car, carefully surveying the crowd. Regrettably, they were powerless to stop certain idiots from cursing and spitting on Armstrong as he passed. The Texan ignored them and pushed toward the finish line.

Finally, with just 3 kilometers (1.9 miles) to go, Armstrong passed Basso, his last remaining obstacle to a sixth Tour victory. The Italian, who had started 2 minutes before Armstrong, was slumped over his bike, hunkered down, near collapse. In stark contrast, the champion sat comfortably and pushed toward the summit.

Now the road was protected by barriers, and the storm calmed. Armstrong finished the time trial in 39:41. Over the standard timed distance, his mark was 37:36, just 46 seconds off Pantani's 1995 record. Ullrich finished second, 1:01 behind. At the top, Armstrong said, "It really wasn't a good idea to have a time trial here. Some of the fans were just too disgusting. But that's life."

"The winner by knockout," declared *L'Équipe* the following morning. In the next breath, it poised the inevitable question: "Will Lance Armstrong be in Noirmoutier in July 2005 to seek a seventh victory?" Overwhelming dominator of the 2004 Tour, claiming a record sixth victory, the American would indeed return the next year to take an unprecedented seventh consecutive victory, finishing ahead of Basso and Ullrich once again. It would be an all-time record.

CHAPTER TWENTY-FIVE

2006

Landis in
Armstrong's Footsteps

L AUGHTER AND TEARS. ON SATURDAY, JULY 1, 2006, FRENCH SOCCER fans celebrated their national team's 1-0 victory over the heavily favored five-time champion Brazil in the World Cup quarterfinals. The victory, engineered by Zinedine Zidane, evoked memories of the blue team's first World Cup title, when it had beaten the same team 3-0 in 1998. An elated France began to dream of another '98 from its newly secured position in the semifinals, a repeat performance that would establish it as an international soccer powerhouse, with idol Zidane leading the way.[1] French soccer was hopeful and appreciative.

French cycling, on the other hand, was discouraged and voicing its discontent. As the Tour prepared to set off, another doping scandal rained down upon it.

A month earlier, Spanish authorities had investigated allegations of drug abuse among professional cyclists. Their findings, known as the Puerto Report, were unsealed just two days before the Tour was to start, and they were explosive. The report claimed that many of the top names in the sport, including most of the Tour favorites, had consulted with the Spanish doctor Eufemiano Fuentes, who had supplied them with treated blood and other doping products. As a result, some racers were asked to stay home, and others voluntarily withdrew from the Tour in tears even as they protested their innocence. Cycling stars Ivan Basso, Armstrong's main challenger, whom everyone was watching; Jan Ullrich (T-Mobile), the big favorite; Oscar Sevilla (T-Mobile); Francisco Mancebo (AG2R Prévoyance); Joseba Beloki (Astana); Alberto Contador (Astana); and Alexander Vinokourov (Astana) were all shown the door.

The French sun was at its zenith at the World Cup while storms and tempests raged at the Tour.

Disgruntled French cycling fans also thought back to 1998, but their memories were not pleasant ones. That summer, the Tour had started with great fanfare from Dublin, Ireland. But shortly thereafter an explosive scandal erupted when a Festina team car was found to contain an impressive quantity of doping paraphernalia. The team was accused of practicing systematic doping and ousted from the race. Its leader, the French climber and public darling Richard Virenque, was barred from a Tour he had been largely favored to win.

In his book *Sauvons le Tour* (Let's save the Tour), published in the summer of 2007, former Tour director Xavier Louy suggested that the timing of the Festina Affair while the World Cup in France was in full swing was no accident. He pointed out that cycling posted doctors at the finish line for immediate testing, but doctors assigned to soccer teams were often unable to check urine samples for several hours after competition. If soccer players were subjected to the same stringent standards as cyclists, Louy maintained, the national team would have hemorrhaged. In his view, the Festina Affair had served to distract attention from soccer's own drug problems. He regretted that so many cyclists had been barred from the 2006 Tour based on rumors alone and decried what he considered a double standard.

Six Candidates for the Yellow Jersey

With so many contenders expelled, who were the remaining pretenders to Armstrong's throne? There were essentially six who had their eye on the yellow jersey: the Americans Floyd Landis (Phonak) and Levi Leipheimer (Gerolsteiner), the Russian Denis Menchov (Rabobank), the German Andreas Klöden (T-Mobile), the Australian Cadel Evans (Davitamon-Lotto), and the Spaniard Alejandro Valverde (Caisse d'Epargne–Iles Baleares). The Portuguese José Azevedo, the leader of Discovery Channel (successor to U.S. Postal as title sponsor), was a dark-horse contender, but without its big boss, who had retired from competition for good, the American team no longer had the same ambitions. "The leader is the team itself, it's Discovery, there is no one leader," declared Johan Bruyneel, the *directeur sportif*.

And yet the Tour started well for the American team. Following stage 1—a loop around Strasbourg won by the Frenchman Jimmy Casper (Cofidis), the last-place finisher in the 2001 and 2004 Tours—George Hincapie donned the yellow jersey. Back in the States, Lance Armstrong was smiling.

La Grande Boucle would travel in a counterclockwise direction in 2006, with stops in Luxembourg, Belgium, and northern France, before heading south. After nine flat stages, it would enter the Pyrénées, then head toward the Alps. Alpe d'Huez, bypassed the year before, was back on the menu as the main course in stage 15.

Following the third stage, the Belgian Tom Boonen (Quick Step–Innergetic), wearing the rainbow jersey of world champion, pulled on the yellow jersey in time for the next stage in his homeland. It was a special occasion because it had been sixteen years since a reigning world champion had worn the yellow jersey: Greg LeMond in 1990.

Valverde had to abandon the Tour 20 kilometers (12.4 miles) from the finish (one less favorite), having suffered a broken collarbone. The year before he had also been forced to leave the Tour due to a knee injury. Two abandons in two years—what bad luck.

The first major event of the Tour was stage 7, a 52-kilometer (32.3-mile) time trial from Saint Grégoire to Rennes in stage 7. The Ukrainian Sergei Honchar (T-Mobile) won the day and brought some hierarchical order to the overall standings. Landis finished second, 1:01 behind Honchar, despite having been forced to change bicycles during the stage after an issue with his handlebars. The 30-year-old American was thereby propelled to second place overall and was now the Tour's big favorite.

Landis, heralded as the next Armstrong—who had miraculously beaten cancer—revealed on the first rest day that he was suffering from avascular necrosis, or bone death, in his right hip, which had been injured in a 2003 training crash. Ever since, the area had caused him severe discomfort, and he planned to undergo a hip replacement at the end of the year. Was Landis also following in Armstrong's footsteps as one battling serious illness? How was it possible to climb mountains while ingesting pain medication to cope, having confessed that he was forced to get on his bicycle from the left side or risk falling to the pavement, thrown off balance by his bad hip?

"Whatever happens, I am focusing on the race itself," Landis replied. "Racing is therapy for my hip. It consumes everything I think about. While I am racing, I have the least problems."

A Tour without a Boss

After stage 11 to Pla-de-Beret in the Pyrénées, Landis became the fifth American to wear the yellow jersey, after Greg LeMond, Armstrong, Dave Zabriskie, and Hincapie. Was it a surprise? Having already won the Tour of California, the Tour of Georgia, and Paris-Nice earlier that season, Landis had positioned himself as Armstrong's successor. In truth, the jersey did not interest him at that point; there was a long way to go, and he still had to face the Alps—in particular the formidable Alpe d'Huez stage, with the Izoard and Lautaret serving as appetizers. He decided to let it go for the time being.

So it was that at this Tour without a true *patron*, a breakaway of lesser-known riders formed on stage 13 and arrived in Montélimar with a 30-minute lead after 209 kilometers (130 miles) of freedom. Now the Spaniard Oscar Pereiro (Caisse d'Epargne–Iles Baléares) was leading the event, followed by Landis (1:29), Menchov (2:30), Evans (2:46), Carlos Sastre (3:21), Klöden (3:58), and Leipheimer (7:08). An indignant *L'Équipe* ran the headline "A Tour of Crazies." Landis actually may have committed a tactical error in granting a hall pass to Pereiro, who was no slouch, having already won a Tour stage (to Pau in 2005) and a variety of respectable events, including the 2004 Classique des Alpes and stages in the Tour de Romandie, the Tour of Switzerland, and the Setmana Catalana. He was a serious candidate for final victory.

The day of Alpe d'Huez had arrived. "We Will Know in the End," declared the *Dauphiné Libéré*—the mountain was about to sort things out. Gracing the inside pages of the newspaper that morning was a photo of none other than Lance Armstrong at a window of Hôtel l'Ours Blanc, in the center of L'Alpe d'Huez. Armstrong had first been spotted a few days earlier near Gap, sporting a jersey as he accompanied some American cycling tourists who were sponsor VIPs. He had even climbed, incognito, the twenty-one switchbacks of the Alpe with former teammate Kevin Livingston—just for fun.

In truth, Armstrong's legacy hovered over the peloton; even the clouds seemed to form in his image. From the start, his spirit had haunted the Tour and had even infiltrated race tactics. For example, following the Discovery riders' debacle in the Pyrénées,[2] some considered Yaroslav Popovych's victory at Carcassonne suspect; it had come at the end of a four-man breakaway that included the formidable sprinter Oscar Freire of Rabobank. Freire and Popovych had been seen conversing briefly, and in the final stretch Freire had seemed to let the Ukrainian go. Had they made some sort of deal, such as the stage victory for Popovych in return for Discovery's promise to help Menchov, Rabobank's leader, on the Alpe?

L'Équipe even suggested that Armstrong was there to wage a personal vendetta against Landis, his former teammate. The magazine intimated that the ex-champion disliked his heir apparent and did not want to see him wear yellow. For three seasons, from 2002 to 2004, Landis had helped Armstrong win the Tour as a member of U.S. Postal. But in 2005, Landis had turned his loyalties to Phonak. Supposedly Armstrong deeply resented the disloyalty and was intent on exacting revenge.

Landis addressed his relations with Armstrong candidly. "Following Lance all those years gave my career a big boost," he said. "I learned a lot by riding at his side even if our relationship was sometimes complicated. Lance was completely obsessed by his goals. He always wanted everything to go in his favor. There came a time when I wanted to take charge of my own career and do things as I saw fit. I was responsible for certain tensions between us, and I recognize that. I'm not always good at being reasonable."

But was Armstrong really Landis's sworn enemy? The press had gotten it wrong. To the *Dauphiné Libéré* Armstrong explained, "Floyd can win this Tour, and I would be delighted. He's an American, and that's great for U.S. cycling. If the first Tour winner after me is American, that would be very positive for cycling and the bike industry."

It was in this fantastical atmosphere that the riders were confronting L'Alpe d'Huez, where Armstrong was staying. Dressed in a khaki shirt, black Discovery cap, and gray jeans, Armstrong spoke briefly with journalists. "Are you going to meet with Jean-Marie Leblanc, the *patron* of the Tour?" he was asked. "I've come to see my friends, team Discovery," he replied. "I'm not planning on meeting with [Leblanc]!" Armstrong laughed, determined to avoid the controversy that had erupted the previous year when *L'Équipe* had leveled fresh drug charges against him, and Tour officials—most notably Leblanc—had failed to defend the departed champion. His mood then had been dark. Now he would let the issue rest.

The race to the Alpe was heated from the start: twenty-five racers broke away just before the Col d'Izoard. The Italian Stefano Garzelli (Liquigas) went to the front of the group of escapees, who built up a lead of 6:30 over the peloton. But the 14 kilometers (8.7 miles) of initial alpine climbing over the rocky, barren landscape would eliminate a number of pretenders.

The second climb of the day, the Lautaret, wore on tired bodies even more. Finally, at the foot of Alpe d'Huez, only two of the original twenty-five breakaway riders remained: the young Italian Damiano Cunego (Lampre), winner of the 2004 Giro, riding his first Tour and in the hunt for the white jersey of best young rider, and Fränk Schleck (CSC) of Luxembourg. They still held a 3:20 lead over the favorites, who had decided once again to contest the yellow jersey over the Alpe's twenty-one legendary switchbacks.

Klöden's Offensive

The most aggressive of the Tour favorites was Andreas Klöden, ranked seventh overall, 3:58 behind Pereiro and 2:29 behind Landis, determined to risk it all. Having already finished second at the 2004 Tour and been promoted to leader of T-Mobile in Ullrich's absence, he attacked as soon as he hit the Alpe. Landis calmly followed, and Cadel Evans (Davitamon-Lotto), who was in fifth overall, latched on. Denis Menchov (Rabobank) couldn't hold their wheels. He was fourth overall and a strong favorite but was being left behind.

Klöden kept the pressure on, his unzipped jersey revealing his torso and dangling gold chain. On his nose, he wore an adhesive strip to open his nostrils and improve his breathing. Evans could not hang on.

On the road to L'Alpe d'Huez, Klöden was wildly urged on by the German colony, who saw him as Ullrich's replacement. Landis, engrossed by his efforts, his face hidden by sunglasses, followed. Ten kilometers (6.2 miles) from the summit, the American decided to attack. Klöden was the only one able to stay on Landis's wheel. It was now a duel. But the

American did not want to fire all his bullets on the Alpe. He prudently slowed the pace, allowing two more to join them: Sastre, sixth overall, and Leipheimer, 15th overall.

Landis caught up with his teammate Axel Merckx, one of the morning breakaways, and the two then worked together. Merckx took the lead, followed by a grimacing Sastre, an attentive Klöden, and a slumped-over Leipheimer. With just 5 kilometers (3.1 miles) to go, Klöden attacked again, and only Landis was able to follow. The duel resumed. Meanwhile, up ahead, Schleck dropped Cunego and was first to the summit of Alpe d'Huez, depriving the young Italian of a prestigious victory.

Fourth on the stage, Landis registered the best time up the Alpe (38:34) and reclaimed the yellow jersey, with a 10-second lead over Pereiro. He was the second American, after Lance Armstrong in 2003, to pull on the jersey on the peaks of L'Oisans.

Above all, Landis had shown that he was now the boss. The world had discovered a new champion. The press wrote about his strict upbringing in Pennsylvania Dutch country. His Mennonite parents rejected modern conveniences such as cars and televisions and even frowned on cycling shorts. In deference to them, Landis trained in sweatpants, but they still weren't happy. "For my parents," Landis explained, "the bicycle was just a means of transportation. And when they realized that it meant something more to me, my father assigned me after-school chores to discourage me from riding." Not to be deterred, Landis trained between 9 P.M. and midnight. He found his salvation on a bicycle.

On the podium in L'Alpe d'Huez, Landis smiled broadly. The yellow jersey lit up his face, including the blond mustache and goatee straight out of the belle epoque. The American dreamed of sweet exoneration, of a Tour victory he would dedicate to his parents, who despite their strict religious beliefs were proud of him.

Landis and Armstrong: The Meeting

Armstrong was also smiling. The next morning, before the stage from Bourg d'Oisans to La Toussuire, he joined Landis for breakfast at his hotel, Club Med La Sarenne, near the alpine airport. As it happened, I was staying at the same hotel and was able to discreetly observe them two tables away from where I sat with journalists from *Vélo* magazine. No doubt the Americans were discussing Landis's battle plans for the imminent mountain stage. In any event, far from the media spotlight, the two chatted amicably amidst smiles and laughter and pats on the back; it was the perfect alliance. Armstrong congratulated Landis, assuring him that he was to be his successor. Then more quips and laughter.

Landis's *directeur sportif*, Jacques Michaud, came and sat at our table. He confided, "Floyd is in super shape and very confident. He did it! I can honestly say that he will win the Tour. It's a done deal! There are still two mountain stages, today and tomorrow, but he's a cut above the rest. And his story is exceptional. He'll be the perfect winner to follow Lance."

And then the drama.

Disappointment: Wednesday, July 19, 4:53 P.M. At kilometer 172 (mile 107), with about 10 more kilometers (6.2 miles) to the summit of La Toussuire, Landis cracked. He slowed almost to a stop, glued to the wide road that rose toward the resort. Behind him was Michaud's car. It might as well have been a hearse. Floyd was dead; he had lost the Tour. His dream was shattered. The media turned their attention far ahead, to the Dane Michael Rasmussen (Rabobank), who would win the stage, and to third-place finisher and new yellow jersey Pereiro. Landis finished 10:04 back and fell to 11th overall, 8:08 behind Pereiro.

Resurrection: The 17th and final mountain stage, from Saint-Jean-de-Maurienne to Morzine, was the next day. On the first climb, at kilometer 71 (mile 44), a little more than a third of the way, Landis broke away from the peloton and set off on a 130-kilometer (81-mile) solo marathon. No one took it seriously. But they made a big mistake. Landis suddenly, miraculously regained his strength and motivation, making up for his inexplicable meltdown the day before. He devoured the climbs of Aravis, Colombière, and Joux-Plane. He reached the finish line in Morzine with a 5:42 lead over second-place finisher Sastre (CSC). He climbed back to third place overall, just 30 seconds behind Pereiro and 18 seconds behind second-place Sastre.

The 18th stage, from Morzine to Mâcon, left the top three places unchanged. The Tour would come down to the 57-kilometer (35.4-mile) time trial from Le Creusot to Montceau-les-Mines, the day before the arrival in Paris. Landis performed magnificently, snatching third place behind Honchar and Klöden. Most importantly, he beat Pereiro by 1:29, grabbing the yellow jersey and opening up a lead of almost 1 minute on Sastre.

Klöden bumped the fading Spaniard out of third place, but with a 1:29 gap and one stage to go, the German had no real shot at the overall. Landis sailed into Paris the next day as the victor. Pereiro took second and Klöden third. The American's achievement was monumental. "Landis deserved it," declared *L'Équipe*. "Landis, a Human God," gushed *Vélo* magazine.

Alas, the celebration was premature, and Landis's fairy-tale comeback was apparently too good to be true. On July 26, just three days after his Parisian triumph, the papers announced the bad news: Floyd Landis had tested positive following his victory in Morzine. The B, or follow-up, test had revealed the presence of exogenous testosterone in his urine.

Ever since that fateful day, Landis has maintained his innocence. He has filed repeated appeals, so far to no avail. The latest decision, issued by an independent American arbitration board on September 20, 2007, by a vote of 2-1, upheld Landis's disqualification and Pereiro's claim to the title.

Landis, who successfully underwent hip replacement surgery two months after finishing the Tour, served a two-year suspension while he sought to exonerate himself. In the meantime, he wrote an autobiography and prepared for an eventual return to professional cycling. To no one's surprise, he condemned the arbitration board's verdict and continues to protest his innocence. "I'm upset by this decision, but it won't keep me up at night," he declared. "I know that I won the 2006 Tour fairly and squarely and I will always consider myself the true winner."

Whether he did or did not, time will tell. And should he return, the Alpe will await, as it awaits all who hope to challenge, and win, the Tour de France.

Appendix A:
The Ascents of Alpe d'Huez

1952

Stage: Lausanne to L'Alpe d'Huez, 266 kilometers (65.3 miles)

1. Fausto Coppi, 8:51:40
   Average speed: 30.18 kilometers (18.75 miles) per hour
2. Jean Robic 1:20
3. Stan Ockers 3:22
4. Antonio Gélabert 3:22
5. Jean Dotto 3:27
6. Andrea Carrea 3:29
7. Pierre Molinéris 4:00
8. Jan Nolten 4:00
9. Fiorenzo Magni 4:13
10. Alex Close 4:15

Final Overall Standings

1. Fausto Coppi
2. Stan Ockers 28:17
3. Bernardo Ruiz 34:38

BEST CLIMBER: Fausto Coppi

1976

Stage: Divonne-les-Bains to L'Alpe d'Huez, 258 kilometers (160.3 miles)

1. Joop Zoetemelk, 8:31:49
   Average speed: 30.304 kilometers (18.83 miles) per hour
2. Lucien van Impe 0:03
3. Francisco Galdos 0:58

4. André Roméro 1:38
5. Fausto Bertoglio 1:45
6. Gianbattista Baronchelli 1:45
7. José Martins 1:50
8. Bernard Thévenet 1:50
9. Raymond Poulidor 1:50
10. Walter Riccomi 2:00

Final Overall Standings

1. Lucien van Impe
2. Joop Zoetemelk 4:14
3. Raymond Poulidor 12:08

GREEN JERSEY: Freddy Maertens
POLKA-DOT JERSEY: Giancarlo Bellini
BEST YOUNG RIDER: Enrique Martinez-Heredia

1977

Stage: Chamonix to L'Alpe d'Huez, 185 kilometers (114.95 miles)

1. Hennie Kuiper, 6:00:20
   Average speed: 30.721 kilometers (19.089 miles) per hour
2. Bernard Thévenet 0:41
3. Lucien van Impe 2:06
4. Francisco Galdos 2:54
5. Joop Zoetemelk 4:40
6. Raymond Martin 8:15
7. Sébastian Pozo 8:34
8. Joaquim Agostinho 8:44
9. Michel Laurent 9:29
10. Pedro Torres 10:49

Final Overall Standings

1. Bernard Thévenet
2. Hennie Kuiper 0:48
3. Lucien van Impe 3:32

GREEN JERSEY: Jacques Esclassan
POLKA-DOT JERSEY: Lucien van Impe
BEST YOUNG RIDER: Dietrich Thurau

1978

Stage: Saint-Étienne to L'Alpe d'Huez, 240 kilometers (149.13 miles)

1. Hennie Kuiper, 7:23:45
    Average speed: 32.40 kilometers (20.132 miles) per hour
2. Bernard Hinault 0:08
3. Joop Zoetemelk 0:41
4. Joaquim Agostinho 1:34
5. Henk Lubberding 2:14
6. Lucien van Impe 2:23
7. Francisco Galdos 2:23
8. Sven-Ake Nilsson 3:25
9. Paul Wellens 3:43
10. Raymond Martin 4:48

Final Overall Standings

1. Bernard Hinault
2. Joop Zoetemelk 3:56
3. Joaquim Agostinho 6:54

GREEN JERSEY: Freddy Maertens
POLKA-DOT JERSEY: Mariano Martinez
BEST YOUNG RIDER: Henk Lubberding

1979: Two Stages to L'Alpe d'Huez

A. Menuires to L'Alpe d'Huez, 167 kilometers (103.77 miles)

1. Joaquim Agostinho, 6:12:55
    Average speed: 27.272 kilometers (16.946) per hour
2. Robert Alban 1:57
3. Paul Wellens 2:45
4. Michel Laurent 2:48
5. Jean-René Bernaudeau 3:17
6. Sven-Ake Nilsson 3:19
7. Giovanni Battaglin 3:19
8. Bernard Hinault 3:19
9. Joop Zoetemelk 3:19
10. Raymond Martin 3:34

B. L'Alpe d'Huez to L'Alpe d'Huez, 119 kilometers (73.94 miles)

1. Joop Zoetemelk, 4:23:28
    Average speed: 26.986 kilometers (16.768 miles) per hour

   2. Lucien van Impe 0:40
   3. Bernard Hinault 0:47
   4. Joaquim Agostinho 1:05
   5. Giovanni Battaglin 2:21
   6. Mariano Martinez 2:21
   7. Paul Wellens 2:23
   8. Hennie Kuiper 2:48
   9. Jean-René Bernaudeau 3:29
  10. Christian Levavasseur 3:29

Final Overall Standings

   1. Bernard Hinault
   2. Joop Zoetemelk 13:07
   3. Joaquim Agostinho 26:53

GREEN JERSEY: Bernard Hinault
POLKA-DOT JERSEY: Giovanni Battaglin
BEST YOUNG RIDER: Jean-René Bernaudeau

1981

Stage: Morzine to L'Alpe d'Huez, 230 kilometers (142.92 miles)

   1. Peter Winnen, 7:38:18
       Average speed: 30.506 kilometers (18.956 miles) per hour
   2. Bernard Hinault 0:08
   3. Lucien van Impe 0:09
   4. Robert Alban 0:12
   5. Johan de Muynck 1:38
   6. Joop Zoetemelk 2:01
   7. Claude Criquielion 3:23
   8. Paul Wellens 3:33
   9. Fons de Wolf 4:14
  10. Jean-René Bernaudeau 4:16

Final Overall Standings

   1. Bernard Hinault
   2. Lucien van Impe 14:34
   3. Robert Alban 17:04

GREEN JERSEY: Freddy Maertens
POLKA-DOT JERSEY: Lucien van Impe
BEST YOUNG RIDER: Peter Winnen

1982

Stage: Orcières-Merlette to L'Alpe d'Huez, 123 kilometers (76.43 miles)

1. Beat Breu, 3:24:22
   Average speed: 36.112 kilometers (22.439 miles) per hour
2. Robert Alban 0:16
3. Alberto Fernandez 1:18
4. Raymond Martin 1:22
5. Bernard Hinault 1:26
6. Joop Zoetemelk 1:26
7. Peter Winnen 1:26
8. Bernard Vallet 2:12
9. Johan van de Velde 2:12
10. Paul Wellens 2:51

Final Overall Standings

1. Bernard Hinault
2. Joop Zoetemelk 6:21
3. Johan van de Velde 8:59

GREEN JERSEY: Sean Kelly
POLKA-DOT JERSEY: Bernard Vallet
BEST YOUNG RIDER: Phil Anderson

1983

Stage: La Tour du Pin to L'Alpe d'Huez, 223 kilometers (138.57 miles)

1. Peter Winnen, 7:21:32
   Average speed: 30.303 kilometers (18.829 miles) per hour
2. Jean-René Bernaudeau, same time
3. Edgar Corredor 0:57
4. Robert Alban 1:22
5. Laurent Fignon 2:07
6. Lucien van Impe 2:09
7. Pedro Delgado 2:10
8. Raymond Martin 2:42
9. Patrocino Jimenez 3:05
10. Gérard Veldscholten 3:07

Final Overall Standings

1. Laurent Fignon
2. Angel Arroyo 4:04
3. Peter Winnen 4:09

GREEN JERSEY: Sean Kelly

POLKA-DOT JERSEY: Lucien van Impe

BEST YOUNG RIDER: Laurent Fignon

1984

Stage: Grenoble to L'Alpe d'Huez, 151 kilometers (93.83 miles)

1. Lucho Herrera, 4:39:24
   Average speed: 32.426 kilometers (20.149 miles) per hour
2. Laurent Fignon 0:49
3. Angel Arroyo 2:27
4. Robert Millar 3:05
5. Rafaël Acevedo 3:09
6. Greg LeMond 3:30
7. Bernard Hinault 3:44
8. Pascal Simon 3:55
9. Gustave Wilches 4:10
10. Pedro Muñoz 4:12

Final Overall Standings

1. Laurent Fignon
2. Bernard Hinault 10:32
3. Greg LeMond 11:46

GREEN JERSEY: Frank Hoste

POLKA-DOT JERSEY: Robert Millar

BEST YOUNG RIDER: Greg LeMond

1986

Stage: Briançon to L'Alpe d'Huez, 163 kilometers (101.28 miles)

1. Bernard Hinault, 5:03:03
   Average speed: 32.17 kilometers (19.989 miles) per hour
2. Greg LeMond, same time
3. Urs Zimmermann 5:15
4. Reynel Montoya 6:06
5. Yvon Madiot 6:21
6. Andy Hampsten 6:22
7. Ronan Pensec 6:26
8. Samuel Cabrera 6:34

9. Pascal Simon 6:45
10. Alvaro Pino 6:48

Final Overall Standings

1. Greg LeMond
2. Bernard Hinault 3:10
3. Urs Zimmermann 10:54

GREEN JERSEY: Eric Vanderaerden
POLKA-DOT JERSEY: Bernard Hinault
BEST YOUNG RIDER: Andy Hampsten

1987

Stage: Villard-de-Lans to L'Alpe d'Huez, 201 kilometers (124.89 miles)

1. Federico Echave, 5:52:11
   Average speed: 34.24 kilometers (21.276 miles) per hour
2. Anselmo Fuerte 1:32
3. Christophe Lavainne 2:12
4. Martin Ramirez 3:00
5. Lucho Herrera 3:19
6. Laurent Fignon 3:25
7. Pedro Delgado 3:44
8. Guido van Calster 3:44
9. Claude Criquielion 4:23
10. Gerhard Zadrobilek 4:43

Final Overall Standings

1. Stephen Roche
2. Pedro Delgado 0:40
3. Jean-François Bernard 2:13

GREEN JERSEY: Jean-Paul van Poppel
POLKA-DOT JERSEY: Lucho Herrera
BEST YOUNG RIDER: Raúl Alcalá

1988

Stage: Morzine to L'Alpe d'Huez, 227 kilometers (141.05 miles)

1. Steven Rooks, 6:55:44
   Average speed: 32.76 kilometers (20.356 miles) per hour

2. Gert-Jan Theunisse, 0:17
3. Pedro Delgado, same time
4. Fabio Parra 0:23
5. Lucho Herrera 1:06
6. Thierry Claveyrolat 2:31
7. Steve Bauer 2:34
8. Éric Boyer 2:34
9. Peter Winnen 3:08
10. Andy Hampsten 4:21

Final Overall Standings

1. Pedro Delgado
2. Steven Rooks 7:13
3. Fabio Parra 9:58

GREEN JERSEY: Eddy Planckaert
POLKA-DOT JERSEY: Steven Rooks
BEST YOUNG RIDER: Erik Breukink

1989

Stage: Briançon to L'Alpe d'Huez, 165 kilometers (102.53 miles)

1. Gert-Jan Theunisse, 5:10:39
   Average speed: 31.86 kilometers (19.80 miles) per hour
2. Pedro Delgado 1:09
3. Laurent Fignon 1:09
4. Abelardo Rondon 2:08
5. Greg LeMond 2:28
6. Marino Lejarreta 2:41
7. Steven Rooks 3:04
8. Gianni Bugno 3:04
9. Robert Millar 3:08
10. Pascal Simon 3:48

Final Overall Standings

1. Greg LeMond
2. Laurent Fignon 0:08
3. Pedro Delgado 3:34

GREEN JERSEY: Sean Kelly
POLKA-DOT JERSEY: Gert-Jan Theunisse
BEST YOUNG RIDER: Fabrice Philipot

1990

Stage: St. Gervais–Mont Blanc to L'Alpe d'Huez, 182 kilometers (113.09 miles)

1. Gianni Bugno, 5:37:51
   Average speed: 32.442 kilometers (20.159 miles) hour
2. Greg LeMond, same time
3. Erik Breukink 0:01
4. Thierry Claveyrolat 0:04
5. Fabio Parra 0:06
6. Abelardo Rondon 0:40
7. Andy Hampsten 0:40
8. Pedro Delgado 0:40
9. Claude Criquielion 0:47
10. Ronan Pensec 0:48

Final Overall Standings

1. Greg LeMond
2. Claudio Chiappucci 2:16
3. Erik Breukink 2:29

GREEN JERSEY: Olaf Ludwig
POLKA-DOT JERSEY: Thierry Claveyrolat
BEST YOUNG RIDER: Gilles Delion

1991

Stage: Gap to L'Alpe d'Huez, 125 kilometers (77.67 miles)

1. Gianni Bugno, 3:25:48
   Average speed: 36.443 kilometers (22.645 miles) per hour
2. Miguel Induráin 0:01
3. Luc Leblanc 0:02
4. Jean-François Bernard 0:35
5. Steven Rooks 0:43
6. Claudio Chiappucci 0:43
7. Thierry Claveyrolat 0:43
8. Pedro Delgado 0:45
9. Laurent Fignon 1:12
10. Alvaro Meija 1:13

Final Overall Standings

1. Miguel Induráin
2. Gianni Bugno 3:36
3. Claudio Chiappucci 5:56

GREEN JERSEY: Djamolidine Abdoujaparov
POLKA-DOT JERSEY: Claudio Chiappucci
BEST YOUNG RIDER: Alvaro Meija

1992

Stage: Sestrières to L'Alpe d'Huez, 186 kilometers (115.58 miles)

1. Andy Hampsten, 5:41:58
    Average speed: 32.722 kilometers (20.333 miles) per hour
2. Franco Vona 1:17
3. Éric Boyer 2:08
4. Jan Nevens 2:46
5. Claudio Chiappucci 3:15
6. Miguel Induráin 3:15
7. Bombin Unzaga 3:28
8. Richard Virenque 4:04
9. Gert-Jan Theunisse 4:13
10. Erik Breukink 4:42

Final Overall Standings

1. Miguel Induráin
2. Claudio Chiappucci 4:35
3. Gianni Bugno 10:49

GREEN JERSEY: Laurent Jalabert
POLKA-DOT JERSEY: Claudio Chiappucci
BEST YOUNG RIDER: Eddy Bouwmans

1994

Stage: Valréas to L'Alpe d'Huez, 224 kilometers (139.19 miles)

1. Roberto Conti, 6:06:45
    Average speed: 36.728 kilometers (22.822 miles) per hour
2. Hernan Buenahora 2:02
3. Udo Bölts 3:49
4. Alberto Elli 3:49
5. Giancarlo Perini 4:03
6. Jörg Müller 4:39
7. Bruno Cenghialta 5:05
8. Marco Pantani 5:41
9. Alberto Torres 5:55
10. Angel Carmago 7:15

Final Overall Standings

1. Miguel Induráin
2. Piotr Ugrumov 5:39
3. Marco Pantani 7:19

GREEN JERSEY: Djamolidine Abdoujaparov
POLKA-DOT JERSEY: Richard Virenque
BEST YOUNG RIDER: Marco Pantani

1995

Stage: Aime La Plagne to L'Alpe d'Huez, 162.5 kilometers (100.97 miles)

1. Marco Pantani, 5:13:14
   Average speed: 31.126 kilometers (19.341 miles) per hour
2. Miguel Induráin 1:24
3. Alex Zülle 1:24
4. Bjarne Riis 1:26
5. Laurent Madouas 1:54
6. Fernando Escartin 2:01
7. Laurent Jalabert 2:26
8. Richard Virenque 2:50
9. Ivan Gotti 2:50
10. Claudio Chiappucci 3:02

Final Overall Standings

1. Miguel Induráin
2. Alex Zülle 4:35
3. Bjarne Riis 6:47

GREEN JERSEY: Laurent Jalabert
POLKA-DOT JERSEY: Richard Virenque
BEST YOUNG RIDER: Marco Pantani

1997

Stage: Saint-Étienne to L'Alpe d'Huez, 203.5 kilometers (126.45 miles)

1. Marco Pantani, 5:21:42
   Average speed: 40.3 kilometers (25.04 miles) per hour
2. Jan Ullrich 0:47
3. Richard Virenque 1:27
4. Francesco Casagrande 2:27

5. Bjarne Riis 2:28
6. Beat Zberg 2:59
7. Udo Bölts 2:59
8. Roberto Conti 2:59
9. Laurent Madouas 2:59
10. Laurent Jalabert 3:22

Final Overall Standings

1. Jan Ullrich
2. Richard Virenque 9:09
3. Marco Pantani 14:03

GREEN JERSEY: Eric Zabel
POLKA-DOT JERSEY: Richard Virenque
BEST YOUNG RIDER: Jan Ullrich

1999

Stage: Sestrières to L'Alpe d'Huez, 220.5 kilometers (137.01 miles)

1. Giuseppe Guerini, 6:42:31
   Average speed: 32.868 kilometers (20.423 miles) per hour
2. Pavel Tonkov 0:21
3. Fernando Escartin 0:25
4. Alex Zülle 0:25
5. Lance Armstrong 0:25
6. Richard Virenque 0:25
7. Laurent Dufaux 0:25
8. Kurt van de Wouwer 0:25
9. Manuel Beltran 0:32
10. Carlos Contreras 0:49

Final Overall Standings

1. Lance Armstrong
2. Alex Zülle 7:37
3. Fernando Escartin 10:26

GREEN JERSEY: Eric Zabel
POLKA-DOT JERSEY: Richard Virenque
BEST YOUNG RIDER: Benoît Salmon

2001

Stage: Aix-les-Bains to L'Alpe d'Huez, 209 kilometers (129.87 miles)

1. Lance Armstrong, 6:23:47
   Average speed: 32.675 kilometers (20.303 miles) per hour
2. Jan Ullrich 1:59
3. Joseba Beloki 2:09
4. Christophe Moreau 2:30
5. Oscar Sevilla 2:54
6. Francisco Mancebo 4:01
7. Laurent Roux 4:03
8. Igor González de Galdeano 4:03
9. Roberto Laiseka 4:03
10. Leonardo Piepoli 4:07

Final Overall Standings

1. Lance Armstrong
2. Jan Ullrich 6:44
3. Joseba Beloki 9:05

GREEN JERSEY: Eric Zabel
POLKA-DOT JERSEY: Laurent Jalabert
BEST YOUNG RIDER: Oscar Sevilla

2003

Stage: Sallanches to L'Alpe d'Huez, 219 kilometers (136.08 miles)

1. Iban Mayo, 5:57:30
   Average speed: 38.685 kilometers (24.038 miles) per hour
2. Alexander Vinokourov 1:45
3. Lance Armstrong 2:12
4. Francisco Mancebo 2:12
5. Haimar Zubeldia 2:12
6. Joseba Beloki 2:12
7. Tyler Hamilton 2:12
8. Ivan Basso 2:12
9. Roberto Laiseka 2:12
10. Pietro Caucchioli 3:36

Final Overall Standings

1. Lance Armstrong
2. Jan Ullrich 1:01
3. Alexander Vinokourov 4:14

GREEN JERSEY: Baden Cooke
POLKA-DOT JERSEY: Richard Virenque
BEST YOUNG RIDER: Denis Menchov

2004

Stage: Bourg d'Oisans to L'Alpe d'Huez, 15.5-kilometer (9.63-mile) individual time trial

1. Lance Armstrong, 39:41
   Average speed: 23.435 kilometers (14.562 miles) per hour
2. Jan Ullrich 1:01
3. Andreas Klöden 1:41
4. José Azevedo 1:45
5. Santos Gonzalez 2:11
6. Giuseppe Guerini 2:11
7. Vladimir Karpets 2:15
8. Ivan Basso 2:23
9. David Moncoutié 2:23
10. Carlos Sastre 2:27

Final Overall Standings

1. Lance Armstrong
2. Andreas Klöden 6:19
3. Ivan Basso 6:40

GREEN JERSEY: Robbie McEwen
POLKA-DOT JERSEY: Richard Virenque
BEST YOUNG RIDER: Vladimir Karpets

2006

Stage: Gap to L'Alpe d'Huez, 187 kilometers (116.2 miles)

1. Fränk Schleck, 4:52:22
   Average speed: 38.376 kilometers (23.846 miles) per hour
2. Damiano Cunego 0:11
3. Stefano Garzelli 1:10
4. Floyd Landis 1:10
5. Andreas Klöden 1:10
6. Ruben Lobato 1:14
7. Sylvain Chavanel 1:18
8. Eddy Mazzoleni 1:28

9. Carlos Sastre 1:35
10. Levi Leipheimer 1:49

*Final Overall Standings**

1. Oscar Pereiro
2. Andreas Klöden 0.32
3. Carlos Sastre 2:16

*Floyd Landis finished first, but on September 20, 2007, he was found guilty of doping and stripped of the title. He has appealed the decision to the Court of Arbitration for Sport.

GREEN JERSEY: Robbie McEwen
POLKA-DOT JERSEY: Michael Rasmussen
BEST YOUNG RIDER: Damiano Cunego

Appendix B:
Statistics

Rankings: Hinault, King of the Mountain

If one considers all twenty-five climbs up Alpe d'Huez to date (twenty-four Tour events, with two climbs in 1979), which racer emerges as the top performer? Devising a ranking formula is a fun little statistical game. For our purposes, we have considered only the top twenty finishers from each ascent and assigned them points in reverse order of their finish (20 points to the 1st-place finisher, 19 to the 2nd, and so forth, down to 1 point for the 20th-place finisher). Then we tallied each individual's points.

Bernard Hinault came out on top. Of course, our barometer favors those who made multiple appearances over the course of a long career; Hinault scaled the Alpe seven times. By comparison, Lance Armstrong, who made two fewer ascents, ranks only ninth. But the results nonetheless give a good sense of who made the greatest impact climbing the legendary twenty-one switchbacks. Hinault, after all, was the dominant force at Alpe d'Huez during his era: second in 1978, eighth and third in 1979 (the year there were two assaults on the Alpe over two consecutive days), second in 1981, fifth in 1982, seventh in 1984, and first in 1986.

It should be noted, too, that our rankings favor riders of the 1980s (1980 and 1985 were the only years the Tour did not climb the Alpe in that decade). In contrast, from 1990 to 2007, this stage was forgotten seven times (in 1993, 1996, 1998, 2000, 2002, 2005, and 2007). The relative infrequency of the stage in recent years—surprising, considering that it has never been more popular with fans or more closely followed by the media—evidently penalizes the generations of Induráin and Armstrong. The American, in fact, is our highest-ranked racer of the post-Hinault era, followed by Richard Virenque (10th).

As is appropriate for a climb nicknamed "Dutch Mountain," our second rider in the standings is Joop Zoetemelk. But arguably, our rankings do not give due credit to the Italians, whose six victories tally only one fewer than the Dutch record yet whose highest-ranked riders have ended up in a three-way tie with Sven-Ake Nilsson, in 22nd. Furthermore, both are two-time winners at Alpe d'Huez: Gianni Bugno (1990 and 1991) and Marco Pantani (1995 and 1997), who also holds the record for the fastest ascent of all time: 36:50.

The Top Fifty-one Riders at Alpe d'Huez from 1952 to 2006

1. Bernard Hinault (France), 119 points
2. Joop Zoetemelk (Netherlands), 116 points
3. Lucien van Impe (Belgium), 110 points
4. Pedro Delgado (Spain), 98 points
5. Laurent Fignon (France), 80 points
6. Greg LeMond (U.S.) and Raymond Martin (France), 76 points
8. Jean-René Bernaudeau (France), 75 points
9. Lance Armstrong (U.S.), 74 points
10. Robert Alban (France), 72 points
11. Joaquim Agostinho (Portugal), Richard Virenque (France), and Paul Wellens (Netherlands), 69 points
14. Peter Winnen (Netherlands), 66 points
15. Jan Ullrich (Germany), 65 points
16. Lucho Herrera (Colombia), 62 points
17. Claude Criquielion (Belgium), 60 points
18. Gert-Jan Theunisse (Netherlands), 59 points
19. Francisco Galdos (Spain), 57 points
20. Hennie Kuiper (Netherlands), 55 points
21. Steven Rooks (Netherlands), 54 points
22. Sven-Ake Nilsson (Sweden), Gianni Bugno (Italy), and Marco Pantani (Italy), 53 points
25. Thierry Claveyrolat (France), 52 points
26. Claudio Chiappucci (Italy), 50 points
27. Robert Millar (Scotland), 44 points
28. Miguel Induráin (Spain) and Michel Laurent (France), 43 points
30. Fabio Parra (Colombia), 41 points
31. Alex Zülle (Switzerland) and Fernando Escartin (Spain), 39 points
33. Ronan Pensec (France), 38 points
34. Pascal Simon (France), 36 points
35. Abelardo Rondon (Colombia) and Giuseppe Guerini (Italy), 35 points
37. Henk Lubberdink (Netherlands) and Andreas Klöden (Germany), 34 points
39. Angel Arroyo (Spain), Roberto Conti (Italy), and Bjarne Riis (Denmark), 33 points

42. Bernard Thévenet (France), 32 points
43. Giovanni Battaglin (Italy), 30 points
44. Mariano Martinez (France) and Beat Breu (Switzerland), 29 points
46. Ivan Basso (Italy), Alarcon Jesus Montoya (Spain), and Urs Zimmermann (Switzerland), 26 points
49. Steve Bauer (Canada), 25 points
50. Carlos Sastre (Spain) and Stefano Garzelli (Italy), 24 points

The Fastest Ascents

Who made the best time up the Alpe's summit road? Official timing began in 1990 at the behest of watchmaker Tissot, the Tour's official timekeeper that year. Six official timers clocked the first thirty racers from Bourg d'Oisans to the finish, a distance of about 15.5 kilometers (9.6 miles). Erik Breukink recorded the best time, 43:19, and received a bracelet and a gold watch valued at 20,000 francs ($3,672 at that time, or $5,664 today). Then came Fabio Parra (43:23), Abelardo Rondon (43:57), Andy Hampsten (43:58), Claude Criquielion (44:00), and Ronan Pensec (44:04). Curiously, the stage winner, the Italian Gianni Bugno, was not among the top six. In fact, the fastest on the final climb is not always the winner of the stage; in this case, Breukink "only" finished third.

Ever since 1990, the final climb has been timed, but at different starting points. The original one at Bourg d'Oisans was eventually moved up to the "false flat" leading to the foot of the Alpe, resulting in a distance of about 14.5 kilometers (9 miles). More recently, however, timekeepers have tended to eliminate that initial stretch from their calculations and have started keeping time at the very foot of the Alpe, a distance of 13.8 kilometers (8.57 miles).

These discrepancies in distances make it difficult to compare performances over the years. In recent years, to facilitate comparisons, chronometers have timed both the 14.5- and 13.8-kilometer stretches. In 1997, for example, Pantani registered 37:35 over the longer course and 36:55 over the actual climb. In 2004, Armstrong, over the same stretches, clocked 39:41 and 37:36, respectively.

The double standard creates some controversy, however, when it comes to bragging rights. A case in point is Pantani's climb in 1995. Over the longer stretch, he was clocked at 38:04; fast, but no record. On the actual climb, however, he registered a blistering 36:50, which is the record to this day. So, which standard is the fairest measure of performance? Most favor the final 13.8 kilometers. Pantani's time is thus generally considered the benchmark. It is all the more remarkable to consider that he set that time while concluding a 162.5-kilometer (101-mile) stage after having climbed the Madeleine and the Croix de Fer. His record even beats Lance Armstrong's winning time in the 2004 individual time trial, covering nothing but the final 13.8 kilometers.

And how does Fausto Coppi's inaugural climb in 1952 compare? Jacques Goddet revealed in *L'Équipe–Élans* that he used his own watch to time the Italian up the final ascent. Goddet clocked Coppi at 45:22, 8:32 slower than Pantani's record forty-three years later. But if one considers the state of the roads in 1952 and the equipment of the period, Coppi's climb was a veritable feat.

The fastest times over the 13.8 kilometers (8.57 miles) are:

1. Marco Pantani, 36:50 in 1995, 22.48 kilometers (13.97 miles) per hour
2. Marco Pantani, 36:55 in 1997
3. Marco Pantani, 37:15 in 1994
4. Lance Armstrong, 37:36 in 2004
5. Jan Ullrich, 37:40 in 1997
6. Lance Armstrong, 38:01 in 2001
7. Miguel Induráin and Alex Zülle, 38:10 in 1995
8. Bjarne Riis, 38:15 in 1995
9. Richard Virenque, 38:20 in 1997
10. Floyd Landis, 38:34 in 2006

The Climb

The climb up Alpe d'Huez measures 13.8 kilometers. The altitude at the base of the mountain is 760 meters (2,493 feet), and it rises to 1,850 meters (6,069 feet) by the summit, a difference of 1,090 meters (3,576 feet). The maximum grade is 10.6 percent along the initial 2-kilometer (1.2-mile) stretch. The road features 21 switchbacks, each with a marker listing the names of one or two past winners of an Alpe stage, and the altitude and the number of each turn in descending order.

Turn 21: Fausto Coppi 1952 and Lance Armstrong 2001, 806 meters of altitude, after 1.4 kilometers

Turn 20: Joop Zoetemelk 1976 and Iban Mayo 2003, 880 meters, after 2.1 kilometers; grade 10.6 percent

Turn 19: Hennie Kuiper 1977, 900 meters, after 2.3 kilometers

Turn 18: Hennie Kuiper 1978, 922 meters, after 2.6 kilometers

Turn 17: Joaquim Agostinho 1979, 965 meters, after 2.9 kilometers

Turn 16: Joop Zoetemelk 1979, 980 meters, after 3.2 kilometers (outskirts of the village La Garde)
Turn 15: Peter Winnen 1981, 1,025 meters, after 3.8 kilometers
Turn 14: Beat Breu 1982, 1,055 meters, after 4.2 kilometers
Turn 13: Peter Winnen 1983, 1,120 meters, after 4.9 kilometers
Turn 12: Lucho Herrera 1984, 1,161 meters, after 5.4 kilometers (start of Ribot d'Huez)
Turn 11: Bernard Hinault 1986, 1,195 meters, after 5.9 kilometers
Turn 10: Federico Echave 1987, 1,245 meters, after 6.5 kilometers
Turn 9: Steven Rooks 1988, 1,295 meters, after 7 kilometers (halfway point)
Turn 8: Gert-Jan Theunisse 1989, 1,345 meters, after 7.6 kilometers
Turn 7: Gianni Bugno 1990, 1,390 meters, after 8.1 kilometers (the cemetery of Huez)
Turn 6: Gianni Bugno 1991, 1,480 meters, after 9.2 kilometers; grade 9.4 percent
Turn 5: Andy Hampsten 1992, 1,512 meters, after 9.8 kilometers
Turn 4: Roberto Conti 1994, 1,553 meters, after 10.2 kilometers (here the road to L'Alpe d'Huez forks; the Tour takes the left branch)
Turn 3: Marco Pantani 1995, 1,626 meters, after 11.1 kilometers
Turn 2: Marco Pantani 1997, 1,669 meters, after 11.5 kilometers
Turn 1: Giuseppe Guerini 1999, 1,713 meters, after 12 kilometers

After Turn 1 comes the final 1.3 kilometers to the summit of the Alpe, where the elevation reaches 1,850 meters.

The Most Victorious Countries

If one considers the nationalities of the winners of those twenty-five stages, the Dutch rank first with eight victories, justifying the nickname "Dutch Mountain." But Italy is close behind with seven victories, followed by the United States (three victories) and Spain (two victories). France has won once, thanks to Bernard Hinault, the celebrated "King of Alpe d'Huez," as have Switzerland and Colombia. The Dutch dominated in the 1970s and 1980s, scoring all of their eight victories before 1990. The Italians ruled in the 1990s, taking six victories, and the Americans figured prominently in this first decade of the 21st century, thanks to Lance Armstrong.

The Most Frequent Appearances

Five racers have figured in the top twenty on seven occasions: Bernard Hinault, Pedro Delgado, Joop Zoetemelk, Lucien van Impe, and Raymond Martin (who just missed setting the record, having finished 21st in 1980). Joop Zoetemelk was present eight times but finished in 45th place in 1983. Induráin likewise was present eight times but finished in the top twenty only four times.

Single Appearances

Fausto Coppi, 1st in 1952
Raymond Poulidor, 9th in 1976
Eddy Merckx, 20th in 1977

Prominent Riders Who Never Appeared or Who Have Yet to Appear (through 2007)

Jacques Anquetil
Federico Bahamontes
Louison Bobet
Alberto Contador
André Darrigade
José-Manuel Fuente
Felice Gimondi
Hugo Koblet
Ferdi Kübler
Alejandro Valverde
Rik van Looy
Rik van Steenbergen

The Climbs of Hinault, Induráin, Pantani, and Armstrong

These are the four great champions who won both an Alpe d'Huez stage and the Tour. The following shows how they placed at the Alpe and, in parentheses, in the overall.

Bernard Hinault

1978: 2nd, 0:08 behind Hennie Kuiper (1st overall)
1979: 8th, 3:19 behind Joaquim Agostinho and 3:47 behind Joop Zoetemelk (1st overall)
1981: 2nd, 0:08 behind Peter Winnen (1st overall)
1982: 5th, 1:26 behind Beat Breu (1st overall)
1984: 7th, 3:44 behind Lucho Herrera (2nd overall behind Laurent Fignon)
1986: 1st (2nd overall behind Greg LeMond)

Miguel Induráin

1987: 107th, 24:23 behind Federico Echave (97th overall)
1988: 63rd, 20:25 behind Steven Rooks (47th overall)
1989: 31st, 9:40 behind Gert-Jan Theunisse (17th overall)
1990: 40th, 11:55 behind Gianni Bugno (10th overall)
1991: 2nd, 0:01 behind Bugno (1st overall)
1992: 6th, 3:15 behind Andy Hampsten (1st overall)
1994: 12th, 7:56 behind Roberto Conti (1st overall)
1995: 2nd, 1:24 behind Marco Pantani (1st overall)

Marco Pantani

1994: 8th, 5:41 behind Roberto Conti (3rd overall)
1995: 1st (13th overall)
1997: 1st (3rd overall)

Lance Armstrong

1995: 56th, 18:44 behind Marco Pantani (36th overall)
1999: 5th, 0:05 behind Giuseppe Guerini (1st overall)
2001: 1st (1st overall)
2003: 3rd, 2:12 behind Iban Mayo (1st overall)
2004: 1st (1st overall)

How Much Does the Winner Make at Alpe d'Huez?

The Tour has three stage categories: the prologue, individual time trials, and regular stages. The winner at Alpe d'Huez pockets the standard stage prize of 7,620 euros ($11,596). In addition, he earns 762 euros ($1,160) for being the first to reach an *hors catégorie* mountaintop, in this case Alpe d'Huez. However, the prestige of winning at the top of the Alpe is priceless!

The Fastest Stages

1997, Saint-Étienne to L'Alpe d'Huez, 203 kilometers (126 miles); won by Marco Pantani with an average speed of 40.3 kilometers (25.04 miles) per hour. The fast pace was due in part to the lack of challenges from other riders before the final ascent.

2006, Gap to L'Alpe d'Huez, 187 kilometers (116.2 miles); won by Fränk Schleck with an average speed of 38.376 kilometers (23.846 miles) per hour.

1994, Valréas to L'Alpe d'Huez, 224 kilometers (139.2 miles); won by Roberto Conti with an average speed of 36.728 kilometers (22.822 miles) per hour.

The Slowest Stages

The time trial in 2004: Lance Armstrong averaged 23.4 kilometers (14.5 miles) per hour over 15.5 kilometers (9.6 miles). But if one considers only non–time trial stages, the slowest winning pace is that of Joop Zoetemelk, who registered 26.986 kilometers (16.768 miles) per hour in 1979 over 119 kilometers (73.9 miles), the shortest of all the stages ending at the summit of the Alpe. The slow pace may reflect the fact that the racers had covered the same stretch the day before.

The Longest Stages

In 1952, Lausanne to L'Alpe d'Huez, 266 kilometers (165.3 miles), with no major challenges before the final ascent. If one considers only the "modern" stages (from 1976 on), the longest was that of 1976, covering 258 kilometers (160.3 miles), followed by those of 1978, 240 kilometers (149.1 miles), and 1981, 230 kilometers (142.9 miles). Since 2000, the stages have been 209 kilometers (129.9 miles) in 2001, 219 kilometers (136.1 miles) in 2003, and 187 kilometers (116.2 miles) in 2006.

The Most Frequently Used "Warm-Up" Climbs

The mountain most frequently traversed to reach the valley of Romanche and the foot of Alpe d'Huez is the Madeleine: 24.5 kilometers (15.2 miles) and 1,993 meters (6,539 feet) in elevation. It has been included seven times: 1977, 1979, 1981, 1988, 1990, 1995, and 2001.

Next comes the Glandon: 21.3 kilometers (13.2 miles) and 1,924 meters (6,312 feet) in elevation. It has been traversed six times: 1977, 1981, 1983, 1988, 1990, and 2001. The Madeleine and the Glandon are often climbed one after the other during the same Alpe d'Huez stage, as was the case in 1977, 1981, 1988, 1990, and 2001.

After these come the Croix de Fer, 29.6 kilometers (18.4 miles) and 2,068 meters (6,784.8 feet), and the Col d'Ornon, 14.4 kilometers (8.9 miles) and 1,367 meters (4,485 feet), traversed five times each, and the Galibier, 18.1 kilometers (11.2 miles) and 2,642 meters (8,668 feet), four times.

The Biggest Margins of Victory

In 1994 Roberto Conti finished 2:02 ahead of his dauphin, Hernan Buenahora. In the 2001 edition, Lance Armstrong finished 1:59 ahead of Jan Ullrich. In 1979, Joaquim Agostinho beat Robert Alban by 1:57.

Those Who Took the Yellow Jersey after the Alpe d'Huez Stage

Eleven riders claimed the yellow jersey after the Alpe stage without necessarily winning the stage or the Tour that year. They are as follows (the name of the previous yellow jersey holder is given in parentheses):

1952: Fausto Coppi (Andrea Carrea, Coppi's *domestique*)
1976: Lucien van Impe (Freddy Maertens)
1978: Michel Pollentier (Joseph Bruyère). Note: Pollentier was disqualified on drug charges the next day; Joop Zoetemelk wore the yellow jersey when the race resumed.
1983: Laurent Fignon (Pascal Simon, who abandoned before the final ascent)
1984: Laurent Fignon (Vincent Barteau)
1987: Pedro Delgado (Stephen Roche)
1988: Pedro Delgado (Steve Bauer)
1989: Laurent Fignon (Greg LeMond)
2001: François Simon (Stuart O'Grady)
2003: Lance Armstrong (Richard Virenque)
2006: Floyd Landis (Oscar Pereiro)

Alpe d'Huez and Yellow Jersey Double

Only Fausto Coppi (1952) has won the stage and taken the yellow jersey with it. In 1986, Greg LeMond was already wearing the yellow jersey and crossed the line with Hinault, but the American officially finished second. In 2001, Lance Armstrong won the stage but was still 20.7 seconds behind François Simon in the overall standings. In 2004, Lance Armstrong won the stage but already had the yellow jersey.

Alpe d'Huez and Tour Double

Only Fausto Coppi (1952) and Lance Armstrong (2001, 2004) have won both the stage and the Tour in the same year.

Alpe d'Huez, Yellow Jersey, and Tour Triple

Fausto Coppi, 1952

In Yellow at Alpe d'Huez and Overall Victory

Ten Tour winners have either donned the yellow jersey at Alpe d'Huez or increased their hold on it there (not including Floyd Landis in 2006 because he was disqualified). Their collective victories total eighteen, underscoring the importance of this key stage.

Fausto Coppi, 1952
Lucien van Impe, 1976
Bernard Thévenet, 1977
Bernard Hinault, 1979, 1981, 1982
Laurent Fignon, 1983, 1984
Greg LeMond, 1986
Pedro Delgado, 1988
Miguel Induráin, 1991, 1992, 1994, 1995
Jan Ullrich, 1997
Lance Armstrong, 1999, 2003, 2004
Floyd Landis, 2006 (later disqualified, with the Tour victory going to Oscar Pereiro)

Two-Time Winners at Alpe d'Huez

Hennie Kuiper (Netherlands), 1977, 1978 (after Michel Pollentier was disqualified on drug charges)
Joop Zoetemelk (Netherlands), 1976, 1979
Peter Winnen (Netherlands), 1981, 1983
Gianni Bugno (Italy), 1990, 1991
Marco Pantani (Italy), 1995, 1997
Lance Armstrong (U.S.), 2001, 2004

Consistency

With five ascents to his credit, Laurent Fignon surpasses Raymond Martin (who nevertheless climbed the Alpe seven times) in our rankings. The Parisian consistently finished strong in this stage: 5th in 1983, 2nd in 1984, 6th in 1987, 5th in 1989, and 9th in 1991.

Greg LeMond also finished consistently well: 6th in 1984, 2nd in 1986, 5th in 1989, 2nd in 1990, and 14th in 1991.

Robert Alban was one of the most consistent performers in this stage, finishing in the top four on four occasions: 2nd in 1979, 4th in 1981, 2nd in 1982, and 4th in 1983.

Raymond Delisle climbed the Alpe only twice, finishing 14th both times (in 1976 and 1977).

Bernard Thévenet also only climbed Alpe d'Huez twice and finished well both times: 8th in 1976 and 2nd in 1977.

Jan Ullrich finished second three out of four times: in 1997 (behind Pantani), in 2001, and in 2004 (both times behind Armstrong). In 2003 he finished 13th.

Rest Days

Of the twenty-five ascents of Alpe d'Huez, four were followed by a rest day at the resort in L'Oisans: in 1952 (there was also a rest day in Toulouse), 1978 (as well as one in Biarritz), 1983, and 1986.

Alpe d'Huez and Television

Television made its debut at the Tour in 1952, thanks to Pierre Sabbagh, a highly regarded French journalist. That same year, the first images of the Tour taken from the back of a motorcycle were shot during the Alpe stage.

In 1976, the first ascent of the modern era, the climb up Alpe d'Huez was transmitted live starting at Bourg d'Oisans. In 1986, when Bernard Hinault and Greg LeMond crossed the line together, holding hands, the race had been broadcast starting at the Croix de Fer.

In 1990, all the great mountain stages were rebroadcast in France, including the stage from Saint-Gervais Mont Blanc to L'Alpe d'Huez. Television was quick to appreciate that the legendary mountain provided a splendid backdrop for irresistible showdowns. It is the stage that you do not want to miss.

Notes

Prologue

1. In 2006, Floyd Landis took the yellow jersey from Oscar Pereiro following the Alpe d'Huez stage. Though the American was celebrated as the final winner in Paris, he was eventually disqualified for using performance-enhancing drugs, in this case testosterone.

2. The Batavians were a tribe of Germanic origin reported by Tacitus to have lived around the Rhine delta in the area now known as the Netherlands.

3. *Bicisport*, "La storia del Tour 97," no. 8.

4. *Le Parisien*, July 24, 1992.

Chapter 1

1. *L'Équipée belle*, Éditions Robert Laffont.

2. Joseph Paganon, who was also a military attaché to Georges Clémenceau, is widely considered a founding father of L'Alpe d'Huez. Georges Rajon explained, "He asked Mr. Laprade, an official with the department of Beaux-arts, to project a resort in the area. Paganon insisted that the site would eventually become a world-famous destination."

3. In the 1930s, there was not yet running water at L'Alpe d'Huez, a fact that complicated construction of the road up to the Alpe's summit. Georges Rajon recalled that, to clear snow off the narrow road to Huez, the inhabitants initially used a large rake pulled by a horse—until Paganon supplied a Caterpillar plow.

Chapter 2

1. *Gregario* is the Italian equivalent of the French term *domestique*. Both refer to a teammate who rides in support of the team leader.

Chapter 3

1. *L'Équipée belle*, Éditions Robert Laffont.

2. "Nanar," slang for "trash" in French, was Thévenet's unflattering nickname.

3. An excellent sporting review of the period refers in its archives to an Alpe d'Huez stage in 1966, the year Lucien Aimar prevailed and a sick Jacques Anquetil quit the race for good. A few racers did in fact spend a night on the Alpe. Nevertheless, that Tour did not navigate the twenty-one turns to the summit. The stage in question, won by the Spaniard Luis Otano, ended at Bourg d'Oisans. The road to the Alpe was not accessible that year, as it was being overhauled in preparation for the 1968 Winter Olympics.

Chapter 4

1. La Grande Boucle, variously translated as "the Big Buckle" or "the Big Loop," is often used in French as a metaphorical label for the encircling Tour de France.

2. In 1976, after the racers had traversed the Alps, they were flown from Manosque to Port Barcares, where they started the first stage in the Pyrénées.

3. *Eddy Merckx*, VeloPress.

4. *Vélo-Legende*, no. 6, November 1988.

Chapter 5

1. *L'Équipée belle*, Éditions Robert Laffont.

2. In 1994, in his book *Eddy Merckx* (VeloPress), Rik Vanwalleghem related Merckx's reaction to this advice. The latter reportedly declared, "When I won the Tour four times in a row, I was keenly aware of the organizers' feigned joy. They had seen enough of me and feared I was killing the suspense. I was very offended that Goddet attacked me in that manner after so many years. His reaction was petty."

3. "Golden fleece" is another metaphor used in reference to the yellow jersey.

4. *L'Équipe*, July 1978.

5. To general surprise, in the 2003 Tirreno-Adriatico, Massimiliano Mori (Formaggi Pinzolo) was booted from the race for attempting to cheat the control in the same manner. Like Pollentier, he hid a bulb filled with urine given him by his *directeur sportif*. It was for a urinary control that was supposed to supplement a blood test conducted the previous evening. The latter had already revealed an excessively high red-blood-cell count.

6. *Massacre à la Chaîne*, Calmann-Lévy.

7. Ironically, one of the sponsors of the contest that year was the water brand Contrexville.

Chapter 6

1. For several years, kilometer 92 was a familiar milestone for the Tour entourage; a refreshment stop was provided there courtesy of Hauts-de-Seine County, the 92nd *département* of France.

Chapter 7

1.   Also known as *pétanque*, *boules* is similar to lawn bowling or Italian boccie. It is traditionally played on a flat dirt surface. The object is to throw each steel ball with an arched trajectory and some backspin as close to a small wooden ball (the *cochonnet*) as possible. The winner is the player with a ball closest to the *cochonnet*.

Chapter 8

1.   The Clásico RCN and Vuelta a Colombia are Colombia's two most important stage races, with the former sponsored by Radio Cadena Nacional and held in October. The first edition was run in 1961.

2.   Joop Zoetemelk, the winner of the 1980 Tour, currently holds the record for participation in the race, with 16 Tours in all from 1970 to 1986. He finished 2nd in 1970, 1971, 1976, 1978, 1979, and 1982; 4th in 1973, 1975, and 1981; 5th in 1972; 8th in 1977; 23rd in 1983; 30th in 1984; 12th in 1985; and 24th in 1986. Next are two Belgians, Lucien van Impe and Guy Nulens, each having participated in 15 Tours.

Chapter 9

1.   According to a poll conducted by l'Institut Français d'Opinion Publique (French Institute of Public Opinion).

2.   Jonathan Boyer reached Paris in 12th place overall.

Chapter 10

1.   Quoted in *Panache*, a booklet dedicated to the glory of Eddy Merckx, childhood, and cycling. Éditions Le Dilettante, 1991.

Chapter 11

1.   "Cohabitation" refers to a power-sharing arrangement in which the president and prime minister belong to different parties.

2.   *Rouleur* is a term used for a rider who can ride all day over rolling hills.

3.   *L'Express Sport*, February 1988.

4.   *Le Peloton des souvenirs*, Éditions Robert Laffont, 1988. English translation: *Memories of the Peloton*, Noel Henderson (translator), Vitesse Press, 1989.

5.   *L'Équipe*, March 1991.

Chapter 12

1. The Tour Cycliste Féminin was launched in 1984 and has since been renamed La Grande Boucle Féminine. Over the years, it has struggled to find sponsorship, forcing multiple cancellations.
2. Eighth-place Miguel Induráin had also caught everyone's attention, but he was not yet "King of Spain."

Chapter 13

1. Antenne 2 became France 2 in 1992 and is the country's largest public television network. It is one of several networks operated by France Télévisions, including France 3, France 5, Réseau France Outre-mer, and the all-digital France 4.
2. The team was put together by Paul Koechli after his departure from La Vie Claire.

Chapter 14

1. Induráin hailed from Navarre, historically a Basque region but an autonomous community today. The Basque region of País Vasco begins one province farther west, but the Basques have always claimed Induráin as one of their own.
2. Gert-Jan Theunisse tested positive in the 1988 Tour, the 1990 Flèche Wallonne, and the 1990 Subita Arrate.

Chapter 15

1. In the postwar period, *L'Équipe*'s main rival was *Miroir du Cyclisme*; many of the latter's journalists also wrote for *L'Humanité* and *La Marseillaise*, two prominent dailies affiliated with the French Communist Party.
2. Ekimov was an hour record-holder, riding 49.672 kilometers (30.865 miles).
3. In the 1990 Tour, the Russian wore the polka-dot jersey of best climber and won the 17th stage.
4. Gianni Bugno had worn the Giro's pink leader's jersey that year from start to finish, a feat accomplished previously only by Costante Girardengo (1919), Alfredo Binda (1927), and Eddy Merckx (1973).

Chapter 16

1. Though Pensec had signed with Seur, he would race the Tour wearing the Amaya Seguros jersey.

2.   A *jour sans* (literally, "day without") is a "bad day"—a day when a rider's form or strength fails him, often for no apparent reason.

3.   At the 1991 Tour, four Italians had already won the previous four consecutive stages: Marco Lietti in Gap, Moreno Argentin in Alès, Bruno Cenghialta in Castres, and Claudio Chiappucci in Val Louron.

Chapter 18

1.   A few months later, during the Coppa Agostini, Gianni Bugno was suspended for caffeine doping.

3.   Only one rider at the start in Valréas had already won at the Alpe: Federico Echave in 1987. This time he would finish 43rd, 13:42 behind the winner, the Italian Roberto Conti.

3.   *Pas de géant* means "giant steps," but *L'Équipe* replaced *Pas* with *Pois*, meaning dots, in reference to the red polka dots on Virenque's jersey of best climber.

Chapter 20

1.   *L'Équipe*, October 22, 1996.
2.   Miguel Induráin finished the 1996 Tour in 11th place.
3.   *L'Équipe*, July 16, 1997.

Chapter 21

1.   *L'Équipe*, June 30, 1999.
2.   *L'Équipe*, July 4, 1999.
3.   Skittles is the ancestor of the sport known today in North America as bowling and throughout history has often been played outdoors. Skittles, or ninepin bowling, was brought to America from Europe during colonial times.

4.   Mario Cipollini started the stage dressed as a Roman emperor. He had won four straight stages, a feat that had not been accomplished since Charles Pélissier had done so in 1930. The stage wins took place in Blois (ahead of Zabel), Amiens (ahead of Steels), Maubeuge (ahead of Zabel), and Thionville (ahead of O'Grady). On the descent from Mongenèvre, he fell and abandoned the race.

5.   Marc Madiot, the *directeur sportif* of La Française des Jeux, blamed Heulot's teammate and drug crusader Christophe Basson for the failure of Heulot's attack, suggesting that the peloton was motivated to deny his team a victory to get back at Basson.

6.   *La Dépêche du Midi*, July 21, 1999.

Chapter 22

1. The Forli court gave Marco Pantani a suspended sentence of three months in prison after tests in the 1995 Milano-Torino revealed an excessively high red-blood-cell count (hematocrit level), reaching 60.1. He registered similar test results at the 1999 Giro and was accused of "sporting fraud" before dropping out of the event.

2. French authorities opened an investigation into this matter and eventually exonerated the U.S. Postal team.

3. Jan Ullrich had finished second at the Tour in 1996, 1998, and 2000, and he would finish second again at this Tour.

4. The thirteen riders were Aitor González (Kelme); Marc Wauters, Erik Dekker, and Bram de Groot (Rabobank); Pascal Chanteur and Sven Teutenberg (Festina); Andreï Kivilev (Cofidis); Jacky Durand (La Française des Jeux); Ludovic Turpin (AG2R Prévoyance); Servais Knaven (Domo); Nicola Loda (Fassa Bortolo); François Simon (Bonjour); and Stuart O'Grady (Crédit Agricole).

5. Andreï Kivilev died at 29 in the second stage of Paris-Nice in 2003, between La Clayette and Saint-Étienne, victim of a fall that put him in a coma.

6. In Europe, whistling is a common expression of spectator disapproval, akin to the North American custom of booing.

Chapter 23

1. *L'Équipe*, July 28, 2003.

2. The first rider to wear the yellow jersey was the Frenchman Eugène Christophe in the stage from Grenoble to Geneva.

3. *L'Équipe*, July 5, 2003.

Chapter 24

1. Besides Marco Pantani in 1997 and Felice Gimondi in 1965, the other Italian winners of the Tour are Gastone Nencini (1960), Fausto Coppi (1949 and 1952), Gino Bartali (1938 and 1948), and Ottavio Bottecchia (1924 and 1925).

Chapter 25

1. As it turned out, France beat Portugal in the semifinal but finished second, losing to Italy in the final on penalty kicks.

2. In the second Pyrenean stage to Pla-de-Beret, Azevedo finished 15th, 4:10 back; Popovych finished 26th at 6:25; Hincapie finished 46th at 21:23; and Savoldelli finished 50th at 23:04, suffering from bronchitis.